THE
VINTAGE
CONTEMPORARIES
READER

THE
VINTAGE
CONTEMPORARIES
READER

VINTAGE CONTEMPORARIES | VINTAGE BOOKS
A DIVISION OF RANDOM HOUSE, INC. | NEW YORK

|||| CONTENTS

Dates given in the Contents indicate the year of the first Vintage Contemporaries publication of each volume.

Yesterday's Discoveries, Today's Classics:
An Introduction

IN THE LAST fourteen years, the earth traveled 353,230,940,000 miles around the sun; the population of the United States grew from 232,904,825 to 268,684,928. We've been through three presidents, and the Toronto Blue Jays and the Minnesota Twins won the World Series the most times. Back in 1984, Milos Forman's *Amadeus* won the Oscar for the Best Film. The number-one song was "When Doves Cry" by Prince and the Revolution, and Ronald Reagan was President. A puppy born back then would now be an elder statesman in the dog world.

And in 1984, a group of young, smart editors at a small imprint within a large publishing house started an enterprise called Vintage Contemporaries. The first list included Raymond Carver, Jay McInerney, Peter Matthiessen, and Thomas McGuane. The most recent list includes Charles Frazier, Amy Tan, and Alice Munro, not to mention all the outstanding books in between.

The volume you hold in your hand contains selections, in some cases complete stories, by some of the most talented writers of the century. From such undeniable classics as Richard Yates's *Revolutionary Road* and Frederick Exley's *A Fan's Notes* to the unique talent of Raymond Carver and Tobias Wolff, to some of our braver writers working the fringes of consciousness, like Nicholson Baker, and Mark Leyner, to the stylistic brillance of Kaye Gibbons and Sandra Cisneros. Not to mention—heck, I think I will mention, the sheer genius of the rest of the authors represented here, including Ann Beattie, Edwidge Danticat, Don DeLillo, Andre Dubus, Bret Easton Ellis, Richard Ford, Ernest J. Gaines, David Guterson, Michelle Huneven, Patrick McGrath, Steven Millhauser, Richard Russo, Sapphire, and Mona Simpson.

You might say the authors included herein represent much of the best that contemporary fiction has had to offer for the past fourteen years. As editor in chief of Vintage Books, I would take your saying that as an indication that you are a reader of great taste and enormous good fortune. Because, in this one volume, you have the opportunity to relive many of fiction's finest moments during this time period and perhaps to be turned on to some you may have missed.

This volume is an opportunity for those of us at Vintage to thank you for your support of our efforts to bring these authors to you.

Enough.

Enjoy.

Marty Asher
Editor in Chief
Vintage Books

THE
VINTAGE
CONTEMPORARIES
READER

|||| JAY MCINERNEY

from *Bright Lights, Big City*

No other novel set the tone for the harrowingly excessive 1980s quite like Jay McInerney's best-selling Bright Lights, Big City, *and McInerney has since become a signature voice for his generation with such Vintage Contemporaries novels as* Ransom, Story of My Life, Brightness Falls, *and* The Last of the Savages. *Jay McInerney is currently working on a collection of stories entitled* Model Behavior, *forthcoming from Knopf.*

■ IT'S SIX A.M. DO YOU KNOW WHERE YOU ARE?

YOU ARE NOT the kind of guy who would be at a place like this at this time of the morning. But here you are, and you cannot say that the terrain is entirely unfamiliar, although the details are fuzzy. You are at a nightclub talking to a girl with a shaved head. The club is either Heartbreak or the Lizard Lounge. All might come clear if you could just slip into the bathroom and do a little more Bolivian Marching Powder. Then again, it might not. A small voice inside you insists that this epidemic lack of clarity is a result of too much of that already. The night has already turned on that imperceptible pivot where two A.M. changes to six A.M. You know this moment has come and gone, but you are not yet willing to concede that you have crossed the line beyond which all is gratuitous damage and the palsy of unraveled nerve endings. Somewhere back there you could have cut your losses, but you rode past that moment on a comet trail of white powder and now you are trying to hang on to the rush. Your brain at this moment is composed of brigades of tiny Bolivian soldiers. They are tired and muddy from their long march through the night.

There are holes in their boots and they are hungry. They need to be fed. They need the Bolivian Marching Powder.

A vaguely tribal flavor to this scene—pendulous jewelry, face paint, ceremonial headgear and hair styles. You feel that there is also a certain Latin theme—something more than the piranhas cruising your bloodstream and the fading buzz of marimbas in your brain.

You are leaning back against a post that may or may not be structural with regard to the building, but which feels essential to your own maintenance of an upright position. The bald girl is saying this used to be a good place to come before the assholes discovered it. You don't want to be talking to this bald girl, or even listening to her, which is all you are doing, but just now you do not want to test the powers of speech or locomotion.

How did you get here? It was your friend, Tad Allagash, who powered you in here, and he has disappeared. Tad is the kind of guy who would be at a place like this at this time of the morning. He is either your best self or you worst self, you're not sure which. Earlier in the evening it seemed clear that he was your best self. You started on the Upper East Side with champagne and unlimited prospects, strictly observing the Allagash rule of perpetual motion: one drink per stop. Tad's mission in life is to have more fun than anyone else in New York City, and this involves a lot of moving around, since there is always the likelihood that where you aren't is more fun than where you are. You are awed by his strict refusal to acknowledge any goal higher than the pursuit of pleasure. You want to be like that. You also think he is shallow and dangerous. His friends are all rich and spoiled, like the cousin from Memphis you met earlier in the evening who would not accompany you below Fourteenth Street because, he said, he didn't have a lowlife visa. This cousin had a girlfriend with cheekbones to break your heart, and you knew she was the real thing when she steadfastly refused to acknowledge your presence. She possessed secrets—about islands, about horses, about French pronunciation—that you would never know.

You have traveled in the course of the night from the meticulous to the slime. The girl with the shaved head has a scar tattooed on her scalp. It looks like a long, sutured gash. You tell her it is very realistic. She takes this as a compliment and thanks you. You meant as opposed to romantic.

"I could use one of those right over my heart," you say.

"You want I can give you the name of the guy that did it. You'd be surprised how cheap."

You don't tell her that nothing would surprise you now. Her voice, for instance, which is like the New Jersey State Anthem played through an electric shaver.

The bald girl is emblematic of the problem. The problem is, for some reason you think you are going to meet the kind of girl who is not the kind of girl who would be at a place like this at this time of the morning. When you meet her you are going to tell her that what you really want is a house in the country with a garden. New York, the club scene, bald women—you're tired of all that. Your presence here is only a matter of conducting an experiment in limits, reminding yourself of what you aren't. You see yourself as the kind of guy who wakes up early on Sunday morning and steps out to cop the *Times* and croissants. Who might take a cue from the Arts and Leisure section and decide to check out an exhibition—costumes of the Hapsburg Court at the Met, say, or Japanese lacquerware of the Muromachi period at the Asia Society. The kind of guy who calls up the woman he met at a publishing party Friday night, the party he did not get sloppy drunk at. See if she wants to check out the exhibition and maybe do an early dinner. A guy who would wait until eleven A.M. to call her, because she might not be an early riser, like he is. She may have been out late, perhaps at a nightclub. And maybe a couple of sets of tennis before the museum. He wonders if she plays, but of course she would.

When you meet the girl who wouldn't et cetera you will tell her that you are slumming, visiting your own six A.M. Lower East Side of the soul on a lark, stepping nimbly between the piles of garbage to the gay marimba rhythms in your head. Well, no, not *gay*. But she will know exactly what you mean.

On the other hand, almost any girl, specifically one with a full head of hair, would help you stave off this creeping sense of mortality. You remember the Bolivian Marching Powder and realize you're not down yet. No way, José. First you have to get rid of this bald girl.

IN THE BATHROOM there are no doors on the stalls, which makes it tough to be discreet. But clearly you are not the only person in here to take on fuel. Lots of sniffling going on in the stalls. The windows are blacked over, and for this you are profoundly grateful.

Hup, two, three, four. The soldiers are back on their feet. They are off and running in formation. Some of them are dancing, and you must follow their example.

Just outside the door you spot her: tall, dark and alone, half hidden behind a pillar at the edge of the dance floor. You approach laterally, moving your stuff like a Bad Spade through the slalom of a synthesized conga rhythm. She jumps when you touch her shoulder.

"Dance?"

She looks at you as if you had just suggested instrumental rape. "I do not speak English," she says, when you ask again.

"Français?"

She shakes her head. Why is she looking at you that way, as if tarantulas were nesting in your eye sockets?

"You are by any chance from Bolivia? Or Peru?"

She is looking around for help now. Remembering a recent encounter with a young heiress's bodyguard at Danceteria—or was it the Red Parrot?—you back off, hands raised over your head.

The Bolivian Soldiers are still on their feet, but they have stopped singing their marching song. You realize that you are at a crucial juncture vis-à-vis morale. What you need is a good pep talk from Tad Allagash, but he is not to be found. You try to imagine what he would say. *Back on the horse. Now we're* really *going to have some fun.* Something like that. You suddenly realize that he has already slipped out with some rich Hose Queen. He is back at her place on Fifth Ave., and they are doing some of her off-the-boat-quality drugs. They are scooping it out of tall Ming vases and snorting it off each other's naked bodies. You hate Tad Allagash.

Go home. Cut your losses.

Stay. Go for it.

You are a republic of voices tonight. Unfortunately, that republic is Italy. All these voices waving their arms and screaming at one another. There's an *ex cathedra* riff coming down from the Vatican: *Repent. Your body is the temple of the Lord and you have defiled it.* It is, after all, Sunday morning, and as long as you have any brain cells left there will be a resonant patriarchal basso echoing down the marble vaults of your churchgoing childhood to remind you that this is the Lord's Day. What you need is another overpriced drink to drown it out. But a search of pockets yields only a dollar bill and change. You paid twenty to get in here. Panic gains.

You spot a girl at the edge of the dance floor who looks like your last chance for earthly salvation. You know for a fact that if you go out into the morning alone, without even your sunglasses—which you have neglected to bring, because who, after all, plans on these travesties?—the harsh, angling light will turn you to flesh and bone. Mortality will pierce you through the retina. But there she is in her pegged pants, a kind of doo-wop Retro ponytail pulled off to the side, as eligible a candidate as you are likely to find this late in the game. The sexual equivalent of fast food.

She shrugs and nods when you ask her to dance. You like the way she moves, the oiled ellipses of her hips and shoulders. After the second song, she says she's tired. She's at a point of bolting when you ask her if she needs a little pick-me-up.

"You've got some blow?" she says.

"Is Stevie Wonder blind?" you say.

She takes your arm and leads you into the Ladies'. A couple of spoons and she seems to like you just fine, and you are feeling very likable yourself. A couple more. This woman is all nose.

"I love drugs," she says, as you march toward the bar.

"It's something we have in common," you say.

"Have you ever noticed how all the good words start with D? D and L."

You try to think about this. You're not quite sure what she's driving at. The Bolivians are singing their marching song, but you can't make out the words.

"You know. Drugs. Delight. Decadence."

"Debauchery," you say, catching the tune now.

"Dexedrine."

"Delectable. Deranged. Debilitated."

"Delinquent."

"Delirium."

"And L," she says. "Lush and luscious."

"Languorous."

"Librium."

"Libidinous."

"What's that?" she says.

"Horny."

"Oh," she says, casting a long, arching look over your shoulder. Her eyes glaze in a way that reminds you precisely of the closing of a sandblasted glass shower door. You can see that the game is over, although you're not sure which rule you broke. Possibly she finds H words offensive. A purist. She is scanning the dance floor for a man with a compatible vocabulary. You have more: *detumescence,* for instance. *Drowning* and *depressed; lost* and *lonesome.* It's not that you're really going to miss this girl who thinks that *decadence* and *Dexedrine* are the high points of the language of Kings James and Lear. But the touch of flesh, the sound of another human voice . . . You know there is a special purgatory waiting for you out there in the dawn's surly light, a desperate half sleep which is like a grease fire in the brainpan.

The girl waves as she disappears into the crowd. There is no sign of the other girl, the girl who would not be here. There is no sign of Tad Allagash. The Bolivians are mutinous. You can't stop their treacherous voices.

IT IS WORSE even than you expected, stepping out into the morning. The glare is like a mother's reproach. The sidewalk sparkles cruelly. Visibility unlimited. The downtown warehouses look serene and restful in this beveled light. An uptown cab passes and you start to wave, then realize you have no money. The cab stops.

You jog over and lean in the window. "I guess I'll walk after all."

"Asshole." He leaves rubber.

You start north, holding a hand over your eyes. Trucks rumble up Hudson Street, bearing provisions into the sleeping city. You turn east. On Seventh Avenue an old woman with a hive of rollers on her head walks a German shepherd. The dog is rooting in the cracks of the sidewalk, but as you approach he stiffens into a pose of terrible alertness. The woman looks at you as if you were something that had just crawled out of the ocean trailing ooze and slime. An eager, tentative growl ripples the shepherd's throat. "Good Pooky," she says. The dog makes a move but she chokes it back. You give them a wide berth.

On Bleecker Street you catch the scent of the Italian bakery. You stand at the corner of Bleecker and Cornelia and gaze at the windows on the fourth floor of a tenement. Behind those windows is the apartment you shared with Amanda when you first came to New York. It was small and dark, but you liked the imperfectly patched pressed-tin ceiling, the claw-footed bath in the kitchen, the windows that didn't quite fit the frames. You were just starting out. You had the rent covered, you had your favorite restaurant on MacDougal where the waitresses knew your names and you could bring your own bottle of wine. Every morning you woke to the smell of bread from the bakery downstairs. You would go out to buy the paper and maybe pick up a couple of croissants while Amanda made the coffee. This was two years ago, before you got married.

DOWN ON THE West Side Highway, a lone hooker totters on heels and tugs at her skirt as if no one had told her that the commuters won't be coming through the tunnels from Jersey today. Coming closer, you see that she is a man in drag.

You cross under the rusting stanchions of the old elevated highway and walk out to the pier. The easterly light skims across the broad expanse of the Hudson. You step carefully as you approach the end of the rotting pier. You are none too steady and there are holes through which you can see the black, fetid water underneath.

You sit down on a piling and look out over the river. Downriver, the Statue of Liberty shimmers in the haze. Across the water, a huge Colgate sign welcomes you to New Jersey, the Garden State.

You watch the solemn progress of a garbage barge, wreathed in a cloud of screaming gulls, heading out to sea.

Here you are again. All messed up and no place to go.

from *A Fan's Notes*

Vintage Contemporaries first published the fiercely comic fictional memoir A Fan's Notes *by Frederick Exley in 1985. Critically praised as "the best novel written in the English language since* The Great Gatsby" (Newsday), *this definitive work of American fiction was a finalist for the National Book Award. Exley wrote two other novels,* Pages from a Cold Island *and* Last Notes from Home. *Frederick Exley died in 1992.*

■ THE NERVOUS LIGHT OF SUNDAY

ON SUNDAY, THE eleventh of November, 196–, while sitting at the bar of the New Parrot Restaurant in my home town, Watertown, New York, awaiting the telecast of the New York Giants–Dallas Cowboys football game, I had what, at the time, I took to be a heart attack.

It wasn't. It—the "seizure" or whatever one chooses to call it—was brought on by the high and delicious anxiety I always experienced just prior to a Giants game, and by a weekend of foodless, nearly heroic drinking. For me it was a common enough drinking; but the amounts consumed had been intensified by the news, received by mail from Scarsdale two days before, that my wife intended to divorce me and to have custody of my two-year-old twin sons. It gives me feeble comfort to report it was not a heart attack. The pain was excruciatingly vivid, and for many moments I was terrified by the fear of death. Illogically, this was one terror I believed I had long since cast off—having cast it off, I thought, with the effortless lunacy of a man putting a shotgun into his mouth and ridding himself of the back of his skull. That the fear of death still owns me is, in its way, a beginning.

Each weekend I traveled the fifty-odd miles from Glacial Falls to Watertown, where I spent Friday night and all day Saturday in some sustained whisky drinking, tapering off Sundays with a few bottles of beer at The Parrot, eyes fixed on the television screen, cheering for my team. *Cheering* is a paltry description. The Giants were my delight, my folly, my anodyne, my intellectual stimulation. With Huff I "stunted" up and down the room among the bar stools, preparing to "shoot the gap"; with Shofner I faked two defenders "out of their cleats," took high, swimming passes over my right shoulder and trotted, dipsy-doodle-like, into the end zone; with Robustelli I swept into backfields and with cruel disdain flung flat-footed, helpless quarterbacks to the turf. All this I did amidst an unceasing, pedantic commentary I issued on the character of the game, a commentary issued with the patronizing air of one who assumed those other patrons incapable of assessing what was taking place before their eyes. Never did I stop moving or talking. Certainly I drove a good many customers away. Most of those who remained had seen the show before and had come back for more, bringing with them the morbid fascination which compels one to stare at a madman.

For the Giants they were exhilarating and lovely afternoons. With Y. A. Tittle passing to Shofner, Webster, Gifford, and Walton, the team was displaying its most adroit and exciting offense in memory; I was giddy with admiration. Despite those few felicitous hours, the weekends were tedious and could as well have taken place at Glacial Falls had I not been earning my drinking money at what my colleagues, with disarming somberness, referred to as "teaching school." It wasn't that teachers weren't permitted to drink in Glacial Falls, or that anyone would have frowned on a teacher's cheering in a local saloon. My case was somewhat different. Prior to his offering me a contract, Mr. A., the superintendent, had told me, half apologetically, half menacingly, that he understood I drank heavily. I should have said,

"Well, friend, if you *understand* that, you'd best not expose me to and run the risk of my polluting the kids"; but I badly needed the job and so found myself in the humiliating position of having to assure the man I'd refrain from "excessiveness" around Glacial Falls, a rural community of ten thousand, buried half the year under leaden skies and heavy snows, and all the year under the weight of its large and intransigent ignorance.

"The children come first," Mr. A. said to me at the time. "You understand that. We have to protect the children at all costs."

He said this sincerely, and I had no reason to doubt him. I wanted to believe him. For me it was another autumn, a time of new beginnings, and I was thirty-two; but I had only to teach a few days to realize the children came anything but first. The curriculum was, as it had been in the two schools where I had substituted, as bland as hominy grits; and there was a faculty that might most kindly be referred to as not altogether cretinous. A freshman had nuns cloistered in a "Beanery," a sophomore thought the characters in *Julius Caesar* talked "pretty damn uppity for a bunch of Wops," a junior defined "in mufti" as the attire worn by "some kind of sexual freak (like a certain ape who sits a few seats from me!)," and a senior considered "Hamlet a fag if I ever saw one. I mean, yak, yak, yak, instead of sticking that Claude in the gizzard, that Claude who's doing all those smelly things to his Mom."

Compounding the touching bewilderment of these students was an English department chairman who clung to such syntactical myths as that either *different from* or *different than* are permissible as the former is used in America and the latter in England. Though I had done some substitute work, this was my first contractual obligation, I was bringing to it a typically asinine and enthusiastic aplomb, and at this point I sought the floor. "I've heard this for years," I said, "have always looked for it, and have found that most English writers use *different from*. Without a

Fowler handy I haven't the foggiest how this argument got started, but I suspect that some prose writer of Dean Swiftian eminence got smashed one day, inadvertently substituted *than* for *from*, and for the past two hundred years the dons at Oxford and Cambridge have been scratching their heads and picking their noses over it. But this professorial bickering has nothing to do with us. Between getting smashed and cracking up their hot rods, initiating each other into their sex clubs, and having their rumbles, these little dears are looking to us for direction"—a loud laugh here from the back of the room, issuing from a Dartmouth man who taught English and Latin—"and we ought to give it to them. Oughtn't we to take a hard and arbitrary line and say it's *different from*, period? Certainly they'll come to us and show us how Hemingway strings together ten compound sentences without employing a single comma, but we'll just have to tell them they *ain't* Hemingway. I doubt there's anything stifling to creativity here. If any of these kids are going to write, they'll write in spite of us, and at least they'll know what rules they're violating."

This tastelessly long-winded monologue occurred at the first department meeting in September. Thinking that the laughter of the Dartmouth man had reflected the sentiments of my colleagues, when I finished, feeling rather proud, I looked round to see how the rest of the English teachers were reacting to the witty and brilliant new addition to their staff. To a man they were glum, somewhat wretched. Immediately after the meeting I discovered why. Approached by a broad-assed, martini-swilling, brazen, and theatrical old termagant, I was informed as a teacher new to the system that one did not enter discussions at department meetings, that "talking took time," and that there were all sorts of places one would rather be. "I'm sorry," I said. "I thought these meetings were for a purpose."

As the year progressed I learned that due to this conspiracy of silence the department chairman was forced to carry single-handedly what were supposed to be give-and-take discussions. Knowing he was no more ignorant than those boobs seated around me patronizing him, I felt sorry for him. At the beginning of each meeting he handed to his English teachers mimeographed sheets containing lettered items *A, B, C, D, E,* reflecting the wisdom of thirty years spent in combat with the language. Unsure of our ability to read (our ability to talk hadn't encouraged him), he read each and every item to us. Beginning with a lovingly theatrical enunciation of *A,* he thereupon was off. Matchlessly vapid, the items were such that I remember only one of them, and that only because to this day I have no notion of what he meant by it: *The best place to make out your lesson plans is at your desk.* In fairness to the man, he did not feel duty-bound to the continuity of his mimeographed sheets and often interrupted his readings to impart to us some newly acquired gem. One day he told us he had come across the word *apostasy* but hadn't bothered to look it up as he had no fear of encountering it again. He was implying that if an English teacher looked up every unknown word he came across, he'd spend half his waking hours poring myopically over the dictionary. Smiling, he then permitted us to nod our heads in acquiescence to his canniness. He beamed. Then he did something unforgivable. Having admitted to not comprehending a word known to most high school seniors, he suddenly chose to group his teachers within the limits of his own scant vision. "Do any of you know the meaning of the word?" he challenged. The silence was awesome. Everyone stared at the floor. I don't know why I chose to speak. It would be the last time I ever did so at a meeting. I defined the word, trying to speak in a matter-of-fact, self-disparaging way, as though I were admitting that nobody but a fool or a freak would know the meaning of such an esoteric work. "Apostasy," I said, "is the disavowal of previously avowed principles." And, oh lord, my impatient, querulous, pompous voice too clearly reflected the long weeks of my anguish at these sessions. Led by the theatrical *grande dame*, all heads cranked round to peer in utter astonishment and loathing at me, loathing not only for having committed the gaffe of entering a discussion but for suggesting that the world wasn't, after all, bordered by the town signs proclaiming Glacial Falls.

Though distressing, these problems seemed not invincible; and I had hopes that by going my own way I could do a good job despite my surroundings. I was wrong. In the Glacial Falls teacher's manual, a booklet I had been assured was Biblical in its authority (chiseled in stone), I one day came across a high-toned and vague clause (very much like a paragraph in any education textbook) calling on teachers to pass with the grade of C any student who was "working to capacity"—a capacity one could, I guessed immediately, determine from the IQ records in the guidance office. With a number of seasoned teachers in the system I tried to discuss this clause, but they seemed reluctant to talk about it—more than reluctant, tired, very tired, as though the clause had been discussed all too many times. There were some obvious questions needing answers. What about the superior student who doesn't make any effort but still manages to get a B? Reversing the principle, do I give him a C, and if I do, does that C, in the eyes of the administration, represent the same as the C of a student capable of doing only 40, 30, 20, percent of the work?

"What the clause means," one young and spirited teacher said finally, winking outrageously, "is that *everybody, but everybody, daddy,* passes."

That outrageous wink answered everything. Through some impossible-to-administer policy, the faculty had been rendered moral monsters. Asked to keep one eye open, cool and detached, in appraising half the students, we were to keep the other eye winking as the rest of the students were passed from grade to grade and eventually into a world that would be all too happy to teach them, as they drifted churlishly from disappointment to disaster, what the school should have been teaching them all along: that even in America *failure is a part of life.* (At Glacial Falls, the *F* had been eliminated altogether on the genteel assumption that the *D,* the—in *Newspeak*—"unpassing" grade, somehow represented a less equivocal failure.) In the end, of course, the policy didn't hurt the student nearly so much as the teacher: a wink eventually becomes a twitch, a twitch the sign of some inner disturbance. Still, everything had now been solved for me. I would go through the motions of teaching and try to prevent my students' believing my contempt was leveled at them. Not succeeding, I found that by the Thanksgiving holiday the majority of my students despised me, I loathed them, and we moved warily about each other snarling like antic cats. So I went each weekend to Watertown to drink and come alive those Sunday afternoon hours before the television screen. At game's end I returned to Glacial Falls, where during the day I continued to snarl and be snarled at, and where during the evening in the isolation of my bleak, eight-dollar room, I fell with incredible ease into profound and lengthy sleep. Occasionally sleeping as much as fourteen hours, I rose as though great lead weights were tied to me and returned to the agitation of the classroom.

But the weeks passed with paradoxical swiftness. It was as if they were no more than prolonged slumbers burdened by nightmares populated with pimple-picking, gum-chewing, pea-brained, sex-overwhelmed adolescents. When I awoke, perspiring, I was in Watertown standing at the bar of the Crystal Restaurant, drinking a beer and looking across the bar at Leo, who was one of the owners and whom I had known since childhood. Occasionally I drank two or three before the perspiration dried and I could speak to him. Then I would say, "How the

Giants going to make out Sunday, Leo?" Having known the question would come, Leo would smile. With that question life would begin again. The nightmare of the week was over.

Why did football bring me so to life? I can't say precisely. Part of it was my feeling that football was an island of directness in a world of circumspection. In football a man was asked to do a difficult and brutal job, and he either did it or got out. There was nothing rhetorical or vague about it; I chose to believe that it was not unlike the jobs which all men, in some sunnier past, had been called upon to do. It smacked of something old, something traditional, something unclouded by legerdemain and subterfuge. It had that kind of power over me, drawing me back with the force of something known, scarcely remembered, elusive as integrity—perhaps it was no more than the force of a forgotten childhood. Whatever it was, I gave myself up to the Giants utterly. The recompense I gained was the feeling of being alive.

THE CHOICE OF The Parrot as a place to view the games was not an arbitrary one. There had been a time, some two or three seasons before, when I had been able to bounce up and down—shouting, "Oh, God, he did it! Gifford did it! He caught the goddam thing!"—in any place, in any company, and feel neither timidity nor embarrassment. But as one year had engulfed another, and still another, each bringing with it its myriad defeats, as I had come to find myself relying on the Giants as a life-giving, an exalting force, I found myself unable to relax in the company of "unbelievers," in the company of those who did not take their football earnestly or who thought my team something less than the One God. At those times, in those alien places, I felt like a holy man attempting to genuflect amidst a gang of drunken, babbling, mocking heretics. I tried a number of places in Watertown before settling on The Parrot; though it was not exactly the cathedral I would have wished for, it was—like certain old limestone churches scattered throughout the north country—not without its quaint charms. It was ideally isolated on a hill above the city; siting at the bar I was seldom aware of the city's presence, and when I was, I could think of it as a nostalgic place beneath me, a place with elm trees and church towers and bone-clean streets; sitting at the bar, the city could be thought of as a place remembered, and remembered as if from a great distance.

This distance was important to me. For a long time I had been unable to engage my home town with any degree of openness. What friends I had had were married, raising families, and had locked themselves, ever so tightly, behind their neat-trimmed lawns and white clapboard houses, their children cute, their wives sexless and anxious, my friends plotting their next moves to achieve the Black River Valley Club, never asking themselves what, if they achieved that—the town's most venerable institution—could possibly be left for them. My friends and I had long proved an embarrassment to one another; I embarrassing them because I drank too much, was unreliable in my debts and working habits, and had been "hospitalized" a number of times; I embarrassed because they were. We never stopped each other on the streets without, eyes avoiding mine, their patronizing me with queries about my health. It was distressing because there was a kind of gloating—undoubtedly a good deal imagined on my part—in these encounters, as though they were telling me that getting myself proclaimed mad and dragged away a number of times was only a childish and petulant refusal to accept their way of life as the right way, that in seeking some other way I had been assuming a courage and superiority I hadn't possessed. After a time these encounters had proved so painful that whenever I found myself compelled to move about the streets in daylight hours, I dropped my eyes to the sidewalk and charged through the streets as though in a hot-brained hurry. A dim-lighted haven for inarticulate young men and women who arrived in the late hours of the evening and, throwing themselves together in mock couplings, struggled energetically about the dance floor to the plaintive, standard tunes rendered by a local trio, a piano, a drum, a first-rate horn, The Parrot was not a place where I feared encountering any of my "friends." Most of these young people I knew by name or by sight, and I felt comfortable with them. They took me for what I was, a youngish-old teacher from Glacial Falls, one who drank too much and who was a little tetched on the subject of the Giants; but they seemed to like me and didn't appear to begrudge me that I was without the desire to achieve the Black River Valley Club. Sunday afternoons were different. Then, with the music stilled and the blinds thrown open allowing the golden autumn sunlight to diffuse and warm the room, I would stand at the bar and sip my Budweiser, my "tapering-off" device; munch popcorn from wooden bowls; and in league with the bartender Freddy, whose allegiance to the Giants was only somewhat less feverish than mine, cheer my team home. Invariably and desperately I wished that the afternoon, the game, the light would never end.

On the night of the tenth—the night before the "seizure"—I stayed late at the bar, drinking heavily and talking with B., a grieving young man of twenty. Having recently been rejected by a girl he loved, he was in a state near hyperesthesia. I don't know why he chose to burden me with his lament. I did not know him well. In high school his brother and I had played football and basketball together; we had at the same time, or I would guess that we had, taken long aching looks at the same girls who were, in some celestial way, blossoming right before our eyes, so that we must once have been "almost friends." But a few years before, when I was without a job, drinking and drifting, I had borrowed twenty dollars from that brother; and many months later, when I

had attempted to repay him, he had steadfastly refused the
money, saying, "If the tables had been reversed, buddy, I know
you'd have helped me." He had said this with a certain "style,"
as though he were not trying to prove how well he was doing in
business (and he was doing well); but *still*—we could, of course,
never again be "almost friends." Perhaps B. had heard his
brother speak of me, and this coupled with my teacher image and
the flecks of gray at my temples, led him to assume that I had
answers, a conclusion that was not without its irony. In the inner
pocket of my jacket was the letter from my wife—"until we are
much more firmly settled on our separate roads"—and only
moments before B. slithered up to me and said, "Jesus, Ex, I
can't eat or nothin'," in an alcoholic fury I had telephoned long-
distance to my wife and got my sister-in-law, who, refusing to call
my wife to the phone, had prompted me to shout "Fuck you!" into
the wire. All I had wanted to do was conform to the role—that of
the drama's villain—my sister-in-law had assigned to me; and
after I had hung up the receiver, and until B. approached me, I
had stood at the bar chuckling pensively at the thought of my sister-in-law's hysterically indignant *I-told-you-so's*. Because I was
unhappy I offered B. no easy consolation. While he kept saying,
"Oh, Jesus, Ex, *Jesus H. Keeriiisst, don't tell me that,*" I told him
the ordeal of my own first love, how it had taken me two years to
alleviate the pain, how I had risen with it, gone to bed with it, and
lived with it all my waking hours until, accepting its naturalness,
it had begun to recede. Doubtless B. thought I was being cruel;
and I really knew no way of convincing him otherwise. I told him
I wished that when I was his age I had sought out some dismal
creature for advice. Having gone to fat-assed, "successful" souls
(making the American mistake of equating success with wisdom),
I was glibly assured that "you'll get over it"; and when I did not, I
despised myself for what I deemed a flimsiness of heart. Seeing a
younger version of myself in B.'s wild eyes, I offered him all I

could. "Look, B., accept your pain as a part of life. There is, really, absolutely no consolation in telling you that I or any man has undergone the same thing. And then, how would I know I've suffered anywhere near what you're going through? And not knowing that, isn't any advice I give you presumptuous?"

We drank together until closing time, one whisky after another, our heads bent close together. We talked through the velvety blue smoke, whispering about isolation and loss; with our sibilant voices we were trying to protect the privacy of our hearts from the ears all about us. Presently the lurid white lights, with almost a violent snap, caught us cheek-to-cheek and Freddy was shouting, "You don't have to go home, gang—*but you can't stay here!*" Reluctantly I rose, finished my drink, put on my raincoat, and walked to the door to wait. B. had moved quickly down the bar and was attempting to pick up a young, snub-nosed, and attractive girl who frequented the place. He picked her up, too; and I had to admire the ease with which he did it, speaking only a few words to her. He was a handsome, sensitive boy, and watching him so facilely "move" the girl I wondered what that other girl was searching for, the one who had tossed him over. The three of us left together. We drove around town for an hour or so nipping on B.'s bottle, then went to an all-night diner, The Red Moon. We had been looking for a girl friend of snub-nose's, one who was, without my being consulted in the matter, supposed to be my date. We found her at The Red Moon. Before getting back into the car, I drew myself up, unzipped my fly, and stood in the middle of the street taking an enormous piss. A car tooted at me, swerved erratically, and just missed me. Speaking out of the corner of her mouth, my new date said, "Jeez, I ain't going with that crazy bastard!" As she was going back into the diner to her leather-jacketed friends, she added, "Some schoolteacher!"

B., the snub-nosed girl, and I ended up at my motel room, where, getting me alone in the bathroom, B. offered me what he called "first shot" at the girl. I declined, thanking him rather too profusely. I fell asleep that night listening to their mating noises from the adjoining bed. My initiation into sex had taken place on the ground behind a billboard sign advertising beer within walking distance from where I was now lying. The girl had received, with neither complaint nor enthusiasm, a good part of Watertown High School's 1945 football team. Afterward I had had to help her up and walk her, while she clung unsteadily to my arm and wept, to her house some distance down the highway. Listening now, it occurred to me that I hadn't come very far over the years—no farther really than from one "gang bang" to another, save that I had learned, as B. had yet to learn, that tomorrow the pain would be even greater.

from *Mohawk*

Vintage Contemporaries first began publishing Richard Russo in 1986 with his debut novel,
Mohawk. *Admired for his keen ability to perform the high-wire walk between hilarity and
heartache, Russo is the author of three other witty and compassionate novels:* The Risk Pool;
Nobody's Fool, *which was made into an acclaimed film starring Paul Newman; and* Straight Man,
forthcoming from Vintage Contemporaries in August 1998.

DALLAS YOUNGER GRUNTED loudly and rolled over in bed. He had
been dreaming vividly and wanted to go back to sleep so he could
find out how the dream ended up. Not knowing would bother him
the rest of the day. He'd waste a lot of time trying to remember the
dream's details, examining them for clues, until consciousness
finally banished the whole thing. Dallas never paid any attention
to completed dreams, but fragments were worrisome.

The alarm clock on his nightstand was quivering and buzzing
weakly, the way it always did when he allowed it to ring for a long
time before shutting it off. Dallas opened one eye and peeked at
the clock suspiciously, not wanting to believe, at least not yet,
that he had overslept again. Then a horrible idea struck him and
he ran his tongue along the roof of his palate, encountering there
nothing but gum. Unwilling to accept the evidence of a mere
tongue which, now that he thought about it, tasted suspiciously
rancid, he stuck his index finger into this mouth and felt around.
No doubt about it. His bridge was gone again.

When he heard something in the hall outside his apartment,
he vaulted out of bed. This was the third bridge he had lost in as
many months, and it occurred to him now with startling clarity

that someone had to be stealing them, actually sneaking into his room and removing them as he slept. Benny D., in all likelihood, as a practical joke. It wouldn't be difficult, for Dallas always slept with his mouth open, one of a dozen personal habits Anne had irrationally held against him, as if he had control over them. He ran to the door and flung it open in time to discover his neighbor, Mrs. Nicolella, after locking the door to her flat, deposit something into her purse. Whatever it was sounded to Dallas Younger a little like teeth, and he regarded the woman suspiciously.

What Mrs. Nicolella saw when she looked up was a thirty-six-year-old man, naked, who looked like he had just awakened with something on his mind. Something to do with her, a middle-aged widow woman, living alone, except when her daughter visited, which was practically never.

For his own part, Dallas became aware of two things simultaneously: first, that he had no clothes on; and second, that Mrs. Nicolella was no teeth thief. The expression on her face was ample testimony. "My teeth," Dallas tried to explain, having difficulty with the *th* sound.

"Your what?" said Mrs. Nicolella, confused, expecting from the naked man another sort of communication entirely.

"Teeth," Dallas repeated. This time the sound he made more closely approximated his meaning, and he succeeded in reducing at least one level of his neighbor's confusion.

"You aren't wearing any," she reported. Then, seeing that he still eyed her purse, his brain refusing to surrender completely the sound it had first recognized as that of falling teeth, she opened the purse wide so he could see. No teeth.

Back in his apartment, Dallas commenced a thorough search of the premises, though he knew in advance it would be futile. He was thinking more clearly now and the former certainty that his teeth had been stolen began to seem rash. His two-room flat was easy to search. Once he examined the sink and shower, stripped the sofa sleeper and plunged his hands down along the seams, he was more or less finished. His quest was not without its immediate rewards, however, for he found, among other things, his nail clippers, a dollar and a half in change, and a paperback Mickey Spillane, its spine broken and pages falling out. But nothing even vaguely porcelain. He gathered up the Spillane and put it in the trash, figuring that if the urge to finish the book ever became unbearable he could pick up another copy. This particular edition had disappeared months ago without his noticing, so that was unlikely. In the long run he would probably worry more about how his unfinished dream was supposed to come out. In the closet by the hall door he went through the pockets of all his clothes, clean and dirty, finding a number of interesting things but not what he was looking for. Giving up, he put on the only clean workshirt in the closet—this one happened to have *Cal* stitched in script over the pocket—and made a mental note that it was time to do his laundry. The last two days he had worn shirts with other people's names on them, and that was a sure sign he was running low on everything.

Actually, the loss of his teeth was not tragic this time, since he had displayed uncustomary foresight in ordering a spare set the last time he woke up toothless. The spares he found in their pink case in the medicine cabinet where he had stashed them behind the bottle of Old Spice someone had given him two Christmases ago and which he'd been meaning to use. He slipped the bridge in place and it fit perfectly, even better than the old one. Instead of angry and embarrassed, he began to feel pleased with himself for the way he had providently provided against mischance.

Since he was already late for work, he decided to stop and see his brother's widow, remembering, for some reason, that today was his niece's birthday. Mother and daughter lived in a small, square house on the outskirts of town near Mohawk Sand and Gravel. Dallas parked at the curb, since the driveway was strewn with children's toys. Although they had been married in their teens, Loraine and Dallas's younger brother David didn't have their child until they were in their late twenties, after they had just about given up. David was so excited about the baby that he spent every spare penny on his daughter, not that there were so many pennies to spare. When Dawn was one and he discovered he had cancer, David went a little crazy, taking out a substantial loan so he could buy the little girl twenty years' worth of presents. They filled up the walk-in closet of the spare bedroom, each package wrapped and dated: Merry Christmas 1985; Happy Birthday 1987. Loraine had shown Dallas the closet the day after David's funeral, and he remembered the way she had stared blankly at all the brightly wrapped gifts, still awed, perhaps, by her husband's great need to enter and enrich his daughter's life over the long years from the grave.

Dallas found Dawn swinging in the back yard, her white-sneakered feet straight out in front of her. She didn't quite have the hang of pumping but was doing the best she could. When she saw her uncle, the little girl scuffed to a stop and ran up to meet him. "Pow!" she said, poking him in the forehead with her index finger when he picked her up.

"How old are you?" he said.

"Two old."

"I'm the one that's too old, you knucklehead. Besides, you're three old today. Don't you know you own birthday?"

Loraine then appeared at the screen door and studied her brother-in-law wearily. She was still in her bathrobe. Actually, it looked like it might have been David's. "You again," she said, holding the door open for Dallas to come in without having to set his niece down.

"That's a nice hello after you don't see me for a month."

Loraine cocked her head and frowned at him suspiciously. "You were here last night in case you forgot. Three in the morning."

Dallas did not know whether to believe her or not. He had no recollection of visiting his sister-in-law last night, but then he had next to no recollection of last night. For some reason though, when he first saw her standing there on the other side of the screen, he had imagined—could it have been a memory?—that she had been wearing a nightgown, the shadowy outline of her breasts just visible behind the fabric. Dallas tried to think why he should have imagined such a sight. "What would I have been doing here," he asked, genuinely curious.

"You were drunk. I told you to get lost. You really don't remember?"

"Did I have my teeth?"

Loraine shot him a pained look that contained little sympathy. "Not again. . . ."

Dallas nodded, pulling a chair from the kitchen table, and sat, the little girl still on his lap. Dawn pulled up her dress to show him her panties, which featured an embroidered pig. She leaned back as far as she could, her knees high in the air, so he could have the full benefit of the pig. "Will you take me to Chickey Fried Chicken?"

"You mean the Kentucky Colonel? All the way to Schenectady?"

Dawn nodded eagerly and smoothed her dress back down.

"At times I still can't believe you and David were brothers," Loraine said.

"Uncle Dallas says it's my birfday."

"How would he know? He doesn't even know where his teeth are." Loraine squinted at him. "What are those in your mouth?"

"Spares. You mean it's not her birthday?"

"You insisted the same thing last night. It isn't till the middle of the month."

"And I had my teeth?"

"It was three in the morning, Dallas. I don't remember. Though I think I would have noticed if you didn't."

Since there now appeared to be a consensus that today was not her birthday, Dawn squirmed down from her uncle's lap and went to her mother, clutching her robe with one hand, inserting the other, nearly the whole fist, in her own mouth.

"Come back here."

"No," the little girl said, coyly refusing to look at him.

"What was that on your underwear?"

"Pig," said Dawn through her fist.

"I don't believe it," Dallas said, but his niece refused to take the bait.

"Go back outside if you're going to sulk," her mother said. "And take your hand out of your mouth."

When Dawn didn't obey, Loraine removed it. "Don't want to go outside," Dawn whined, her eyes filling with tears. "It's my birf-day."

"Thanks a lot," Loraine said.

"Come here," Dallas clapped his hands. "Be my girl." But instead the child ran outside and let the screen door slam behind her. In a minute the swing squeaked into motion.

"I could make you some eggs," Loraine offered.

Dallas shook his head. "I'm late for work."

He didn't object to the cup of coffee, though, which Loraine poured without asking him. "Then I lost them someplace between here and home. Assuming I went home."

"You promised you would," Loraine said. "You were talking about stopping by the grave, but I made you promise not to."

Dallas frowned. "Grave. What grave?"

"Your brother's. Whose do you think?" She sat down opposite him and put the cream pitcher between them.

"Why would I go there?"

"You were in one of your maudlin moods. I really wish you'd stay away when you get like that. I feel the same way half the time myself, and I don't need any encouragement."

Dallas said he was sorry, and he was, too, though in much the same way he was sorry about a rainy day or something else he had no control over. When he drank too much, he nearly always blacked out and had to depend on people to tell him what he'd been up to, and because he was often told that he became senti-mental at such times, he supposed it must be true, though he couldn't say for sure.

"My daughter doesn't need to be woke up in the middle of the night either," Loraine went on. "She's got enough on her mind. She's been scared as hell ever since David."

"Scared of what?"

"She doesn't know. Who ever needed a reason?"

Loraine looked a little scared herself right then, and Dallas felt ashamed of his behavior. He wished he could remember his behavior, so he could feel even worse about it. It wasn't fair that Loraine should feel frightened, and even more unfair that little Dawn should be. When he finished his coffee, Loraine quickly cleared the cups and saucers, and he watched her at the sink, trying to think if there was something he could do for her or the little girl. He had promised his brother he would do what he could for them, but even at the time he hadn't any idea what that might be.

Loraine rinsed the cups in the sink and dried them carefully with a thin dish towel before putting them back in the cupboard. When she and David had married, Loraine was a very pretty girl with soft skin and lovely brown hair. People had wondered out loud how such a shy, studious boy like David had done so well, especially since in addition to being pretty Loraine had a reputa-tion for being a little wild. Those who made book on other people's chances gave them long odds. But David was kind and attentive, qualities that were more or less new to Loraine and that she discovered she liked. According to those who knew her best, she simply changed overnight, returning her husband's devotion as if, without a word of discussion, he had somehow convinced her to forget about wildness in favor of himself and the life he had to offer, which was pleasant and satisfying if not always terribly exciting.

Loraine also discovered early in their marriage that there was nothing she could do to alter his love for her, and when she first noticed that she'd put on a few pounds, that the curves of her body were straightening, she refused to be disappointed in herself. Since he didn't appear to notice the way she was thickening, she repaid the favor by telling herself that she did not mind her young husband's receding hairline, nor that the drain was always full of his dark hair after he showered. Only Dallas, who often visited them on Sundays, made her feel a little self-conscious about her appearance, because he was an unmerciful tease. After a while, though, he stopped ribbing her. She never knew why. At first she thought maybe David made him stop, but then a more plausible explanation occurred to her—that Dallas stopped the ribbing when what he was saying became too true to be good fun any more. She had got very big with Dawn and somehow never quite lost the shapelessness of postpregnancy. Now she thought it might be nice if Dallas would start teasing her again, but he never did. When he commented at all, it was to say that she looked well, and since she knew that wasn't true, the compliment had the opposite effect of what was intended.

Indeed, as he watched her at the sink, he did feel bad for Loraine. With her husband gone and more than half her life ahead of her, it seemed to him that she needed to be prettier than she was. "So," he said when she turned around and discovered him looking at her, "how are you making out?"

She dried her hands on the dish towel and looped it through the refrigerator door handle. "Fine. How can you look at these lavish surroundings and ask such a question?" Her sweeping gesture included not just the kitchen, but the rest of the house, the yard, the neighborhood, and probably all of Mohawk.

"I'm serious," Dallas said, feeling immediately the silliness of his remark, since Loraine was obviously serious too. Her attitude in this respect was inexplicable to him, partly because her surroundings *were* quite lavish compared to his. Admittedly, there was a threadbare quality to the house. Even when David was alive, they had been forced by necessity to make do with things until they were used up. Now what had once been simply thin was close to transparent, like the dish towel Loraine had used to dry her hands. But that was one of the things Dallas had always liked about his brother's house. Dallas himself never wore anything out. He lost it before wear-and-tear became an issue. His clothing was never ragged, because when he went to the laundromat he always managed to leave at least one load in one of the machines. Loss was perhaps the central feature of his existence, and he had learned to accept it the way one does a scraped knuckle or skinned knee. In the long run things equaled out anyway. For every load of clothing he forgot in the washing machine, he gained another in the dryer. Tumbling towels and shirts inside one dryer often bore a striking resemblance to those in the next, and more than once Dallas had discovered, after shoving the spun-dry contents into his duffle bag and going home, that it was some other man's wardrobe he had inherited. Provided the clothes fit, or near enough, Dallas was content and his life various.

Only when he visited his brother's house and saw the sameness of things, the continuity of familiar objects, did he feel keenly dissatisfied with the lack of control he exercised over his daily affairs. He had always liked Loraine's house and was more comfortable there than just about any place he knew, except maybe the track or Greenie's Tavern after work. He was so comfortable in his brother's house that he disliked even the smallest changes or additions, and on those rare occasions when Loraine bought something small and bright and new for the house, he couldn't help but wonder what she wanted with it. Fortunately, she wasn't one of those women who liked to move furniture around. She was far too sensible to suppose that rearranging resulted in improvement.

"You never see anything," she told him, "but the whole place needs work. The cold seeps in everywhere during the winter. The lower cabinets are rotting where the plumbing leaks. None of the doors hang right anymore. I can't even close the one in the bathroom. Not that it matters."

"I could—" Dallas began.

"Don't go making offers. I'm just fed up, that's all."

"I—"

"Don't," she insisted. "You'll promise and then half an hour from now you'll forget, and then I'll dislike you for a while until I forget. Then in a few weeks you'll remember and be mad at yourself until you forget again. So spare us both."

Dallas could tell that she was already angry with him, and he knew, of course, that what she said was true.

from *The Sportswriter*

Considered one of the most important writers of his generation, Richard Ford is the author of five novels, among them A Piece of My Heart, The Ultimate Good Luck, and Wildlife, as well as a volume of short stories, Rock Springs, and, most recently, a collection of three novellas, Women With Men, all available from Vintage Contemporaries. His 1995 novel Independence Day won both the Pulitzer Prize and the PEN/Faulkner Award. Its main character, Frank Bascombe, first appeared in Ford's 1986 novel, The Sportswriter. Richard Ford is at work on a new novel, forthcoming from Knopf.

MY NAME IS Frank Bascombe. I am a sportswriter.

For the past fourteen years I have lived here at 19 Hoving Road, Haddam, New Jersey, in a large Tudor house bought when a book of short stories I wrote sold to a movie producer for a lot of money, and seemed to set my wife and me and our three children—two of whom were not even born yet—up for a good life.

Just exactly what that good life was—the one I expected—I cannot tell you now exactly, though I wouldn't say it has not come to pass, only that much has come in between. I am no longer married to X, for instance. The child we had when everything was starting has died, though there are two others, as I mentioned, who are alive and wonderful children.

I wrote half of a short novel soon after we moved here from New York and then put it in the drawer, where it has been ever since, and from which I don't expect to retrieve it unless something I cannot now imagine happens.

Twelve years ago, when I was twenty-six, and in the blind way of things then, I was offered a job as a sportswriter by the editor of a glossy New York sports magazine you have all heard of, because of a free-lance assignment I had written in a particular way he liked. And to my surprise and everyone else's I quit writing my novel and accepted.

And since then I have worked at nothing but that job, with the exception of vacations, and one three-month period after my son died when I considered a new life and took a job as an instructor in a small private school in western Massachusetts where I ended up not liking things, and couldn't wait to leave and get back here to New Jersey and writing sports.

My life over these twelve years has not been and isn't now a bad one at all. In most ways it's been great. And although the older I get the more things scare me, and the more apparent it is to me that bad things can and do happen to you, very little really worries me or keeps me up at night. I still believe in the possibilities of passion and romance. And I would not change much, if anything at all. I might not choose to get divorced. And my son, Ralph Bascombe, would not die. But that's about it for these matters.

Why, you might ask, would a man give up a promising literary career—there were some good notices—to become a sportswriter?

It's a good question. For now let me say only this: if sportswriting teaches you anything, and there is much truth to it as well as plenty of lies, it is that for your life to be worth anything you must sooner or later face the possibility of terrible, searing regret. Though you must also manage to avoid it or your life will be ruined.

I believe I have done these two things. Faced down regret. Avoided ruin. And I am still here to tell about it.

I HAVE CLIMBED over the metal fence to the cemetery directly behind my house. It is five o'clock on Good Friday morning, April 20. All other houses in the neighborhood are shadowed, and I am waiting for my ex-wife. Today is my son Ralph's birthday. He would be thirteen and starting manhood. We have met here these last two years, early, before the day is started, to pay our respects to him. Before that we would simply come over together as man and wife.

A spectral fog is lifting off the cemetery grass, and high up in the low atmosphere I hear the wings of geese pinging. A police car has murmured in through the gate, stopped, cut its lights and placed me under surveillance. I saw a match flare briefly inside the car, saw the policeman's face looking at a clipboard.

At the far end of the "new part" a small deer gazes at me where I wait. Now and then its yellow tapetums blink out of the dark toward the old part, where the trees are larger, and where three signers of the Declaration of Independence are buried in sight of my son's grave.

My next-door neighbors, the Deffeyes, are playing tennis, calling their scores in hushed-polite early-morning voices. "Sorry." "Thanks." "Forty-love." Pock. Pock. Pock. "*Ad* to you, dear." "Yes, thank you." "Yours." Pock, pock. I hear their harsh, thrashing nose breaths, their feet scraping. They are into their eighties and no longer need sleep, and so are up at all hours. They have installed glowless barium-sulphur lights that don't shine in my yard and keep me awake. And we have stayed good neighbors if not close friends. I have nothing much in common with them now, and am invited to few of their or anyone else's cocktail parties. People in town are still friendly in a distant way, and I consider them fine people, conservative, decent.

It is not, I have come to understand, easy to have a divorced man as your neighbor. Chaos lurks in him—the viable social contract called into question by the smoky aspect of sex. Most people feel they have to make a choice and it is always easier to choose the wife, which is what my neighbors and friends have mostly done. And though we chitter-chatter across the driveways and hedges and over the tops of each other's cars in the parking lots of grocery stores, remarking on the condition of each other's

soffits and down-drains and the likelihood of early winter, sometimes make tentative plans to get together, I hardly ever see
them, and I take it in my stride.

Good Friday today is a special day for me, apart from the other
specialness. When I woke in the dark this morning, my heart
pounding like a tom-tom, it seemed to me as though a change
were on its way, as if this dreaminess tinged with expectation,
which I have felt for some time now, were lifting off of me into the
cool tenebrous dawn.

Today I'm leaving town for Detroit to begin a profile of a
famous ex-football player who lives in the city of Walled Lake,
Michigan, and is confined to a wheelchair since a waterskiing
accident, but who has become an inspiration to his former team-
mates by demonstrating courage and determination, going back
to college, finishing his degree in communications arts, marrying
his black physiotherapist and finally becoming honorary chap-
lain for his old team. "Make a contribution" will be my angle. It
is the kind of story I enjoy and find easy to write.

Anticipation rises higher, however, because I'm taking my
new girlfriend Vicki Arcenault with me. She has recently moved
up to New Jersey from Dallas, but I am already pretty certain I'm
in love with her (I haven't mentioned anything about it for fear of
making her wary). Two months ago, when I sliced up my thumb
sharpening a lawnmower blade in my garage, it was Nurse Arcenault who stitched me up in the ER at Doctors Hospital, and
things have gone on from there. She did her training at Baylor in
Waco, and came up here when her marriage gave out. Her family,
in fact, lives down in Barnegat Pines, not far away, in a subdivi-
sion close to the ocean, and I am scheduled to be exhibit A at
Easter dinner—a vouchsafe to them that she has made a successful transition to the northeast, found a safe and good-hearted
man, and left bad times including her dagger-head husband
Everett far behind. Her father, Wade, is a toll-taker at Exit 9 on
the Turnpike, and I cannot expect he will like the difference in

our ages. Vicki is thirty. I am thirty-eight. He himself is only in his fifties. But I am in hopes of winning him over and eager as can be under the circumstances. Vicki is a sweet, saucy little black-hair with a delicate width of cheekbone, a broad Texas accent and a matter-of-factness with her raptures that can make a man like me cry out in the night for longing.

You should never think that leaving a marriage sets you loose for cheery womanizing and some exotic life you'd never quite grasped before. Far from true. No one can do that for long. The Divorced Men's Club I belong to here in town has proven that to me if nothing else—we don't talk much about women when we are together and feel relieved just to be men alone. What leaving a marriage released me—and most of us—to, was celibacy and more fidelity than I had ever endured before, though with no one convenient to be faithful to or celibate for. Just a long empty moment. Though everyone should live alone at some time in a life. Not like when you're a kid, summers, or in a single dorm room in some crappy school. But when you're grown up. *Then* be alone. It can be all right. You can end up more within yourself, as the best athletes are, which is worth it. (A basketball player who goes for his patented outside jumper becomes nothing more than the simple wish personified that the ball go in the hole.) In any case, doing the brave thing isn't easy and isn't supposed to be. I do my work and do it well and remain expectant of the best without knowing in the least what it will be. And the bonus is that a little bundle like Nurse Arcenault seems sent straight from heaven.

For several months now I have not taken a trip, and the magazine has found plenty for me to do in New York. It was stated in court by X's sleaze-ball lawyer, Alan, that my travel was the cause of our trouble, especially after Ralph died. And though that isn't technically true—it was a legal reason X and I invented together—it is true that I have always loved the travel that accompanies my job. Vicki has only seen two landscapes in her entire life: the flat, featureless gloom-prairies around Dallas, and New Jersey—a strange unworldliness these days. But I will soon show her the midwest, where old normalcy floats heavy on the humid air, and where I happen to have gone to college.

It is true that much of my sportswriter's work is exactly what you would think: flying in airplanes, arriving and departing airports, checking into and out of downtown hotels, waiting hours in corridors and locker rooms, renting cars, confronting unfriendly bellmen. Late night drinks in unfamiliar bars, up always before dawn, as I am this morning, trying to get a perspective on things. But there is also an assurance to it that I don't suppose I could live happily without. Very early you come to the realization that nothing will ever take you away from yourself. But in these literal and anonymous cities of the nation, your Milwaukees, your St. Louises, your Seattles, your Detroits, even your New Jerseys, something hopeful and unexpected can take place. A woman I met at the college where I briefly taught, once told me I had too many choices, that I was not driven enough by dire necessity. But that is just an illusion and her mistake. Choices are what we all need. And when I walk out into the bricky warp of these American cities, that is exactly what I feel. Choices aplenty. Things I don't know anything about but might like are here, possibly waiting for me. Even if they aren't. The exhilaration of a new arrival. Good light in a restaurant that especially pleases you. A cab driver with an interesting life history to tell. The casual, lilting voice of a woman you don't know, but that you are allowed to listen to in a bar you've never been in, at a time when you would otherwise have been alone. These things are waiting for you. And what could be better? More mysterious? More worth anticipating? Nothing. Not a thing.

THE BARIUM-SULPHUR lights die out over the Deffeyes' tennis court. Delia Deffeyes' patient and troubleless voice, still hushed, begins assuring her husband Caspar that he played well, while they walk toward their dark house in their pressed whites.

The sky has become a milky eye and though it is spring and nearly Easter, the morning has a strangely winter cast to it, as though a high fog is blotting its morning stars. There is no moon at all.

The policeman has finally seen enough and idles out the cemetery gate onto the silent streets. I hear a paper slap on a sidewalk. Far off, I hear the commuter train up to New York making its belling stop at our station—always a consoling sound.

X's brown Citation stops at the blinking red light at Constitution Street, across from the new library, then inches along the cemetery fence on Plum Road, her lights on high beam. The deer has vanished. I walk over to meet her.

X is an old-fashioned, solidly Michigan girl from Birmingham, whom I met in Ann Arbor. Her father, Henry, was a Soapy Williams best-of-his-generation liberal who still owns a plant that stamps out rubber gaskets for a giant machine that stamps out car fenders, though he is now a Republican and rich as a Pharaoh. Her mother, Irma, lives in Mission Viejo, and the two of them are divorced, though her mother still writes me regularly and believes X and I will eventually reconcile, which seems as possible as anything else.

X could choose to move back to Michigan if she wanted to, buy a condominium or a ranch-style home or move out onto the estate her father owns. We discussed it at the divorce, and I did not object. But she has too much pride and independence to move home now. In addition, she is firmly behind the idea of family and wants Paul and Clarissa to be near me, and I'm happy to think she has made a successful adjustment of her new life. Sometimes we do not really become adults until we suffer a good whacking loss, and our lives in a sense catch up with us and wash over us like a wave and everything goes.

Since our divorce she has bought a house in a less expensive but improving section of Haddam called The Presidents by the locals, and has taken a job as teaching pro at Cranbury Hills C.C. She co-captained the Lady Wolverines in college and has lately begun entering some of the local pro-ams, now that her short game has sharpened up, and even placed high in a couple last summer. I believe all her life she has had a yen to try something like this, and being divorced has given her the chance.

What was our life like? I almost don't remember now. Though I remember *it*, the space of time it occupied. And I remember it fondly.

I suppose our life was the generic one, as the poet said. X was a housewife and had babies, read books, played golf and had friends, while I wrote about sports and went here and there collecting my stories, coming home to write them up, mooning around the house for days in old clothes, taking the train to New York and back now and then. X seemed to take the best possible attitude to my being a sportswriter. She thought it was fine, or at least she said she did and seemed happy. She thought she had married a young Sherwood Anderson with movie possibilities, but it didn't bother her that it didn't turn out that way, and certainly never bothered me. I was happy as a swallow. We went on vacations with our three children. To Cape Cod (which Ralph called Cape God), to Searsport, Maine, to Yellowstone, to the Civil War battlefields at Antietam and Bull Run. We paid bills, shopped, went to movies, bought cars and cameras and insurance, cooked out, went to cocktail parties, visited schools, and romanced each other in the sweet, cagey way of adults. I looked out my window, stood in my yard sunsets with a sense of solace and achievement, cleaned my rain gutters, eyed my shingles, put up storms, fertilized regularly, computed my equity, spoke to my neighbors in an interested voice—the normal applauseless life of us all.

Though toward the end of our marriage I became lost in some dreaminess. Sometimes I would wake up in the morning and open my eyes to X lying beside me breathing, and not recognize her! Not even know what town I was in, or how old I was, or what life it was, so dense was I in my particular dreaminess. I would lie there and try as best I could to extend not knowing, feel that pleasant soaring-out-of-azimuth-and-attitude sensation I grew to like as long as it would last, while twenty possibilities for who, where, what went by. Until suddenly I would get it right and feel a sense of—what? Loss, I think you would say, though loss of what I don't know. My son had died, but I'm unwilling to say that was the cause, or that anything is ever the sole cause of anything else. I know that you can dream your way through an otherwise fine life, and never wake up, which is what I almost did. I believe I have survived that now and nearly put dreaminess behind me, though there is a resolute sadness between X and me that our marriage is over, a sadness that does not feel sad. It is the way you feel at a high school reunion when you hear an old song you used to like played late at night, only you are all alone.

X APPEARS OUT of the agate cemetery light, loose-gaited and sleepy, wearing deck shoes, baggy corduroys and an old London Fog I gave her years ago. Her hair has been cut short in a new-style way I like. She is a tall girl, big and brown-haired and pretty, who looks younger than she is, which is only thirty-seven. When we met fifteen years ago in New York, at a dreary book signing, she was modeling at a Fifth Avenue clothing store, and sometimes even now she has a tendency to slouch and walk about long-strided in a loose-limbed, toes-out way, though when she takes a square stance up over a golf ball, she can smack it a mile. In some ways she has become as much of a genuine athlete as anyone I know. Needless to say, I have the greatest admiration for her, and love her in every way but the strictest one. Sometimes I see her on the street in town or in her car without expecting to and without her knowing it, and I am struck by wonder: what can she want from life now? How could I have ever loved her and let her go.

"It's chilly, still," she says, in a small, firm voice when she is close enough to be heard, her hands stuffed down deep inside her raincoat. It is a voice I love. In many ways it was her voice I loved first, the sharpened midwestern vowels, the succinct glaciated syntax: Binton Herbor, himburg, Gren Repids. It is a voice that knows the minimum of what will suffice, and banks on it. In general I have always liked hearing women talk more than men.

I wonder, in fact, what my own voice will sound like. Will it be a convincing, truth-telling voice? Or a pseudo-sincere, phony, ex-husband one that will stir up trouble? I have a voice that is really mine, a frank, vaguely rural voice more or less like a used car salesman: a no-frills voice that hopes to uncover simple truth by a straight-on application of the facts. I used to practice it when I was in college. "Well, okay, look at it this way," I'd say right out loud. "All right, all right." "Yeah, but look here." As much as any, this constitutes my sportswriter voice, though I have stopped practicing by now.

X leans herself against the curved marble monument of a man named Craig—at a safe distance from me—and presses her lips inward. Up to this moment I have not noticed the cold. But now that she said it, I feel it in my bones and wish I'd worn a sweater.

These pre-dawn meetings were my idea, and in the abstract they seem like a good way for two people like us to share a remaining intimacy. In practice they are as uncomfortable as a hanging, and it's conceivable we will just forgo it next year, though we felt the same way last year. It is simply that I don't know how to mourn and neither does X. Neither of us has the vocabulary or temperament for it, and so we are more prone to pass the time chatting, which isn't always wise.

"Did Paul mention our rendezvous last night?" I say. Paul, my son, is ten. Last night I had an unexpected meeting with him standing in the dark street in front of his house, when his mother was inside and knew nothing of it, and I was lurking about outside. We had a talk about Ralph, and where he was and about how it might be possible to reach him—all of which caused me to go away feeling better. X and I agree in principle that I shouldn't sneak my visits, but this was not that way.

"He told me Daddy was sitting in the car in the dark watching the house like the police." She stares at me curiously.

"It was just an odd day. It ended up fine, though." It was in fact much more than an odd day.

"You could've come in. You're always welcome."

I smile a winning smile at her. "Another time I will." (Sometimes we do strange things and say they're accidents and coincidences, though I want her to believe it *was* a coincidence.)

"I just wondered if something was wrong," X says.

"No. I love him very much."

"Good," X says and sighs.

I have spoken in a voice that pleases me, a voice that is really mine.

X brings a sandwich bag out of her pocket, removes a hard-boiled egg and begins to peel it into the bag. We actually have little to say. We talk on the phone at least twice a week, mostly about the children, who visit me after school while X is still out on the teaching tee. Occasionally I bump into her in the grocery line, or take a table next to hers at the August Inn, and we will have a brief chairback chat. We have tried to stay a modern, divided family. Our meeting here is only by way of a memorial for an old life lost.

Still it is a good time to talk. Last year, for instance, X told me that if she had her life to live over again she would probably wait to get married and try to make a go of it on the LPGA tour. Her father had offered to sponsor her, she said, back in 1966—something she had never told me before. She did not say if she would marry me when the time came. But she did say she wished I had finished my novel, that it would have probably made things better, which surprised me. (She later took that back.) She also told me, without being particularly critical, that she considered me a loner, which surprised me too. She said that it was a mistake to have made as few superficial friends as I have done in my life, and to have concentrated only on the few things I have concentrated on—her, for one. My children, for another. Sportswriting and being an ordinary citizen. This did not leave me well enough armored for the unexpected, was her opinion. She said this was because I didn't know my parents very well, had gone to a military school, and grown up in the south, which was full of betrayers and secret-keepers and untrustworthy people, which I agree is true, though I never knew any of them. All that originated, she said, with the outcome of the Civil War. It was much better to have grown up, she said, as she did, in a place with no apparent character, where there is nothing ambiguous around to confuse you or complicate things, where the only thing anybody ever thought seriously about was the weather.

"Do you think you laugh enough these days?" She finishes peeling her egg and puts the sack down deep in her coat pocket. She knows about Vicki, and I've had one or two other girlfriends since our divorce that I'm sure the children have told her about. But I do not think she thinks they have turned my basic situation around much. And maybe she's right. In any case I am happy to have this apparently intimate, truth-telling conversation, something I do not have very often, and that a marriage can really be good for.

"You bet I do," I say. "I think I'm doing all right, if that's what you mean."

"I suppose it is," X says, looking at her boiled egg as if it posed a small but intriguing problem. "I'm not really worried about you." She raises her eyes at me in an appraising way. It's possible my talk with Paul last night has made her think I've gone off my bearings or started drinking.

"I watch Johnny. He's good for a laugh," I say. "I think he gets funnier as I get older. But thanks for asking." All this makes me feel stupid. I smile at her.

X takes a tiny mouse bite out of her white egg. "I apologize for prying into your life."

"It's fine."

X breathes out audibly and speaks softly. "I woke up this morning in the dark, and I suddenly got this idea in my head about Ralph laughing. It made me cry, in fact. But I thought to myself that you have to strive to live your life to the ultimate. Ralph lived his whole life in nine years, and I remember him laughing. I just wanted to be sure you did. You have a lot longer to live."

"My birthday's in two weeks."

"Do you think you'll get married again?" X says with extreme formality, looking up at me. And for a moment what I smell in the dense morning air is a swimming pool! Somewhere nearby. The cool, aqueous suburban chlorine bouquet that reminds me of the summer coming, and all the other better summers of memory. It is a token of the suburbs I love, that from time to time a swim-ming pool or a barbecue or a leaf fire you'll never ever see will drift provocatively to your nose.

"I guess I don't know," I say. Though in truth I would love to be able to say *Couldn't happen, not on a bet, not this boy.* Except what I do say is nearer to the truth. And just as quick, the silky-summery smell is gone, and the smell of dirt and stolid monu-ments has won back its proper place. In the quavery gray dawn a window lights up beyond the fence on the third floor of my house. Bosobolo, my African boarder, is awake. His day is beginning and I see his dark shape pass the window. Across the cemetery in the other direction I see yellow lights in the caretaker's cottage, beside which sits the green John Deere backhoe used for dredging graves. The bells of St. Leo the Great begin to chime a Good Friday prayer call. "Christ Died Today, Christ Died Today" (though I believe it is actually "Stabat Mater Dolorosa").

"I think I'll get married again," X says matter-of-factly. Who to, I wonder?

"Who to?" Not—please—one of the fat-wallet 19th-hole clubsters, the big hale 'n' hearty, green-sports-coat types who're always taking her on weekends to the Trapp Family Lodge and getaways to the Poconos, where they take in new Borscht Belt comedians and make love on waterbeds. I hope against all hope not. I know all about those guys. The children tell me. They all drive Oldsmobiles and wear tasseled shoes. And there is every good reason to go out with them, I grant you. Let them spend their money and enjoy their discretionary time. They're decent fellows, I'm sure. But they are not to be married.

"Oh, a software salesman, maybe," X says. "A realtor. Somebody I can beat at golf and bully." She smiles at me a mouthdown smirky smile of unhappiness, and bunches her shoulders to wag them. But unexpectedly she starts to cry through her smile, nodding toward me as if we both knew about it and should've expected this, and that in a way I am to blame, which in a way I am.

The last time I saw X cry was the night our house was broken into, when, in the search for what might've been stolen, she found some letters I'd been getting from a woman in Blanding, Kansas. I don't know why I kept them. They really didn't mean anything to me. I hadn't seen the woman in months and then only once. But I was in the thickest depths of my dreaminess then, and needed—or thought I did—something to anticipate away from my life, even though I had no plans for ever seeing her and was in fact intending to throw the letters away. The burglars had left Polaroid pictures of the inside of our empty house scattered about for us to find when we got back from seeing *The Thirty-Nine Steps* at the Playhouse, plus the words, "We are the stuffed men," spray-painted onto the dining room wall. Ralph had been dead two years. The children were with their grandfather at the Huron Mountain Club, and I was just back from my teaching position at Berkshire College, and was hanging around the house more or less dumb as a cashew, but otherwise in pretty good spirits. X found the letters in a drawer of my office desk while looking for a sock full of silver dollars my mother had left me, and sat on the floor and read them, then handed them to me when I came in with a list of missing cameras, radios and fishing equipment. She asked if I had anything to say, and when I didn't, she went into the bedroom and began tearing apart her hope chest with a claw hammer and a crowbar. She tore it to bits, then took it to the fireplace and burned it while I stood outside in the yard mooning at Cassiopeia and Gemini and feeling invulnerable because of dreaminess and an odd amusement I felt almost everything in my life could be subject to. It might seem that I was "within myself" then. But in fact I was light years away from everything.

In a little while X came outside, with all the lights in the house left shining and her hope chest going up the chimney in smoke—it was June—and sat in a lawn chair in another part of the dark yard from where I was standing and cried loudly. Lurking behind a large rhododendron in the dark, I spoke some hopeful and unconsoling words to her, but I don't think she heard me. My voice had gotten so soft by then as to be inaudible to anyone but myself. I looked up at the smoke of what I found out was her hope chest, full of all those precious things: menus, ticket stubs, photographs, hotel room receipts, place cards, her wedding veil, and wondered what it was, what in the world it *could've been* drifting off into the clear spiritless New Jersey nighttime. It reminded me of the smoke that announced a new Pope—*a new Pope!*—if that is believable now, under those circumstances. And in four months I was divorced. All this seems odd now, and far away, as if it had happened to someone else and I had only read about it. But that was my life then, and it is my life now, and I am in relatively good spirits about it. If there's another thing that sportswriting teaches you, it is that there are no transcendent themes in life. In all cases things are here and they're over, and that has to be enough. The other view is a lie of literature and the liberal arts, which is why I did not succeed as a teacher, and another reason I put my novel away in the drawer and have not taken it out.

"Yes, of course," X says and sniffs. She has almost stopped crying, though I have not tried to comfort her (a privilege I no longer hold). She raises her eyes up to the milky sky and sniffs again. She is still holding the nibbled egg. "When I cried in the dark, I thought about what a big nice boy Ralph Bascombe should be right now, and that I was thirty-seven no matter what. I wondered about what we should all be doing." She shakes her head and squeezes her arms tight against her stomach in a way I have not seen her do in a long time. "It's not your fault, Frank. I just thought it would be all right if you saw me cry. That's my idea of grief. Isn't that womanish?"

She is waiting for me to say a word now, to liberate us from that old misery of memory and life. It's pretty obvious she feels something is odd today, some freshening in the air to augur a permanent change in things. And I am her boy, happy to do that very thing—let my optimism win back a day or at least the morning or a moment when it all seems lost to grief. My one redeeming strength of character may be that I am good when the chips are down. With success I am worse.

"Why don't I read a poem," I say, and smile a happy old rejected suitor's smile.

"I guess I was supposed to bring it, wasn't I?" X says, wiping her eyes. "I cried instead of bringing a poem." She has become girlish in her tears.

"Well, that's okay," I say and go down into my pants pockets for the poem I have Xeroxed at the office and brought along in case X forgot. Last year I brought Housman's "To an Athlete Dying Young" and made the mistake of not reading it over beforehand. I had not read it since I was in college, but the title made me remember it as something that would be good to read. Which it wasn't. If anything, it was much too literal and dreamily so about real athletes, a subject I have strong feelings about. Ralph in fact had not been much of an athlete. I barely got past "townsman of a stiller town," before I had to stop and just sit staring at the little headstone of red marble, incised with the little words RALPH BASCOMBE.

"Housman hated women, you know," X had said into the awful silence while I sat. "That's nothing against you. I just remembered it from some class. I think he was an old pederast who would've loved Ralph and hated us. Next year I'll bring a poem if that's okay."

"Fine," I had answered miserably. It was after that that she told me about my writing a novel and being a loner, and having wanted to join the LPGA back in the sixties. I think she felt sorry for me—I'm sure of it, in fact—though I also felt sorry for myself.

"Did you bring another Housman poem?" she says now and smirks at me, then turns and throws her nibbled egg as far as she can off into the gravestones and elms of the old part, where it hits soundlessly. She throws as a catcher would, snapping it by her ear in a gainly way, on a tape-line into the shadows. I admire her positive form. To mourn the loss of one child when you have two others is a hard business. And we are not very practiced, though we treat it as a matter of personal dignity and affection so that Ralph's death and our loss will not get entrapped by time and events and ruin our lives in a secret way. In a sense, we can do no wrong here.

Out on Constitution Street an appliance repair truck has stopped at the light. Easler's Philco Repair, driven by Sid (formerly of Sid's Service, a bankrupt). He has worked on my house many times and is heading toward the village square to hav-a-cup at The Coffee Spot before plunging off into the day's kitchens and basements and sump pumps. The day is starting in earnest. A lone pedestrian—a man—walks along the sidewalk, one of the few Negroes in town, walking toward the station in a light-colored, wash-and-wear suit. The sky is still milky, but possibly it will burn off before I leave for the Motor City with Vicki.

"No Housman today," I say.

"Well," X says and smiles, and seats herself on Craig's stone to listen. "If you say so." Lights are numerous and growing dim with the daylight along the backs of houses on my street. I feel warmer.

It is a "Meditation" by Theodore Roethke, who also attended the University of Michigan, something X will be wise to, and I start it in my best, most plausible voice, as if my dead son could hear it down below:

"I have gone into the waste lonely places behind the eye. . . ."

X has already begun to shake her head before I am to the second line, and I stop and look to her to see where the trouble is.

She punches out her lower lip and sits on her stone. "I don't like that poem," she says matter-of-factly.

I knew she would know it and have a strong opinion about it. She is still an opinionated Michigan girl, who thinks about things with certainty and is disappointed when the rest of the world doesn't. Such a big strapping things-in-order girl should be in every man's life. They alone are reason enough for the midwest's existence, since that's where most of them thrive. I feel tension rising off me like a fever now. It is possible that reading a poem over a little boy who never cared about poems is not a good idea.

"I thought you'd know it," I say in a congenial voice.

"I shouldn't really say I don't like it," X says coldly. "I just don't believe it, is all."

It is a poem about letting the everyday make you happy—insects, shadows, the color of a woman's hair—something else I have some strong beliefs about. "When I read it, I always think it's me talking," I say.

"I don't think those things in that poem would make anybody happy. They might not make you miserable. But that's all," X says and slips down off the stone. She smiles at me in a manner I do not like, tight-lipped and disparaging, as if she believes I'm wrong about everything and finds it amusing. "Sometimes I don't think anyone can be happy anymore." She puts her hands into her London Fog. She probably has a lesson at seven, or a follow-through seminar, and her mind is ready to be far, far away.

"I think we're all released to the rest of our lives, is my way of looking at it," I say hopefully. "Isn't that true?"

She stares at our son's grave as if he were listening and would be embarrassed to hear us. "I guess."

"Are you really getting married?" I feel my eyes open wide as if I knew the answer already. We are like brother and sister suddenly, Hansel and Gretel, planning their escape to safety.

"I don't know." She wags her shoulders a little, like a girl again, but in resignation as much as anything else. "People want to marry me. I might've reached an age, though, when I don't need men."

"Maybe you *should* get married. Maybe it would make you happy." I do not believe it for a minute, of course. I'm ready to marry her again myself, get life back on track. I miss the sweet specificity of marriage, its firm ballast and sail. X misses it too, I can tell. It's the thing we both feel the lack of. We are having to make everything up now, since nothing is ours by right.

She shakes her head. "What did you and Pauly talk about last night? I felt like it was all men's secrets and I wasn't in on it. I hated it."

"We talked about Ralph. Paul has a theory we can reach him by sending a carrier pigeon to Cape May. It was a good talk."

X smiles at the idea of Paul, who is as dreamy in his own way as I ever was. I have never thought X much liked that in him, and preferred Ralph's certainty since it was more like hers and, as such, admirable. When he was fiercely sick with Reye's, he sat up in bed in the hospital one day, in a delirium, and said, "Marriage is a damnably serious business, particularly in Boston"— something he'd read in Bartlett's, which he used to leaf through, memorizing and reciting. It took me six weeks to track the remark down to Marquand. And by then he was dead and lying right here. But X liked it, thought it proved his mind was working away well underneath the deep coma. Unfortunately it became a kind of motto for our marriage from then till the end, an unmeant malediction Ralph pronounced on us.

"I like your new hair," I say. The new way was a thatch along the back that is very becoming. We are past the end of things now, but I don't want to leave.

X fingers a strand, pulls it straight away from her head and cuts her eyes over at it. "It's dikey, don't you think?"

"No." And indeed I don't.

"Well. It'd gotten to a funny length. I had to do something. They screamed at home when they saw it." She smiles as if she's realized this moment that children become our parents, and we just become children again. "You don't feel old, do you, Frank?" She turns and stares away across the cemetery. "I don't know why I've got all these shitty questions. I feel old today. I'm sure it's because you're going to be thirty-nine."

The black man has come to the corner of Constitution Street and stands waiting as the traffic light flicks from red to green across from the new library. The appliance truck is gone, and a yellow minibus stops and lets black maids out onto the same corner. They are large women in white, tentish maid-dresses, talking and swinging big banger purses, waiting for their white ladies to come and pick them up. The man and women do not speak. "Oh, isn't that the saddest thing you ever saw," X says, staring at the women. "Something about that breaks my heart. I don't know why."

"I really don't feel a bit old," I say, happy to be able to answer a question honestly, and possibly slip in some good advice on the side. "I have to wash my hair a little more often. And sometimes I wake up and my heart's pounding to beat the band—though Fincher Barksdale says it isn't anything to worry about. I think it's a good sign. I'd say it was some kind of urgency, wouldn't you?"

X stares at the maids who are talking in a group of five, watching up the street where their rides will come from. Since our divorce she has developed the capability of complete distraction. She will be talking to you but be a thousand miles away. "You're very adaptable," she says airily.

"I am. I know you don't have a sleeping porch in your house, but you should try sleeping with all your windows open and your clothes on. When you wake up, you're ready to go. I've been doing it for a while now."

X smiles at me again with a tight-lipped smile of condescension, a smile I don't like. We are not Hansel and Gretel anymore. "Do you still see your palmist, what's-her-name?"

"Mrs. Miller. No, less often." I'm not about to admit I tried to see her last night.

"Do you feel like you're at the point of understanding everything that's happened—to us and our life?"

"Sometimes. Today I feel pretty normal about Ralph. It doesn't seem like it's going to make me crazy again."

"You know," X says, looking away. "Last night I lay in bed and thought bats were flying around my room, and when I closed my eyes I just saw a horizon line a long way off, with everything empty and flat like a long dinner table set for one. Isn't that awful?" She shakes her head. "Maybe I should lead a life more like yours."

A small resentment rises in me, though this is not the place for resentment. X's view of my life is that it is a jollier, more close to the grain business than hers, and certainly more that way than I know it to be. She'd probably like to tell me again that I should've gone ahead and written a novel instead of quitting and being a sportswriter, and that she should've done some things differently herself. But that would not be right, at least about me—there were even plenty of times when she thought so herself. Everything looks old gloomy to her now. One strain in her character that our divorce has touched is that she is possibly less resilient than she has been before in her life, and worry about getting older is proof of it. I'd cheer her up if I could, but that is one of the talents I lost a long time ago.

"I'm sorry again," she says. "I'm just feeling blue today. There's something about your going away that makes me feel like you're leaving for a new life and I'm not."

"I hope I am," I say, "though I doubt it. I hope you are." Nothing, in fact, would I like better than to have a whole new colorful world open up to me today, though I like things pretty well as they are. I will settle for a nice room at the Pontchartrain, a steak Diane and a salad bar in the rotating rooftop restaurant, seeing the Tigers under the lights. I am not hard to make happy.

"Do you ever wish you were younger?" X says moodily.

"No. I'm fairly happy this way."

"I wish it all the time," she says. "That seems stupid, I know."

I have nothing I can say to this.

"You're an optimist, Frank."

"I hope I am." I smile a good yeoman's smile at her.

"Sure, sure," she says, and turns away from me and begins making her way quickly out through the tombstones, her head up toward the white sky, her hands deep in her pockets like any midwestern girl who's run out of luck for the moment but will soon be back as good as new. I hear the bells of St. Leo the Great chime six o'clock, and for some reason I have a feeling I won't see her for a long time, that something is over and something begun, though I cannot tell you for the life of me what those somethings might be.

from *Anywhere But Here*

Mona Simpson's triumphant 1986 debut novel, Anywhere But Here, *became a national bestseller upon publication, and established Simpson as one of the most promising and refreshing new writers in years. Now a Vintage Contemporaries veteran for over a decade, Simpson has published two more critically praised novels,* The Lost Father, *and, most recently,* A Regular Guy. *She is at work on a new novel, forthcoming from Knopf.*

■ ANYWHERE

WE FOUGHT. WHEN my mother and I crossed state lines in the stolen car, I'd sit against the window and wouldn't talk. I wouldn't even look at her. The fights came when I thought she broke a promise. She said there'd be an Indian reservation. She said that we'd see buffalo in Texas. My mother said a lot of things. We were driving from Bay City, Wisconsin, to California, so I could be a child star while I was still a child.

"Talk to me," my mother would say. "If you're upset, tell me."

But I wouldn't. I knew how to make her suffer. I was mad. I was mad about a lot of things. Places she said would be there, weren't. We were running away from family. We'd left home.

Then my mother would pull to the side of the road and reach over and open my door.

"Get out, then," she'd say, pushing me.

I got out. It was always a shock the first minute because nothing outside was bad. The fields were bright. It never happened on a bad day. The western sky went on forever, there were a few clouds. A warm breeze came up and tangled around my legs. The road was dull as a nickel. I stood there at first amazed that there was nothing horrible in the landscape.

But then the wheels of the familiar white Continental turned, a spit of gravel hit my shoes and my mother's car drove away. When it was nothing but a dot in the distance, I started to cry.

I lost time then; I don't know if it was minutes or if it was more. There was nothing to think because there was nothing to do. First, I saw small things. The blades of grass. Their rough side, their smooth, waxy side. Brown grasshoppers. A dazzle of California poppies.

I'd look at everything around me. In yellow fields, the tops of weeds bent under visible waves of wind. There was a high steady note of insects screaking. A rich odor of hay mixed with the heady smell of gasoline. Two or three times, a car rumbled by, shaking the ground. Dry weeds by the side of the road seemed almost transparent in the even sun.

I tried hard but I couldn't learn anything. The scenery all went strange, like a picture on a high billboard. The fields, the clouds, the sky; none of it helped because it had nothing to do with me.

My mother must have watched in her rearview mirror. My arms crossed over my chest, I would have looked smaller and more solid in the distance. That was what she couldn't stand, my stubbornness. She'd had a stubborn husband. She wasn't going to have a stubborn child. But when she couldn't see me anymore, she gave up and turned around and she'd gasp with relief when I was in front of her again, standing open-handed by the side of the road, nothing more than a child, her child.

And by the time I saw her car coming back, I'd be covered with a net of tears, my nose running. I stood there with my hands hanging at my sides, not even trying to wipe my face.

My mother would slow down and open my door and I'd run in, looking back once in a quick good-bye to the fields, which turned ordinary and pretty again. And when I slid into the car, I was different. I put my feet up on the dashboard and tapped the round tips of my sneakers together. I wore boys' sneakers she thought I was too old for. But now my mother was nice because she knew I would talk to her.

"Are you hungry?" was the first thing she'd say.

"A little."

"I am," she'd say. "I feel like an ice cream cone. Keep your eyes open for a Howard Johnson's."

WE ALWAYS READ the magazines, so we knew where we wanted to go. My mother had read about Scottsdale and Albuquerque and Bel Air. But for miles, there was absolutely nothing. It seemed we didn't have anything and even air that came in the windows when we were driving fast felt hot.

We had taken Ted's Mobil credit card and we used it whenever we could. We scouted for Mobil stations and filled up the tank when we found one, also charging Cokes on the bill. We dug to our elbows in the ice chests, bringing the cold pop bottles up like a catch. There was one chain of motels that accepted Mobil cards. Most nights we stayed in those, sometimes driving three or four hours longer to find one, or stopping early if one was there. They were called Travel Lodges and their signs each outlined a bear in a night cap, sleepwalking. They were dull motels, lonely, and they were pretty cheap, which bothered my mother because she would have liked to charge high bills to Ted. I think she enjoyed signing *Mrs. Ted Diamond*. We passed Best Westerns with hotel swimming pools and restaurants with country singers and we both wished and wished Ted had a different card.

Travel Lodges were the kind of motels that were set a little off the highway in a field. They tended to be one or at the most two stories, with cement squares outside your room door for old empty metal chairs. At one end there would be a lit coffee shop and a couple of semis parked on the gravel. The office would be near the coffee shop. It would have shag carpeting and office furniture, always a TV attached by metal bars to the ceiling.

Those motels depressed us. After we settled in the room, my mother looked around, checking for cleanliness. She took the bedspreads down, lifted curtains, opened drawers and the medicine cabinet, and looked into the shower. Sometimes she took the paper off a water glass and held the glass up to see that it was washed.

I always wanted to go outside. My mother would be deliberating whether it was safer to leave our suitcase in the room or in the locked car; when she was thinking, she stood in the middle of the floor with her hands on her hips and her lips pursed. Finally, she decided to bring it in. Then she would take a shower to cool off. She didn't make me take one if I didn't want to, because we were nowhere and she didn't care what I looked like in the coffee shop. After her shower, she put on the same clothes she'd been driving in all day.

I went out to our porch and sat in the one metal chair. Its back was a rounded piece, perhaps once designed to look like a shell. I could hear her shower water behind me, running; in front, the constant serious sound of the highway. A warm wind slapped my skin lightly, teasing, the sound of the trucks on the highway came loud, then softer, occasionally a motorcycle shrank to the size of a bug, red taillights ticking on the blue sky.

I acted like a kid, always expecting to find something. At home, before supper, I'd stood outside when the sky looked huge and even the near neighbors seemed odd and distant in their occupations. I'd watched the cars moving on the road, as if by just watching you could understand, get something out of the world.

At the motel, I would walk around to the back. I'd stand looking at the field, like any field. The back of the building was ordinary, brick, with glass meter gauges. There was a gas tank lodged on a cement platform, pooled with rusty water. The field went on to where you could see trailers and a neon sign for Dairy Queen in the distance.

The near and the far, could have been anywhere, could have been our gas tank, our fields and sky at home. Our yard had the same kinds of weeds. Home could have been anywhere too.

"Ann. A-yun," my mother would be yelling, then. It all ended, gladly, when she called me from the door. She was finished with her shower and wanted to go for supper at the coffee shop. Our day was almost done. And we enjoyed the dinners in those coffee shops. We ordered the most expensive thing on the menu and side dishes and beverages and desserts. We were anxious, trying to plan to get all the best of what they had. We rolled up our sleeves, asked for extra sour cream and butter. We took pleasure in the scrawled figures added up on the green-lined bill.

Mornings, we always started out later than we'd planned. The manager ran the credit card through the machine and filled the form out slowly. My mother drummed her nails on the counter top, waiting. Then she sighed, holding the credit card form in both hands, examining it a second before signing. "Okay," she said every time she handed the paper back, as if she were giving away one more thing she'd once had.

We'd drive off in the morning and I'd look again, at the plain building, the regular field. I'd forget the land. It was like so much other land we'd seen.

MY MOTHER HAD clipped out pictures of houses in Scottsdale, Arizona. We loved the colors: pink, turquoise, browns, rich yellow. The insides of the houses had red tiled floors, clay bowls of huge strawberries on plain, rough wooden tables.

We went out of our way to go to Scottsdale. When we got there, my mother drove to the Luau, a good hotel, one they'd listed in *Town and Country*. I sat in a chair on one side of the lobby while she went up to the desk. She came back and whispered me the price.

"What do you think? It's a lot but maybe it's worth it once to just relax."

"I think we should find somewhere cheaper."

"There might not be a Travel Lodge in town," she said. "Well, think, Pooh-bear-cub. It's up to you. What would you like to do?"

"Let's find out if there's a Travel Lodge."

She sighed. "Okay. I don't know how we're going to find out. There's probably not. In fact, I'm pretty sure. So what do you think? What should we do?"

I worried about money. And I knew it was a bigger system than I understood. I tried to pick the cheaper thing, like a superstition.

"There's a telephone. Maybe they have a phone book." We were standing in the dark Polynesian lobby. A phone hung in the corner.

She did the looking and it was there, Travel Lodge, with a boxed ad showing the bear sleepwalking, in the yellow pages, listed as being on Route 9. "Nine where?" my mother said, biting her fingernail, clicking the other hand on the metal shelf. "Now, how the heck am I going to find that? It says right out of town, yeah, I'll bet. I didn't see anything, coming in."

"We don't have to go there." I felt like I'd done my duty, checking. I looked around the lobby. It seemed nice. I was beginning to hope she picked here.

"Well, come on." She pulled her purse strap over her shoulder. "Let's go. We'll go there. We should." She had that much worry, apparently.

But driving to the Travel Lodge, not even halfway there, in

town, at an intersection near a gas station, we had an accident. My mother rear-ended a car on a red light.

I WAS SITTING on a curb of the intersection, pulling at grass behind me banking the closed filling station. Nearby, the cars were pulled over to one side and a police car with a flashing red light was parked, making traffic go around them. The policeman stood writing things down as he talked to my mother.

She was moving her hands all around her hair and face. Then she folded her arms across her chest, but one hand couldn't stand it, it reached up to tug at her collar.

"I was going to just stay at that hotel, I *knew* I was tired. I know myself. Now, God, tell me, really, how long do you think it will take to be fixed?" She bit a nail.

The policeman looked into the dark gas station. "Problem is, it's a weekend," he said.

My mother looked at me and shook her head. The policeman walked over to the other driver. She was a woman in shorts and a sleeveless shirt. She seemed calm.

"See, I'm not going to listen to you anymore," my mother said. "Because I know best. You try and save a few pennies and you end up spending thousands." She exhaled, shoving out a hip.

It was ten o'clock and finally getting cooler. We were hungry, we still hadn't eaten dinner. The other woman, having taken the numbers she needed, left, waving good-bye to us and to the policeman.

"Calm down, Adele," she said to my mother.

My mother pulled a piece of her hair. "Calm down, well, that's easy for you to say. Jeez, calm down, she says, when she's going to sue, she'll get her kids' college educations out of this, I know how it's done."

The woman laughed and slammed her car door shut. She

rolled down her window. "Barry's Hanover might have a mechanic in on Saturday," she called to the policeman.

"Mom, I'm hungry." My rump was cold and it seemed we might be there all night.

"Well, we have to stay," she said. "If we'd just checked in, then we'd be there now, probably eating, no, we'd be finished. We'd probably be having dessert. But now we have to wait."

"For how long?"

"I don't know."

The policeman came over to us, still holding his notebook. "We've done all we can do until tomorrow," he said. "Now, I'll take you wherever you want to go and you can just leave the car here and call in the morning and have her towed."

"They're probably not even going to have room left at the hotel now," she said to me.

The policeman had freckles on his arms and hands, like my mother. He put the notebook in his back pocket. "Now, you are both welcome to stay with my wife and I for the night, if you're worried. There's plenty of extra room."

"Oh, no, thank you, though, we couldn't."

"Because it wouldn't be any trouble. And my wife makes a mean apple pie." He looked at me.

"Thank you, but no, really." My mother inspired offers like that, often. I didn't know until I was older how unusual that is. "But would you mind dropping us off at the Luau?"

"Yes, ma'am," he said. "Nice place."

We both sat in the backseat while he drove. The windows were covered with chicken wire. "I just hope they still have room," my mother said, stretching her fingers out on the seat and looking down at her nails.

THE THING ABOUT my mother and me is that when we get along, we're just the same. Exactly. And at the Luau Hotel, we were happy. Waiting for our car to be fixed, we didn't talk about money. It was so big, we didn't think about it. We lay on our stomachs on the king-sized bed, our calves tangling up behind us, reading novels. I read *Gone With the Wind.* Near the end, I locked myself in the bathroom, stopping up my face with a towel. After a while she knocked on the door.

"Honey, let me in, I want to tell you something!" I made myself keep absolutely still. "Don't worry, Honey, she gets him back later. She gets him again in the end."

We loved the swimming pool. Those days we were waiting for our car to be fixed, we lay out from ten until two, because my mother had read that those were the best tanning hours. That was what we liked doing, improving ourselves: lying sprawled out on the reclining chairs, rubbed with coconut suntan oil, turning the pages of new-bought magazines. Then we'd go in the pool, me cannonballing off the diving board for the shock of it, my mother starting in one corner of the shallow end, both her arms out to the sides, skimming the surface as she stepped in gradually, smiling wide, saying, "Eeeeeeeee."

My mother wore a white suit, I swam in gym shorts. While I was lying on a chair, once, she picked up my foot and looked down my leg. "Apricot," she said.

At home, one farmer put in a swimming pool, fenced all around with aluminum. That summer, Ben and I sat in the fields outside, watching through the diamond spaces of the fence. Sometimes the son would try and chase us away and throw rocks at us, little sissy pieces of gravel.

"Public property!" we screamed back at him. We were sitting in Guns Field. We kids all knew just who owned what land.

EVERY AFTERNOON, LATE, after the prime tanning hours, we went out. Dressing took a long time. My mother called room service for a pitcher of fresh lemonade, told them not too much sugar, but some sugar, like yesterday, a pinch, just enough so it was sweet. Sweet, but a little tart, too. Come to think of it, yesterday tasted a little too tart, but the day before was perfect. This was on the telephone. My mother was the kind of customer a waitress would like to kill.

We'd each take showers and wash our hair, squeezing lemons on it before the cream rinse. We touched up our fingernails and toenails with polish. That was only the beginning. Then came the body cream and face cream, our curlers and hair sprays and makeup.

All along, I had a feeling we couldn't afford this and that it would be unimaginably bad when we had to pay. I don't know what I envisioned: nothing, no luck, losing everything, so it was the absolute worst, no money for food, being stopped on a plain cement floor in the sun, unable to move, winding down, stopping like a clock stopped.

But then it went away again. In our sleeveless summer dresses and white patent leather thongs, we walked the district of small, expensive shops. There was an exotic pet store we visited every day. We'd been first drawn in by a sign on the window for two defumed skunks.

"But you can never really get the smell completely out," the blond man inside had told us. He showed us a baby raccoon and we watched it lick its paws, with movements like a cat but more delicate, intricate features.

More than anything, I wanted that raccoon. And my mother wasn't saying no. We didn't have to make any decisions until we left the Luau. And we didn't know yet when that would be.

In a china store, my mother held up a plain white plate. "Look at this. See how fine it is?" If she hadn't said that, I wouldn't have noticed anything, but now I saw that it was thin and there was a pearliness, like a film of water, over the surface.

"Granny had a whole *set* like this." She turned the plate upside down and read the fine printing. "Yup, this is it. Spode."

I remembered Granny almost bald, carrying oats and water across the yard to feed Hal's pony. But still, I didn't know.

"Mmhmm. You don't know, but Granny was very elegant. Gramma isn't, she could be, but she isn't. We're like Granny. See, we belong here, Pooh-bear-cub. We come from this."

I didn't know.

A WEEK AFTER the accident, we had good news. The bill for our car was far less than we'd thought and my mother paid ninety dollars, off the record, to fix the other woman's fender. They both agreed not to contact insurance companies.

This was all great except it meant we were leaving. The car would be ready in a day. My mother sat on the edge of the bed, filing her nails, when she put down the telephone receiver, gently. "There's still a few things I'd like to see here," she said.

We went out to the pool and tried not to think. It seemed easy, lying on towels over warm cement. I'd gotten tan, very dark, the week we'd been there. My mother had freckles and pink burns on her cheeks and shoulders, and her hair was streaked lighter from the sun. That day, my mother got up and went inside before I did. She had to be careful in the sun.

I was in the pool, holding on to the side, kicking my legs in the water behind me. I was worried about my knees. Lately, I'd noticed they were fat, not knobby and horselike, the way my mother's were. So I was doing kicks to improve them. Around the pool, other women slouched in deck chairs. I thought about my knees again. At least tan fat looked better than white fat, I was thinking.

Then my mother called me. "We're going to see a house," she said, shoving a towel into my hand. "Hurry up and jump in the shower."

We waited, clean and dressed, outside the Luau. My mother told me that a real estate agent named Gail was picking us up.

There was something in her tone, she didn't want to explain. So I went along with it as if it was nothing out of the ordinary. And there in Scottsdale, it really wasn't. It had been so long since anything was regular.

Suddenly, Gail was there and she honked. I climbed into the backseat and my mother sat next to her in the front. They talked quickly, getting to know each other. My mother said we were just moving, from Bay City, Wisconsin, and that she was looking forward to the warm air.

"I couldn't stand another winter." She rolled down her window and glanced outside. "I love Scottsdale, the dryness."

Gail Letterfine was very tan with light gray hair, bright clothes and turquoise Indian jewelry. "You're going to love this house, it's absolutely cream of the crop. I haven't had anything like this to show for over a year."

She drove us to the top of a hill. The land was brown, dirt. There were no lawns. I just sat in the backseat, not saying anything. I wished I had *Gone With the Wind*. I knew I shouldn't say anything, in case I contradicted my mother. I could tell she was lying, but I wasn't sure. And I didn't know why. She liked me to talk, around strangers, like a kid. But I was mad, sort of. So I just stared out the window.

Gail Letterfine parked the Mustang on the pebbled lot near a fountain. Pennies overlapped and glittered on the bottom. Just from where we were, I could tell this was something we'd never seen before. We didn't have houses like this in Bay City. A maid opened the door, a woman I knew was a maid from her black short dress and white apron. We'd never seen a maid before, in person, at least I hadn't, I didn't know anymore about my mother. When we got along, it seemed we knew everything about each other. But now, I felt like my mother glossed over things. She knew how nervous I could be.

The maid went to get someone else. Gail Letterfine opened a

door and it was a closet. "Coat closet," she said, loudly, as if it were her own house.

The living room was huge, with red clay tile floors and high ceilings. There were long windows on two walls and you could see outside, down the hill. There was no furniture except a black grand piano and chairs against the walls.

The woman of the house came to meet us. Considering where she lived, she looked like an ordinary person. She had plain brown permanented hair and a nice face. She was wearing a gray dress and stockings.

Gail Letterfine introduced her and the woman took us through her house. Out windows, we saw the backyard, brown and dry, with an oval turquoise swimming pool. Clay pots of strawberry plants stood with thick, heavy berries hanging down over their rims. Every time we entered a room, the woman stood in the doorway while Gail Letterfine pointed out features. In the kitchen, Gail opened every cupboard, where we saw canned soup and Jell-O mixes just like in my grandmother's house. Gail went on about the sink, the refrigerator and the stove. Then she started in on the plumbing. From the way my mother shifted, you could tell she was less than interested.

"What about your appointments?" My mother cupped her hand around a painted Mexican candleholder on the kitchen table. "Are they for sale, too? Because they all go so well, they're what *make* the house."

I wondered where she'd learned that word. The woman shook her head. "No, I'm sorry." My mother liked the woman who lived here, her quietness. There was something tough in Gail Letterfine. With her espadrille, she was now pointing to the molding around the kitchen floor. My mother would rather have talked to the woman in the gray dress. Perhaps that's why we'd come here, because my mother missed her friends.

The bedrooms and bathrooms were regular-sized.

"Our daughter's room," the woman said, in the last doorway on the hall. "She's gone off to college."

My mother nudged me, "This would be yours." We wandered into the adjoining bathroom, which had a vanity and a makeup mirror. Starfish and shells cluttered the tile rim of the sunken tub. My mother frowned at me, "Not bad."

They walked back down the hallway to the dining room. The woman in the gray dress had, quietly, offered them tea, and my mother answered quick and loud, "I'd love some."

I stayed in the room. Outside, water slapped the edges of the swimming pool. A light breeze was making waves. I sat on the hard single bed with stuffed animals bunched up by the pillow. Two pompons fluttered on the bulletin board.

I leaned back and imagined the girl away at college. I thought if I lived here, with this bed and this bulletin board, the regular desk and dresser, I would have this kind of life. Nothing to hide. The girl left her room and went to college and people could walk through and see it.

I actually breathed slower and believed my mother had changed her mind about California, that we were really going to live here, in this house.

It was nice lying on that bed, listening to the soft shuffle of water through the window screen. I felt like sleeping. Then a few minutes later, I woke up hungry. I got up and went down the hall. I was thinking of the woman in the gray dress. For some reason, I thought she would give me cookies and a glass of milk.

They were sitting around the dining room on beige chairs. My mother's knees rested together and her calves slanted down, parallel, mirroring the woman's across the room. My mother was sipping her tea, holding it a long time to her lips, appreciating it.

"Could we put in a bathhouse? I'd love a little cabana out there."

Gail Letterfine lifted her silver glasses, which were attached and hooked behind her ears on a thin silver chain, and wrote down my mother's questions in a hand-sized notebook.

"You'd need a permit." She tapped the arm of her chair with a pen. "That's not hard."

"But I would like to know."

"Who can I call? Let me see. Oh, I got it. Mangold."

My mother floated up to where I was at the sliding glass doors. She rummaged her hand through my hair.

"But you like it," Gail Letterfine said, slamming the notebook closed.

"Well, my husband's coming in next week, and of course, he'll have to see it, too."

"Of course," said the woman in the gray dress, nodding as if she understood perfectly.

"But I'm sure he'll like it." My mother nodded, too. "I think this is the one." She lifted her eyes to the high corners of the room. "Mmhmm, I'm sure of it. What do you think, Ann?"

I was reeling, as if I'd just woken up to trouble, when she said her husband. The sentence went through me like a toy train, three times around the track and no time, coming in, could I picture it right. Ted sure wasn't coming. Not after we'd used his credit card like we had.

"I'm hungry, Mom," I said. I was disappointed by the woman in the gray dress, too. I felt like I'd been promised food and then not given it.

My mother ran her hand through my hair again. "Well, we better be off and get this little one something to eat." She smiled. She liked it when I said bratty, kid things in front of other people. We both did. It made us feel normal. She liked people to think she spoiled me.

On the way back to town, Gail Letterfine drove us to see Frank Lloyd Wright's work site in the desert, Taliesin West. I didn't see what the big deal was. They were excavating. There were huge piles of dirt, like you saw at home where they were developing for the new highway, and dust around everywhere. It was so hot, the piece of thong between my toes stung the skin.

"I love the atmosphere," my mother said, tilting her face up to the sun before naturally drifting indoors, to the air-conditioned gift shop. That was one thing about my mother, why she was fun; she valued comfort. We never had to stay in museums too long. If we didn't like something, we left and went somewhere else, like a restaurant. She wasn't too strict about discipline.

Metal bells of all sizes hung from the gift shop ceiling. "People come from all over the world to buy these bells," Gail Letterfine said. "You're lucky to get them at that price. They're going to be collector's items."

My mother bought one, taking a long time to pick the size. "Won't it look nice in the house?" She winked at me.

I scowled.

Gail took us out to a late lunch. We ate a lot, we each had desserts, extras. We acted the way we did at motel diners, not minding the prices, but this was an elegant restaurant, and expensive. They weren't going to take our Mobil credit card. My mother argued primly when Gail tried to pay the bill and I kicked her, hard, under the table. That night, my mother made me watch while she rolled down her stockings and put her fingers on the bruises. She said she'd known all along Gail would insist. And Gail had, tearing the bottom strip off the bill. "It's a write-off, you know," she'd said. "No prob."

She'd left us in front of the Luau.

"So tomorrow morning, I'll bring a contract to breakfast. Just a work sheet. So we can start talking terms. Toot-a-loo," Gail called, waving her plump hand as she drove away.

We watched her car go. All of a sudden it seemed sad, leaving Scottsdale. Suddenly, I really did like Gail.

"Well," my mother shrugged. "We really don't need dinner, that was plenty. Should we just walk around a little?"

We ambled down the streets slowly, because we were full from eating too much and because it was late afternoon and there was a light, warm breeze and because we were leaving tomorrow. My mother led me through an archway, to some shops on an inside courtyard. She found a perfume maker, a blind man, who blended custom fragrances. He showed us essences of oils, leaves, grasses and flowers.

"All natural," he told us.

He kept the essences in small glass bottles lined up on glass shelves. I dawdled while he worked with my mother. He mixed drops of oils on a glass plate, then rubbed them on the inside of my mother's arm with the tip of an eyedropper.

Finally, they got what they wanted. I had to laugh. The mixture was lily of the valley, wild penny rose, lilac and ordinary lawn grass.

"It's like my childhood," my mother said, holding out her arm. "What I grew up around. Smell."

They decided to call it Joie d'Adele and my mother ordered a hundred and fifty dollars' worth, eight little bottles, the smallest batch he made. She asked if he could mix them overnight, because we had to leave Scottsdale the next morning. He was an odd-looking man. His face hung large and white, creamy. He wore brown clothes and he moved slowly, with his head turned down. But he liked my mother, you could tell. Some people did. You could see it. Strangers almost always love my mother. And even if you hate her, can't stand her, even if she's ruining your life, there's something about her, some romance, some power. She's absolutely herself. No matter how hard you try, you'll never get to her. And when she dies, the world will be flat, too simple, reasonable, too fair.

As soon as we got out of the store, we started fighting about the money.

"We can't afford *that*," I whined, turning on one foot to face her. "A hundred and *fifty* dollars! For perfume! Plus the car and the hotel!"

"Well, you should talk, how much do you think your raccoon is!"

We'd made our way, walking and yelling, to the pet store, where the baby raccoon hunched in the window, his paw stalled in a bowl of water.

"He's a hundred and he eats! He'd eat up fifteen dollars a week in food, at least! The perfume would last, it would last me five years probably. I take care of things and they last. You see what I wear. I haven't bought one new thing in years. But they were all good to start with."

That was a total lie. She bought things all the time. I stood knocking on the glass, trying to make the raccoon look at me. I'd been thinking of starting my new school with the raccoon, riding a bike with him wrapped around my shoulders.

"So, I guess we can't afford him either, then," I said.

"Just remember, I'm the one who has to catch a man in this family. I'm the one who has to find you a father."

"You can buy perfume in California."

"No, not like this. There are only three in the world like him. One is in Italy and the other is in France. He's the only one in the United States."

"According to him."

"Stop kicking stones like that, you're ruining your sandals. And when they go, we can't afford another pair."

We both understood that neither of us would get what she wanted, the raccoon or Joie d'Adele. It was fair that way, both deprived.

That night we packed. My mother wrapped the Taliesin bell with care, bundling it several layers thick in hotel towels. When she paid our bill it was higher than we expected. "Three hundred." She frowned, raising her eyebrows. "It's a good thing we didn't get that raccoon, you know?"

Gail Letterfine was due to pick us up at nine o'clock for breakfast. We were gone, far away in Nevada, before the sun came up.

A LOT OF times, I've thought about it and I feel bad that I didn't let my mother buy her perfume. For one thing, I feel bad for the guy, early in the morning, trusting, having his eight bottles of Joie d'Adele carefully wrapped. Now I'd like to smell it: lily of the valley, penny rose, lilac and grass. It's been years since we've been home. He must have been very hurt that we duped him. He might have assumed the worst and he would have been wrong about that; my mother really had liked him. It was only me.

Years later, when we were living in California, we read his obituary in *Vogue*. It said he'd been the only living custom perfume maker in the States, so he had been telling us the truth. Apparently, he hadn't trained anyone under him. If they'd listed the name of an apprentice, I'd have sent away and surprised her.

"Awww, we should have bought some from him, remember when I wanted to get some of his perfume?" my mother said, when she showed me the little article. "It would probably be worth something now."

"By now, it'd be all gone."

The weather changes quickly on my mother's face. She shrugged, nose wrinkling. "You're right."

But I do feel bad about it, still. That bell is precious to her. She's moved it everywhere; that bell has hung, prominently, in the now-long series of her apartments.

"People come from all over the world for the Taliesin bells. We're lucky to have one. They're collector's items." I've heard my mother say that fifty times. She believed every word Gail Letterfine told us, as if we were the only people in the world who lied.

—

IT DID SOMETHING for my mother, every time she let me off on the highway and then came back and I was there. She was proving something to herself. When she drove back, she'd be nodding, grateful-looking, as if we had another chance, as if something had been washed out of her.

Years ago, when I was small, she chased me to the kitchen table and swiveled between her long arms on each side of it.

"Now where are you going to go?" she'd said.

This was when we were all living in my grandmother's house back at home.

I ducked under the table and saw everyone's legs. Jimmy's blue uniform slacks, Ben's bare knees with scrapes and white scars, my grandmother's stiff, bagging, opaque, seamed orange stockings in black tie-up shoes, my mother's tall freckled legs in nylons. The muscles in her calves moved like nervous small animals. I knew I couldn't get away. So I lunged out and grabbed my uncle's blue legs, holding on hard, sobbing in yelps, not letting go. I thought Jimmy was the strongest one there. Carol stood with her back to us, wiping the counter with a sponge.

Jimmy ran his hand over my head and down my spine. He hugged me hard, but then he pried my fingers off and pulled me away from him. His face was blank and large. "I have to let your mother have you."

My mother was screaming, "Jimmy, you give her to me. She's my child. Mine."

Jimmy pushed me forward with his knuckles on my back, and then she had me. When she shook me against the refrigerator, Ben ran out the door. None of them looked while we fought. They turned their backs. Jimmy left then, too, the screen door slamming. Carol followed, shaking her head, and they were gone—a family.

I fought back, I kicked and bit and pulled hair. I fought as if I were fighting to live. She always said I turned animal, wild. And there was something in that. I could feel something, the way my lips went curled on my teeth, the backs of my knees.

Later, I'd be in bed, swollen and touchy, not moving, and the house would seem absolutely still. The sheet felt light, incredibly light on my skin. My grandmother made up her own bed for me, with new sheets dried out on the line. They helped me after, but then I didn't care anymore.

When I was better again, up and running around, my mother still hadn't forgiven me. She drew it out. Those days she ignored me, came in the house like a stranger, as if she had no relation. She left me to my grandmother's care. She'd roll up her pants from the ankles and push up her shirt sleeves to show her cuts and bruises.

"Look what she did to me," she told the mailman on the porch. "She's wild. A little vicious animal."

Maybe it was the same as later, for her it was all one circle, coming back to the same place, when we made up. In the middle of the night, she woke me and wanted to talk. She looked hard into my eyes, sincere and promising, touched me where I didn't want her to touch, told me again and again that she'd never leave me, when I wasn't worried that she would.

"Okay," I always said.

THE LAST TIME my mother let me out by the side of the road was in Nevada. I don't know why she stopped after that, maybe just because we were almost to California. It was different to let me out on the highway than it would be someplace we lived. I was old enough to get in trouble.

That last time in Nevada was different, too. Because she left me out on the road just a mile or two up past an Arco station. I could see the building in the distance. She let me off and drove out of sight, but this time I didn't cry. I started walking, in the ditch, back towards the filling station. I wanted to make a phone call.

There are more important things than love, I was thinking. Because I didn't want to talk to Benny then, he was just a year older, there was nothing he could do.

I got to the gas station. I didn't have any money, but my mind was made up. I went over to a teenage boy who was leaning against a pump, sucking an empty Coke bottle, and asked if I could borrow a dime. He dug into his jeans pocket and pulled one out.

"Don't have to pay me back. You can keep it." When I was walking to the corner of the lot, to the telephone, he said, "Hey. Hey, girl. Where're you from?"

The dime activated the telephone and I told the operator collect call from Ann. Then I stood there waiting for the phone to ring. The static of the line was enough: I could see the old black phone, where it sat on the kitchen counter, breathing silently before it rang. I knew the light there this time of day, the way the vinyl chairs felt, warm and slick from the sun, on your thighs. I thought of the cut cake under the clear glass cover, frosting melting down onto the plate, like candle wax. The empty hallways were clean, roses in the carpet down the middle, strips of wood floor showing at the edges. Clean white lace covered all the dark wood surfaces in the house. Out windows, the yard moved, never still, shimmering, the fields rustled a little, the old barn that used to be a butter factory just on the edge of view.

The phone rang once. I heard it going through the empty house. Maybe my grandmother was out in the yard or at the Red Owl. She could be watering at the cemetery. I was sure, then, no one would be home. And Ted would be working, Jimmy might be on the road.

"Hullo?" My grandmother's voice sounded so exactly like her

that I almost hung up. For the first time, the telephone seemed miraculous to me. I looked around at the poles and wires on the dry hills. We were anywhere. I didn't know where.

"Collect call from Ann?" the operator said. "Will you accept the charges?"

"Why sure. Ann, tell me, where are you?"

"I'm fine. I'm in Nevada."

Then the operator clicked off the phone. It was like other people on the old party line, hanging up.

"Well, tell me what you've been doing." She was perplexed. I could hear, she was trying to find out if I was in trouble.

"I don't know. Nothing much. Driving."

There was a billboard across the highway, the paper peeling off, flapping. It was a family, in a red car, advertising the state of Nevada.

"Well, are you having fun?"

"Yeah, I guess."

"Tell me, is there anything you need, Ann?"

That made me wince, so I couldn't say a word. I held the phone a foot away from me. I wanted to go home, but I couldn't ask for a thing. It was too hard to explain.

The house there seemed small then, still and away from everything. I tried to get my normal voice.

"No, I just called to say hello."

"Well, good. That's fine. We sure do miss you around here." She was tapping something. She kept her nails long, filed in ovals and unpolished. She tapped them against her front teeth. "Is your ma nearby?"

"She's in the bathroom," I said.

"Well, I love you. We all do." Then she was quiet from the embarrassment of having said that.

"Bye."

"Shouldn't I hold on a second and talk to your ma?"

"Nah, she takes a long time in there. With her makeup, you know."

"I suppose she hasn't changed then."

"No."

I hung up the phone and the house back at home closed again, silent and private. I couldn't see inside anymore. It was small and neat, far away. I sank back against the outside wall of the phone booth, letting the wind come to my face. There were low blue hills in the distance.

"Hey, girl, wanna take a ride?"

I crossed my arms and began to say no, but just then my mother's car started coming back over the horizon and so I turned and waited. She slowed down up the road where she'd left me.

Maybe that was why this was the last time it happened: because I wasn't there. The car crawled, slowly, towards the station. She was looking for me. I stood kicking the pavement, in no hurry for her to get there. The fields were plain and dry. Air above the tar pavement shimmered in ankle-deep waves. In a bucket by the pumps, water sparkled, dark and bright.

When my mother saw me, she stopped the car and got out.

"Ann, you nearly scared me to—"

The boy whistled. I smiled and stared down at the blacktop. He was looking at my legs.

"Ann. Get in the car," my mother said.

In my seat, I still saw him. I closed my fist around the dime.

"Who were you calling, tell me."

She was looking at me, waiting. I had to answer.

"No one."

She sighed and started the car.

"Just hold your horses until we get there, okay? Your grandmother's old, leave her be. She hasn't got that long anymore."

I dragged my cupped hand out the window and the moving air felt solid, like a breast.

She was better. I could tell. She drove evenly and her shoulders dropped. Her foot pumped gradually, modulating the speed.

"Are you hungry?" she said. "'Cause I am. I could go for a little something."

All those times on the highway, it was doing something. I lost time there in the ditches, waiting. Minutes out of my life. It was as if I had millions of clocks ticking inside me and each time one stopped. I left one clock, dead and busted, on the gravel by the side of the road, each time.

I didn't say anything. The highway was clean and straight. I rested back in my seat.

"Huh, what do you say, Pooh?" She was trying to make up.

I held out, I was quiet. She clutched the steering wheel and the blood drained from her knuckles. I squeezed my fist. I could feel my palm sweating as if it would rust the metal of the dime. I wouldn't look at her.

But thinking was too hard. She was my mother and she was driving and we were almost to California.

I was quiet as long as I could be, but she would still have me for a long time. It was easier to talk.

"There's a sign," I said finally. "A Travel Inn Hobo Joe's."

"Hungry?" she said, glad and loud.

I thought of the french fries, the chocolate malteds, as much as I wanted from the menu. "Starving," I said.

Kaye Gibbons's first novel, Ellen Foster, *was published to great acclaim when the author was just twenty-seven years old. The novel won the praise of such writers as Eudora Welty, Alice Hoffman, and Walker Percy; was awarded the Sue Kaufman Prize of the American Academy and Institute of Arts and Letters; and accorded a special citation by the Ernest Hemingway Foundation. Kaye Gibbons is the author of six books, including the novels* A Virtuous Woman *and* A Cure for Dreams, *available from Vintage Contemporaries.*

■ One

WHEN I WAS little I would think of ways to kill my daddy. I would figure out this or that way and run it down through my head until it got easy.

The way I liked best was letting go a poisonous spider in his bed. It would bite him and he'd be dead and swollen up and I would shudder to find him so. Of course I would call the rescue squad and tell them to come quick something's the matter with my daddy. When they come in the house I'm all in a state of shock and just don't know how to act what with two colored boys heaving my dead daddy onto a roller cot. I just stand in the door and look like I'm shaking all over.

But I did not kill my daddy. He drank his own self to death the year after the County moved me out. I heard how they found him shut up in the house dead and everything. Next thing I know he's in the ground and the house is rented out to a family of four.

All I did was wish him dead real hard every now and then.

And I can say for a fact that I am better off now than when he was alive.

I live in a clean brick house and mostly I am left to myself. When I start to carry an odor I take a bath and folks tell me how sweet I look.

There is plenty to eat here and if we run out of something we just go to the store and get some more. I had me a egg sandwich for breakfast, mayonnaise on both sides. And I may fix me another one for lunch.

Two years ago I did not have much of anything. Not that I live in the lap of luxury now but I am proud for the schoolbus to pick me up here every morning. My stylish well-groomed self standing in the front yard with the grass green and the hedge bushes square.

I figure I made out pretty good considering the rest of my family is either dead or crazy.

Every Tuesday a man comes and gets me out of social studies and we go to a room and talk about it all.

Last week he spread out pictures of flat bats for me to comment on. I mostly saw flat bats. Then I saw big holes a body could fall right into. Big black deep holes through the table and the floor. And then he took off his glasses and screwed his face up to mine and tells me I'm scared.

I used to be but I am not now is what I told him. I might get a little nervous but I am never scared.

Oh but I do remember when I was scared. Everything was so wrong like somebody had knocked something loose and my family was shaking itself to death. Some wild ride broke and the one in charge strolled off and let us spin and shake and fly off the rail. And they both died tired of the wild crazy spinning and wore out and sick. Now you tell me if that is not a fine style to die in. She sick and he drunk with the moving. They finally gave in to the motion and let the wind take them from here to there.

Even my mama's skin looked tired of holding in her weak self. She would prop herself up by the refrigerator and watch my daddy go round the table swearing at all who did him wrong. She looked all sad in her face like it was all her fault.

She could not help getting sick but nobody made her marry him. You see when she was my size she had romantic fever I think it is called and since then she has not had a good heart.

She comes home from the hospital sometimes. If I was her I would stay there. All laid up in the air conditioning with folks patting your head and bringing you fruit baskets.

Oh no. She comes in and he lets into her right away. Carrying on. Set up in his E-Z lounger like he is King for a Day. You bring me this or that he might say.

She comes in the door and he asks about supper right off. What does she have planned? he wants to know. Wouldn't he like to know what I myself have planned? She would look at him square in the face but not at his eyes or mouth but at his whole face and the ugliness getting out through the front. On he goes about supper and how come weeds are growed up in the yard. More like a big mean baby than a grown man.

I got her suitcase in my hand and I carry it to the bedroom. But while I walk I listen to him and to her not saying a word back to him. She stands between his mean highness and the television set looking at him make words at her.

Big wind-up toy of a man. He is just too sorry to talk back to even if he is my daddy. And she is too limp and too sore to get up the breath to push the words out to stop it all. She just stands there and lets him work out his evil on her.

Get in the kitchen and fix me something to eat. I had to cook the whole time you was gone, he tells her.

And that was some lie he made up. Cook for his own self. Ha. If I did not feed us both we had to go into town and get take-out chicken. I myself was looking forward to something fit to eat but I was not about to say anything.

If anybody had asked me what to do I would have told us both to feed on hoop cheese and crackers. Somebody operated on needs to stay in the bed without some husband on their back all the time. But she does not go on to the bedroom but turns right back around and goes to the kitchen. What can I do but go and reach the tall things for her? I set that dinner table and like to take a notion to spit on his fork.

NOBODY YELLS AFTER anybody to do this or that here.

My new mama lays out the food and we all take a turn to dish it out. Then we eat and have a good time. Toast or biscuits with any-thing you please. Eggs any style. Corn cut off the cob the same day we eat it. I keep my elbows off the table and wipe my mouth like a lady. Nobody barks, farts, or feeds the dogs under the table here. When everybody is done eating my new mama puts the dishes in a thing, shuts the door, cuts it on, and Wa-La they are clean.

MY MAMA DOES not say a word about being tired or sore. She did ask who kept everything so clean and he took the credit. I do not know who he thinks he fooled. I knew he lied and my mama did too. She just asked to be saying something.

Mama puts the food out on the table and he wants to know what am I staring at. At you humped over your plate like one of us is about to snatch it from you. You old hog. But I do not say it.

Why don't you eat? he wants to know.

I don't have a appetite, I say back.

Well, you better eat. Your mama looks like this might be her last supper.

He is so sure he's funny that he laughs at his own self.

All the time I look at him and at her and try to figure out why he hates her so bad. When he is not looking I give him the evil eye. And my mama looks like she could crawl under the table and cry.

We leave his nasty self at that table and go to bed. She is sore all up through her chest and bruised up the neck. It makes me want to turn my head.

We peel her dress off over the head and slip on something loose to sleep in. I help her get herself laid in the bed and then I slide in beside her. She just turns her head into the pillow.

I will stay here with you. Just for a nap I will stay here with you.

NOW AT MY new mama's I lay up late in the day and watch the rain fall outside. Not one thing is pressing on me to get done here.

I have a bag of candy to eat on. One piece at a time. Make it last. All I got left to do is eat supper and wash myself.

Look around my room. It is so nice.

When I accumulate enough money I plan to get some colored glass things that you dangle from the window glass. I lay here and feature how that would look. I already got pink checkerboard curtains with dingleballs around the edges. My new mama sewed them for me. She also sewed matching sacks that I cram my pillows into every morning.

Everything matches. It is all so neat and clean.

When I finish laying here with these malted milk balls I will smooth the covers down and generally clean up after myself. Maybe then I will play with the other people. But I might just lay here until the chicken frying smells ready to eat.

I DO NOT know if she hears him go out the back door. She is still enough to be asleep. He goes off in the truck like he has some business to tend to. And you know and I know he's gone to get himself something to drink. Then he brings it into this house like he is Santa Claus. He sets his package beside his chair and then eases his lazy self into place. Yelling at somebody, meaning myself, to turn on the television set. I could chew nails and spit tacks.

The yelling makes my mama jump and if she was asleep she is awake now. Grits her teeth every time he calls out damn this or that. The more he drinks the less sense he makes.

By the time the dog races come on he's stretched out on the bathroom floor and can't get up. I know I need to go in there and poke him. Same thing every Saturday. This week in particular she does not need to find some daddy hog rooted all up against the toilet stool.

I get up and go in there and tell him to get up that folks got to come in here and do their business. He can go lay in the truck.

He just grunts and grabs at my ankle and misses.

Get on up I say again to him. You got to be firm when he is like this. He'd lay there and rot if I let him so I nudge him with my foot. I will not touch my hands to him. Makes me want to heave my own self seeing him pull himself up on the sink. He zigs-zags out through the living room and I guess he makes it out the door. I don't hear him fall down the steps.

And where did she come from? Standing in the door looking at it all.

Get back in the bed, I say to my mama.

Mama's easy to tend to. She goes back in the bedroom. Not a bit of trouble. Just stiff and hard to move around. I get her back in the bed and tell her he's outside for the night. She starts to whimper and I say it is no reason to cry. But she will wear herself out crying.

I ought to lock him out.

A grown man that should be bringing her food to nibble on and books to look at. No but he is taking care of his own self tonight. Just like she is not sick or kin to him.

A storm is coming up. And I will lay here with my mama until

I see her chest rise up and sink down regular. Deep and regular and far away from the man in the truck.

I can smell the storm and see the air thick with the rain coming.

He will sleep through the thunder and rain. And oh how I have my rage and desire for the lightning to come and strike a vengeance on him. But I do not control the clouds or the thunder.

And the way the Lord moves is his business.

■ Two

WHEN IT IS morning I hear my daddy come in the house. He does not sneak. If he had a horse he would have ridden it right up the steps. He has forgotten last night and he is foolish enough to think we have too.

My mama has got her own self out of the bed. I must have slept hard not to hear her. All my clothes are on that I wore yesterday. It will save me some trouble this morning.

He's got her in the kitchen by herself. I know he won't hurt her with his hands. He might throw a cup or a fork at her but he won't touch her to leave a mark.

I try not to leave her by herself with him. Not even when they are both asleep in the bed. My baby crib is still up in their bedroom so when I hear them at night I throw a fit and will not stop until I can sleep in the baby bed. He will think twice when I am around.

And I have to see now but the door is shut. There is something in the kitchen I need so I go in there to get it.

She is sitting at one end of the table and he is sitting at the other end going through her pocketbook. Some of her heart pills are on the table rolling around loose and the bottle is in her lap.

Give the bottle to me and let me put the pills back in it. They cost money, I say to her.

That's all the pills she's got left. She took almost the whole goddamn bottle, he looks at her and tells me.

Vomit them up, mama. I'll stick my finger down your throat and you can vomit them up. She looks at me and I see she will not vomit. She will not move.

Well I'll just go to the store and use the telephone.

But my daddy says he will kill me if I try to leave this house. All the time I knew he was evil and I did not have the proof.

He would kill me and my mama both with a knife. He looks at the two of us and rubs her pocketbook, patient, like he sits and waits for folks to die all the time. He wants me to put her back in the bed.

Hell, all she needs is some sleep, he says. Take her back there and see if she don't sleep it off. And he gave me a guarantee the pills would not hurt her bad.

We will rest some more. The day is early and we need some more rest.

I ALWAYS LOVE to eat a good supper, brush my teeth and go to bed early. If I am not sleepy I can always find something to do.

Lately I lay up in the bed and read old books. I told the library teacher I wanted to read everything of some count so she made me a list. That was two years ago and I'm up to the Brontë sisters now. I do not read comic books or the newspaper. I find what news I need off the television.

I can hardly tolerate the stories we read for school. Cindy or Lou with the dog or cat. Always setting out on some adventure. They might meet a bandit or they might hop a freight but the policeman or the engineer always brings them home and they are still good children.

I myself prefer the old stories. When I started my project I enjoyed the laughing Middle Ages lady that wore red boots. She was on a trip with a group of people swapping stories, carrying on, slapping each other on the back.

What I am reading now is a little fancy for me but it is on the list. Just men and women sneaking around in a big dark house with one all into the other's business. The library teacher said the author and her sisters wrote books because in their day they could not go out and get jobs. I bet they were just well off and did not need to work.

I could lay here and read all night. I am not able to fall asleep without reading. You have that time when your brain has nothing constructive to do so it rambles. I fool my brain out of that by making it read until it shuts off. I just think it is best to do something right up until you fall asleep.

I ALWAYS WANT to lay here. And she moves her arm up and I push my head down by her side. And I will crawl in and make room for myself. My heart can be the one that beats.

And hers has stopped.

Damn him to the bottom of hell damn him.

What to do now when the spinning starts people will come and they will want to know why and I cannot tell them why. They will not come yet no not for a while. I have her now while she sleeps but just is not breathing. I do not have to tell him so let him sit and wonder at the quiet in here. Why this house is so still and people all over everywhere are glad for the day.

Guilty and held down in his chair by God and fear of a sweet dead woman.

You can rest with me until somebody comes to get you. We will not say anything. We can rest.

—

I DESPISE THAT dress and get your hands off me is what she needs to be told. But I push the bathroom door and leave my aunt on the other side and me to myself.

Is this my lipstick now? I do not think I should put a dab on to wear to the church. She would let me. But somebody would say something.

Put it back put it back just like it was. When I am old I can come back and wear it. When it is not for play. They didn't need this to dress her up with? Somebody must have got her another stick. She left this one at home. To be sure they don't paint everybody they do business with with the same stick.

I will just wash my mouth and sit on the toilet to look. I can see them all through the crack in the door. Everybody I have not seen since last Christmas sitting around patting their hands together.

My daddy is thinking about how good a tall glass of anything would be. Before they all got here he rounded up all his beer cans and pitched them under the back porch.

Somebody must have given him that suit. All he ever wears is gray work outfits. I want to sew a little patch over the pockets that says his name BILL. He could be like the Esso man. Can I help you, ma'am? Check your tires? Change your oil? Throw a knife at you?

All he has done since Sunday morning is open the door for folks and shake his head yes or no. His brother Rudolph put him in the car and took him to town to pick out the coffin. I know when he got there my mama's sisters chased him off. They are the ones with the taste.

He sits there with both feet on the floor and his eyes are red but not from crying. When somebody goes by and leans forward to his ear he touches them on the shoulder. Still king. Now quiet.

She finally shut him up.

from *Revolutionary Road*

Richard Yates was considered one of the best, and most overlooked, American writers, praised by such legends as Tennessee Williams, Kurt Vonnegut, William Styron, Robert Stone, and Larry McMurtry. His prize-winning stories began to appear in 1953 and his first novel, Revolutionary Road, was a finalist for the National Book Award in 1961, becoming an instant classic. Richard Yates died of emphysema at the age of sixty-six in 1992.

THE FINAL DYING sounds of their dress rehearsal left the Laurel Players with nothing to do but stand there, silent and helpless, blinking out over the footlights of an empty auditorium. They hardly dared to breathe as the short, solemn figure of their director emerged from the naked seats to join them on stage, as he pulled a stepladder raspingly from the wings and climbed halfway up its rungs to turn and tell them, with several clearings of his throat, that they were a damned talented group of people and a wonderful group of people to work with.

"It hasn't been an easy job," he said, his glasses glinting soberly around the stage. "We've had a lot of problems here, and quite frankly I'd more or less resigned myself not to expect too much. Well, listen. Maybe this sounds corny, but something happened up here tonight. Sitting out there tonight I suddenly knew, deep down, that you were all putting your hearts into your work for the first time." He let the fingers of one hand splay out across the pocket of his shirt to show what a simple, physical thing the heart was; then he made the same hand into a fist, which he shook slowly and wordlessly in a long dramatic pause, closing one eye and allowing his moist lower lip to curl out in a grimace of triumph and pride. "Do that again tomorrow night," he said, "and we'll have one hell of a show."

They could have wept with relief. Instead, trembling, they cheered and laughed and shook hands and kissed one another, and somebody went out for a case of beer and they all sang songs around the auditorium piano until the time came to agree, unanimously, that they'd better knock it off and get a good night's sleep.

"See you tomorrow!" they called, as happy as children, and riding home under the moon they found they could roll down the windows of their cars and let the air in, with its health-giving smells of loam and young flowers. It was the first time many of the Laurel Players had allowed themselves to acknowledge the coming of spring.

The year was 1955 and the place was a part of western Connecticut where three swollen villages had lately been merged by a wide and clamorous highway called Route Twelve. The Laurel Players were an amateur company, but a costly and very serious one, carefully recruited from among the younger adults of all three towns, and this was to be their maiden production. All winter, gathering in one another's living rooms for excited talks about Ibsen and Shaw and O'Neill, and then for the show of hands in which a common-sense majority chose *The Petrified Forest*, and then for preliminary casting, they had felt their dedication growing stronger every week. They might privately consider their director a funny little man (and he was, in a way: he seemed incapable of any but a very earnest manner of speaking, and would often conclude his remarks with a little shake of the head that caused his cheeks to wobble) but they liked and respected him, and they fully believed in most of the things he said. "Any play deserves the best that any actor has to give," he'd told them once, and another time: "Remember this. We're not just putting on a play here. We're establishing a community theater, and that's a pretty important thing to be doing."

The trouble was that from the very beginning they had been afraid they would end by making fools of themselves, and they had compounded that fear by being afraid to admit it. At first their rehearsals had been held on Saturdays—always, it seemed, on the kind of windless February or March afternoon when the sky is white, the trees are black, and the brown fields and hummocks of the earth lie naked and tender between curds of shriveled snow. The Players, coming out of their various kitchen doors and hesitating for a minute to button their coats or pull on their gloves, would see a landscape in which only a few very old, weathered houses seemed to belong; it made their own homes look as weightless and impermanent, as foolishly misplaced as a great many bright new toys that had been left outdoors overnight and rained on. Their automobiles didn't look right either— unnecessarily wide and gleaming in the colors of candy and ice cream, seeming to wince at each splatter of mud, they crawled apologetically down the broken roads that led from all directions to the deep, level slab of Route Twelve. Once there the cars seemed able to relax in an environment all their own, a long bright valley of colored plastic and plate glass and stainless steel—KING KONE, MOBILGAS, SHOPORAMA, EAT—but eventually they had to turn off, one by one, and make their way up the winding country road that led to the central high school; they had to pull up and stop in the quiet parking lot outside the high-school auditorium.

"Hi!" the Players would shyly call to one another.

"Hi! . . ." "Hi! . . ." And they'd go reluctantly inside.

Clumping their heavy galoshes around the stage, blotting at their noses with Kleenex and frowning at the unsteady print of their scripts, they would disarm each other at last with peals of forgiving laughter, and they would agree, over and over, that there was plenty of time to smooth the thing out. But there wasn't plenty of time, and they all knew it, and a doubling and redoubling of their rehearsal schedule seemed only to make matters worse. Long after the time had come for what the director called "really getting this thing off the ground; really making it happen," it remained a static, shapeless, inhumanly heavy weight; time and again they read the promise of failure in each other's eyes, in the apologetic nods and smiles of their parting and the spastic haste with which they broke for their cars and drove home to whatever older, less explicit promises of failure might lie in wait for them there.

And now tonight, with twenty-four hours to go, they had somehow managed to bring it off. Giddy in the unfamiliar feel of makeup and costumes on this first warm evening of the year, they had forgotten to be afraid: they had let the movement of the play come and carry them and break like a wave; and maybe it sounded corny (and what if it did?) but they had all put their hearts into their work. Could anyone ever ask for more than that?

THE AUDIENCE, ARRIVING in a long clean serpent of cars the following night, were very serious too. Like the Players, they were mostly on the young side of middle age, and they were attractively dressed in what the New York clothing stores describe as Country Casuals. Anyone could see they were a better than average crowd, in terms of education and employment and good health, and it was clear too that they considered this a significant evening. They all knew, of course, and said so again and again as they filed inside and took their seats, that *The Petrified Forest* was hardly one of the world's great plays. But it was, after all, a fine theater piece with a basic point of view that was every bit as valid today as in the thirties ("Even more valid," one man kept telling his wife, who chewed her lips and nodded, seeing what he meant; "even more valid, when you think about it"). The main thing, though, was not the play itself but the company—the brave idea of it, the healthy, hopeful sound of it: the birth of a really good community theater right here, among themselves. This was what had drawn them, enough of them to fill more than half the auditorium, and it was what held them hushed and tense in readiness for pleasure as the house lights dimmed.

The curtain went up on a set whose rear wall was still shaking with the impact of a stagehand's last-minute escape, and the first few lines of dialogue were blurred by the scrape and bang of accidental offstage noises. These small disorders were signs of a mounting hysteria among the Laurel Players, but across the footlights they seemed only to add to a sense of impending excellence. They seemed to say, engagingly: Wait a minute; it hasn't really started yet. We're all a little nervous here, but please bear with us. And soon there was no further need for apologies, for the audience was watching the girl who played the heroine, Gabrielle.

Her name was April Wheeler, and she caused the whispered word "lovely" to roll out over the auditorium the first time she walked across the stage. A little later there were hopeful nudges and whispers of "She's *good,*" and there were stately nods of pride among the several people who happened to know that she had attended one of the leading dramatic schools of New York less than ten years before. She was twenty-nine, a tall ash blonde with a patrician kind of beauty that no amount of amateur lighting could distort, and she seemed ideally cast in the role. It didn't even matter that bearing two children had left her a shade too heavy in the hips and thighs, for she moved with the shyly sensual grace of maidenhood; anyone happening to glance at Frank Wheeler, the round-faced, intelligent-looking young man who sat biting his fist in the last row of the audience, would have said he looked more like her suitor than her husband.

"Sometimes I can feel as if I were sparkling all over," she was saying, *"and I want to go out and do something that's absolutely crazy, and marvelous . . ."*

Backstage, huddled and listening, the other actors suddenly loved her. Or at least they were prepared to love her, even those who had resented her occasional lack of humility at rehearsals, for she was suddenly the only hope they had.

The leading man had come down with a kind of intestinal flu that morning. He had arrived at the theater in a high fever, insisting that he felt well enough to go on, but five minutes before curtain time he had begun to vomit in his dressing room, and there had been nothing for the director to do but send him home and take over the role himself. The thing happened so quickly that nobody had time to think of going out front to announce the substitution; a few of the minor actors didn't even know about it until they heard the director's voice out there in the lights, speaking the familiar words they'd expected to hear from the other man. He was doing his fervent best and delivering each line with a high semi-professional finish, but there was no denying that he looked all wrong in the part of Alan Squiers—squat and partly bald and all but unable to see without his glasses, which he'd refused to wear on stage. From the moment of his entrance he had caused the supporting actors to interrupt each other and forget where to stand, and now in the middle of his important first-act speech about his own futility—*"Yes, brains without purpose; noise without sound; shape without substance—"* one of his gesturing hands upset a glass of water that flooded the table. He tried to cover it with a giggle and a series of improvised lines—*"You see? That's how useless I am. Here, let me help you wipe it up—"* but the rest of the speech was ruined. The virus of calamity, dormant and threatening all these weeks, had erupted now and spread from the helplessly vomiting man until it infected everyone in the cast but April Wheeler.

"Wouldn't you like to be loved by me?" she was saying.

"Yes, Gabrielle," said the director, gleaming with sweat. *"I should like to be loved by you."*

"You think I'm attractive?"

Under the table the director's leg began to jiggle up and down on the spring of its flexed foot. *"There are better words than that for what you are."*

"Then why don't we at least make a start at it?"

She was working alone, and visibly weakening with every line. Before the end of the first act the audience could tell as well as the Players that she'd lost her grip, and soon they were all embarrassed for her. She had begun to alternate between false theatrical gestures and a white-knuckled immobility; she was carrying her shoulders high and square, and despite her heavy make-up you could see the warmth of humiliation rising in her face and neck.

Then came the bouncing entrance of Shep Campbell, the burly young red-haired engineer who played the gangster, Duke Mantee. The whole company had worried about Shep from the beginning, but he and his wife Milly, who had helped with the props and the publicity, were such enthusiastic and friendly people that nobody'd had the heart to suggest replacing him. The result of this indulgence now, and of Campbell's own nervous guilt about it, was that he forgot one of his key lines, said others in a voice so quick and faint that it couldn't be heard beyond the sixth row, and handled himself less like an outlaw than an obliging grocery clerk, bobbing head, rolled-up sleeves and all.

At intermission the audience straggled out to smoke and wander in uncomfortable groups around the high-school corridor, examining the high-school bulletin board and wiping damp palms down their slim-cut trousers and their graceful cotton skirts. None of them wanted to go back and go through with the second and final act, but they all did.

And so did the Players, whose one thought now, as plain as the sweat on their faces, was to put the whole sorry business behind them as fast as possible. It seemed to go on for hours, a cruel and protracted endurance test in which April Wheeler's performance was as bad as the others, if not worse. At the climax, where the stage directions call for the poignance of the death scene to be *punctuated with shots from outside and bursts from* DUKE's *Tommy gun,* Shep Campbell timed his bursts so sloppily, and the answering off-stage gunfire was so much too loud, that all the lovers' words were lost in a deafening smoky shambles. When the curtain fell at last it was an act of mercy.

The applause, not loud, was conscientiously long enough to permit two curtain calls, one that caught all the Players in motion as they walked to the wings, turned back and collided with one another, and another that revealed the three principals in a brief tableau of human desolation: the director blinking myopically, Shep Campbell looking appropriately fierce for the first time all evening, April Wheeler paralyzed in a formal smile.

Then the house lights came up, and nobody in the auditorium knew how to look or what to say. The uncertain voice of Mrs. Helen Givings, the real-estate broker, could be heard repeating *"Very nice,"* over and over again, but most of the people were silent and stiff, fingering packs of cigarettes as they rose and turned to the aisles. An efficient high-school boy, hired for the evening to help with the lights, vaulted up onto the stage with a squeak of his sneakers and began calling instructions to an unseen partner high in the flies. He stood posing self-consciously in the footlights, managing to keep most of his bright pimples in shadow while proudly turning his body to show what the tools of the electrician's trade—knife, pliers, coils of wire—were slung in a professional-looking holster of oiled leather and worn low on one tense buttock of his dungarees. Then the bank of lights clicked off, the boy made a pale exit and the curtain became a dull wall of green velvet, faded and streaked with dust. There was nothing to watch now but the massed faces of the audience as they pressed up the aisles and out the main doors. Anxious, round-eyed, two by two, they looked and moved as if a calm and

orderly escape from this place had become the one great necessity of their lives; as if, in fact, they wouldn't be able to begin to
live at all until they were out beyond the rumbling pink billows of
exhaust and the crunching gravel of this parking lot, out where
the black sky went up and up forever and there were hundreds of
thousands of stars.

from *The Names*

Award-winning novelist Don DeLillo is the author of eleven highly acclaimed novels and several plays, including such Vintage Contemporaries classics as Great Jones Street, Players, Ratner's Star, Running Dog, *and* The Names. *DeLillo won the 1985 National Book Award for* White Noise, *the 1992 PEN/Faulkner for* Mao II, *and was a National Book Award finalist for his 1997 novel* Underworld.

WE STOOD BY the side of the road, pissing in the wind. A hunter in a camouflage jacket came up out of the woods, called a greeting. Steam drifted up from the riverbed.

"Where do we go next?"

"We cross this range, we eat lunch, then we drive south."

"Good," he said.

"You like that idea."

"As long as we drive. I want to keep driving. I like the driving."

The mountains here contained a sense of time, geologic time. Rounded, colorless, unwooded. They lay in embryo, a process unfolding, or a shriveled dying perhaps. They had the look of naked events. But what else? It took me awhile to understand in what precise way these pale masses, southwest of Argos, seemed so strange and irreducible, in what way they worked a mental labor in me, forcing me to shift my eyes time and again, keep to the wheel, look to the road. They were mountains as semantic rudiments, barest definitions of themselves.

"Maybe it'll be warmer down there."

"How far down?"

"All the way," I said. "Where Europe ends."

"I don't mind the cold."

Tap had nothing to say about the landscape. He seemed interested in what we saw, even engrossed at times, but said nothing,
looked out the window, tramped the hills. Eventually I did the
same, talking about anything but what was out there. We let the
features gather, the low skies and mists, the hilltops edged with
miles of old walls, fallen battlements, that particular brooding
woe of the Peloponnese. It hovers almost everywhere, war memory, a heaviness and death. Frankish castles, Turkish fortresses,
ruined medieval towns, the gateways and vaulted cisterns, the
massive limestone walls, the shaft graves, the empty churches
with their faded All-Creator floating in the dome, the curved
Lord, the non-Euclidean, and the votive lamps below, the walnut
throne, the icons in the side galleries, Byzantine blood and gold.
All we did was climb, drive and climb. For three days the
weather was overcast and cold. We climbed the rubble trails, the
goat and donkey paths, the tunnel stairways, the rutted spiral
tracks to upper towns, we climbed the Gothic towers, the broad
ramps of Mycenaean palace mounds.

"When I'm swimming, Dad."

"Yes."

"And I put my head under the water."

"Yes."

"How come the water doesn't rush into my ears and nose and
fill my whole body, sending me to the bottom, where I'm crushed
by the pressure?"

South. The plains and orchards. Bare poplars in the distance,
a combed silk shimmer. This wasn't a bad road. Others unsur-
faced, some half washed off the edge of mountains or rock-
scattered, or ending in a pile of gravel, machines scaled with
gray mud.

"That's it," he said. "That's the question. I'm finished."

Now, ahead, high above us, the hammered sheet, the broad snowy summit of Taygetus. This is the range that thrusts down through the Mani, the middle peninsula of the southern Peloponnese, the middle tit, Owen had called it, all mountain and wild coast.

That whole afternoon we saw half a dozen cars, as many men with dogs and guns. A man riding a horse, a woman who walked behind him holding the horse's tail.

The towns were small, with empty streets and squares. Wind blew across the olive groves, causing a wild tremor, a kind of panic, treetops going silver. We passed rubble fields, rock walls, groups of whale-back boulders, hillsides covered with enclosures of rough stone.

We waited out a downpour in a deserted village square. An old church, a well, a cut-back mulberry tree. The rain was continuous, a single wavering surface, beating on the roof and hood. It was Christmas Day.

A mountain cloud kept rolling toward a white village, then merged with warmer air and vanished. Again it fell, like a rush or slide of timeless snow, disappearing in the air above the village.

In our mood of reticent observation, of speaking of other things, the journey through the Mani became something like a pure rite of seeing. This was appropriate, I thought. If Athens is a place where people breathe the spoken word, if much of Greece is this, then the Mani forms an argument for silence, for finding a way to acknowledge the bleakness that carries something human in it. Tap peered through the windshield, he looked at things with an odd thoughtfulness. We would see what was here, see clearly through the rain shrouds that hung in the gorges, through the bluish smoke high-piled on the coast.

We came to a town that was larger than the others, built at a crossroads, a hotel on the edge of it, two-story cement, boarded shut. I drove slowly down a narrow street to what I thought might be the main square, small as it was, halfhearted, oddly shaped, an historical pause. In the narrowness of this place the stone houses loomed. We got out in a light rain, flexing our legs, and walked toward a cobbled street that seemed to lead down to the water. Doors opened in abandoned houses, wind-swayed. We heard goat-bells nearby and passed a church, seeing three goats come over a broken wall. There were more houses with swinging doors, a butcher shop with an empty meat case, a man standing in the dark near the counter.

When we started down the stone path a wind came cutting up to meet us and we looked at each other and turned around. At the end of a street, bulking high over the road we'd just been on, was a massive anvil rock, maybe five hundred feet tall, a dark presence, a power like a voice in the sky. I spotted a café, tall windows, someone moving about. I told Tap to wait in the car and I went inside.

It was a shabby place, two tables occupied. A man stood in a doorway at the back. It wasn't clear whether he was in charge or just hanging around. It was that kind of place, run by someone who drops in when he thinks of it. I asked the man, in Greek, about hotels nearby. He made a barely perceptible sign, a head movement, the smallest action of eyes and lips. Total disdain. Utter and aloof and final dismissal of all subject matter pertaining to this question, now and forever. A soul shrug. A gesture that placed the question outside the human environment, the things men will rouse themselves to discuss.

He was a grave man with wavy black hair, a thick mustache. I crowded him, as I tended to do when speaking Greek, in order to avoid being overheard by others, and said in an earnest halting way that I had three maps of the area south of here, the area where the main road makes its deepest penetration, then turns to go up the opposite coast. And the maps were all different. And I wondered if he could look at the maps and tell me which one was accurate, if any. The people at the nearest table, not Greeks, stopped talking when I was halfway through my recitation. This made me nervous, of course. Not that it mattered to the black-haired man. He said something I didn't understand, three, maybe four words, looking past me to the front window.

The voices resumed. I bought some chocolate bars for Tap. Then I asked if there was a toilet. The man looked to his left and I asked if this meant outside and he looked again and I saw that it did.

I walked through an alley, across a muddy yard to the toilet. It was the terminal shithouse of the Peloponnese. The walls were splattered with shit, the bowl was clogged, there was shit on the floor, on the toilet seat, on the fixtures and pipes. An inch of exhausted piss lay collected around the base of the toilet, a minor swamp in the general wreckage and mess. In the chill wind, the soft sweet rain, this doleful shed was another plane of experience. It had a history, a reek of squatting armies, centuries of war, plunder, siege, blood feuds. I stood five feet from the bowl to urinate tip-toed. How strange that people used this place, still. It was like an offering to Death, to stand there directing my stream toward that porcelain hole.

Driving slowly, nosing the car out of town, I passed the café, aware we were being watched, although I wasn't sure by whom. We headed south again, in misty light, sharing some chocolate. Soon we began seeing tower houses, tall narrow structures, flat-roofed except where broken near the top. They stood in the bare landscape, solitary pieces, chess pieces, unfigured, raised straight in the dead afternoon. They looked less like houses, former houses, than some mysterious use of the local stone.

"Was I born during the Vietnam war?"

"Don't sound so depressed. You're not scarred for life, I don't think."

"But was I?"

"Yes. It was our favorite war, your mother's and mine. We were both against it but she insisted on being more against it than I

was. It got to be a contest, a running battle. We used to have ter-
rific arguments."

"Not smart."

This is what he said on those occasions when another kid
might say "dumb" or "pretty stupid." Not smart. A whole world
existed in this distinction.

He was belted in, wearing a watch cap, suspended in one of
his inward states. He possessed an eerie calm at such times and
was capable of the most unsettling questions about himself, his
degree of sanity, his chances of living past the age of twenty, figured against world conflicts, new diseases, in a studious mono-
tone. It was almost a talent, a knack he had, these elaborate
balances, the way he dwelt in his own mind as a statistician, a
neutral weigher of destinies.

"What do Sherpas do?" I said.

"Climb mountains."

"What's in Arecibo?"

"The radio telescope. The big dish."

"Let me think of some more."

"Think of some more."

"Let me think," I said.

On a plateau in the distance, separated by open sky, were two
clusters of tower houses, long gray forms rising out of the rocks
and scrub. The houses were set at varying heights so that in
aggregate they resembled a modern skyline seen from a certain
distance, a certain elevation, in the rain and haze, in ruins. I felt
we were coming upon something no one had approached in a
thousand years. A lost history. A pair of towered cities set at the
end of the continent.

They were only villages, of course, and there was nothing very
lost about them. It only seemed that way, here, in the Mani, in a
landscape of rocks. We found a dirt road and drove into the first
of the towns. The road was unpaved all the way in, turned to mud
in some places, deep pools in others. Some of the buildings were

clearly inhabited, although we saw no one. There were several recent structures, made of the same stone, among the broken towers. Walled cactus gardens. House numbers in green paint. Utility poles.

"Who am I named after?"

"You know the answer to that."

"But he died."

"That has nothing to do with it. When you go back to London, ask your mother and your aunt to tell you about his eccentricities. He had some juicy quirks. That's a local fruit you ought to try. And when you go back to Victoria, write me a letter now and then."

"But why am I named after him?"

"Your mother and I both loved him. He was a sweet man, your grandfather. Even your nickname comes from him. Some of his business associates called him Tap. Thomas Arthur Pattison, get it? But the family didn't use the name much. We called him Tommy. He was Tommy, you were Tap. A couple of funny guys. Even though you're Thomas Arthur Axton and not Pattison, we wanted to call you Tap, after him."

"How did he die?"

"You want to know how he died so you can decide whether or not that's how you're going to die. Well there's no connection, so forget it."

A dog slept on a mound of olive pulp. We went a short distance, then turned off the main road again, left this time, and drove slowly up into the other towered hamlet. We saw a woman and child retreat from a doorway, heard gunshots in the hills, two soft bursts, hunters again. Stones were arranged in circular figures, threshing floors. Some houses had slate roofs topped with stones. Stones were crammed into window spaces.

"Here's one for you. What goes on at the Bonneville salt flats?"

"Rocket cars. High-speed tests."

"What do you think of when I say Kimberley?"

"Wait, let me think."

Who are they, the people in the café? Are they *members?* At one table an old man, a chipped white cup. At the other table a group, three or four, not Greeks. They listened when I asked about the maps. How do I know they aren't Greek? Who are they, what are they doing here, this desolate place, in winter? What am I doing here, and have I stumbled across them, and do I want to go back, to look again, to be sure, one way or the other, with my son in hand?

"South Africa."

"Now if I get it, it's because you gave me a hint."

"Mining."

"Thanks for practically telling me."

"What is it then?"

Morose, slumped in his seat. "Diamond mining," he said.

Minutes later we approached the coast again. The last ridge of Taygetus fell to the sea, a clean line of descent in the fading light. I stopped the car to look at the maps. Tap pointed north, catching sight of something through my side of the windshield, and after a moment I was able to see a dark mass of towers set among the terraced hills.

"I think we ought to find a hotel or rooming house. At least figure out where we are."

"Just this last place," he said.

"You like the tower houses."

He kept peering through the glass.

"Or is it the driving you like?"

"This one last place," he said. "Then I promise we can stop."

The road up was a dirt track, all stones and mud. Three or four runnels came splashing past the car, merged in places, and I began to think about the jagged rocks, the deep mud, the force of the racing water, the growing dark. Tap broke a section of chocolate from the bar, then subdivided, a piece for each of us. It was raining hard again.

"No signs. If we knew the name of this place, we could find it on the map. Then we'd know where we are for a change."

"Maybe there's someone up there we can ask."

"Although it's probably not on the map anyway."

"We can ask," he said.

The muddy streams jumped ruts and smaller stones. I spotted dead cypress trees above us. The road kept turning, there was cactus hanging off the edges, stunted brush.

"First you see something in front of the car and then it goes past the way it really is."

"Like a tree," I said.

"Then you look in the mirror and you see the same thing, only it looks different and it moves faster, a lot faster. Whoby obis thobat."

"Too bad your mother isn't here. You could have a long talk in your native tongue. Have they given her a hole in the ground yet?"

"She has an office."

"It's only a matter of time. There's a hole in the ground somewhere in British Columbia that she's determined to end up in. Is that a question you were asking?"

"There are no questions in Ob. You can ask a question but you don't say it like a question in English. You say it like a regular sentence."

The last loop in the road took us away from our destination, momentarily, and provided a look at another towered hamlet, set along a distant ridge, and still another, a smaller cluster, silhouetted on a headland way below us. We turned up onto a long straight approach to the village and then I saw something that sent a chill through me, a delayed chill (I had to think, to translate). I stopped the car and sat there, staring out over the textured fields.

It was a fallen rock, a ten-foot boulder standing by the roadcut to our left, a flat-faced reddish block with two white words painted across its width, the pigment running down off the letters in rough trickles, the accent mark clearly in place.

Ta Onómata.

"Why are we stopping?"

"It was stupid, coming up here. My fault. We ought to be finding a place to stay, some food."

"We're turning around, you mean, just when we get here?"

"You had your drive up. Now you'll have your drive back down."

"What's painted on that rock? Do you think that's what they use for road signs here?"

"No. It's not a road sign."

"What is it?"

"Just someone writing. We've seen writing on walls and buildings everywhere we've gone. Politics. We've even seen crowns, long live the king. If there's no wall around, I guess they use the nearest thing. A rock in this case."

"Is it politics?"

"No. It's not politics."

"What is it?"

"I don't know, Tap."

"Do you know what it means?"

"The Names," I said.

▐▐▐▐ NICHOLSON BAKER

from *The Mezzanine*

Vintage Contemporaries began publishing the inventive, often hilarious work of Nicholson Baker in January 1990 with his first novel, The Mezzanine. *He is the author of three other novels, including* Room Temperature, Vox, *and* The Fermata, *and two nonfiction books,* U and I *and* The Size of Thoughts, *all available from Vintage. His essays have appeared in* The New Yorker, The Atlantic Monthly, The New York Review of Books, Esquire, *and* The Best American Essays.

■ One

AT ALMOST ONE o'clock I entered the lobby of the building where I worked and turned toward the escalators, carrying a black Penguin paperback and a small white CVS bag, its receipt stapled over the top. The escalators rose toward the mezzanine, where my office was. They were the free-standing kind: a pair of integral signs swooping upward between the two floors they served without struts or piers to bear any intermediate weight. On sunny days like this one, a temporary, steeper escalator of daylight, formed by intersections of the lobby's towering volumes of marble and glass, met the real escalators just above their middle point, spreading into a needly area of shine where it fell against their brushed-steel side-panels, and adding long glossy highlights to each of the black rubber handrails which wavered slightly as the handrails slid on their tracks, like the radians of black luster that ride the undulating outer edge of an LP.[1]

When I drew close to the up escalator, I involuntarily trans-

---

[1] I love the constancy of shine on the edges of moving objects. Even propellers or desk fans will glint steadily in certain places in the grayness of their rotation; the

ferred my paperback and CVS bag to my left hand, so that I could take the handrail with my right, according to habit. The bag made a little paper-rattling sound, and when I looked down at it, I discovered that I was unable for a second to remember what was inside, my recollection snagged on the stapled receipt. But of course that was one of the principal reasons you needed little bags, I thought: they kept your purchases private, while signaling to the world that you led a busy, rich life, full of pressing errands run. Earlier that lunch hour, I had visited a Papa Gino's, a chain I rarely ate at, to buy a half-pint of milk to go along with a cookie I had bought unexpectedly from a failing franchise, attracted by the notion of spending a few minutes in the plaza in front of my building eating a dessert I should have outgrown and reading my paperback. I paid for the carton of milk, and then the girl (her name tag said "Donna") hesitated, sensing that some component of the transaction was missing: she said, "Do you want a straw?" I hesitated in turn—did I? My interest in straws for drinking anything besides milkshakes had fallen off some years before, probably peaking out the year that all the major straw vendors switched from paper to plastic straws, and we entered that uncomfortable era of the floating straw;[1] although I did still like plastic elbow straws, whose pleated necks resisted bending in a

---

curve of each fan blade picks up the light for an instant on its circuit and then hands it off to its successor.

[1] I stared in disbelief the first time a straw rose up from my can of soda and hung out over the table, barely arrested by burrs in the underside of the metal opening. I was holding a slice of pizza in one hand, folded in a three-finger grip so that it wouldn't flop and pour cheese-grease on the paper plate, and a paperback in a similar grip in the other hand—what was I supposed to do? The whole point of straws, I had thought, was that you did not have to set down the slice of pizza to suck a dose of Coke while reading a paperback. I soon found, as many have, that there was a way to drink no-handed with those new floating straws: you had to bend low to the table and grasp the almost horizontal straw with your lips, steering it back down into the can every time you wanted a sip, while straining your eyes to keep them trained on the line of the page you were reading. How could the straw engineers have made so elementary a mistake, designing a straw that weighed less than the sugar-water in which it was intended to stand? Madness! But later, when I gave the subject more thought, I decided that, though the straw engineers were probably blameworthy for

way that was very similar to the tiny seizeups your finger joints will undergo if you hold them in the same position for a little while.[1]

So when Donna asked if I would like a straw to accompany my

---

failing to foresee the straw's buoyancy, the problem was more complex than I had first imagined. As I reconstruct that moment of history, circa 1970 or so, what happened was that the plastic material used in place of paper was in fact heavier than Coke—their equations were absolutely correct, the early manufacturing runs looked good, and though the water-to-plastic weight ratio was a little tight, they went ahead. What they had forgotten to take into account, perhaps, was that the bubbles of carbonation attach themselves to invisible asperities on the straw's surface, and are even possibly generated by turbulence at the leading edge of the straw as you plunge it in the drink; thus clad with bubbles, the once marginally heavier straw reascends until its remaining submerged surface area lacks the bubbles to lift it further. Though the earlier paper straw, with its spiral seam, was much rougher than plastic, and more likely to attract bubbles, it was porous: it soaked up a little of the Coke as ballast and stayed put. All right—an oversight; why wasn't it corrected? A different recipe for the plastic, a thicker straw? Surely the huge buyers, the fast-food companies, wouldn't have tolerated straws beaching themselves in their restaurants for more than six months or so. They must have had whole departments dedicated to exacting concessions from Sweetheart and Marcal. But the fast-food places were adjusting to a novelty of their own at about the same time: they were putting slosh caps on every soft drink they served, to go *or* for the dining room, which cut down on spillage, and the slosh caps had a little cross in the middle, which had been the source of some unhappiness in the age of paper straws, because the cross was often so tight that the paper straw would crumple when you tried to push it through. The straw men at the fast-food corporations had had a choice: either we (a) make the crossed slits easier to pierce so that the paper straws aren't crumpled, or we (b) abandon paper outright, and make the slits even *tighter*, so that (1) any tendency to float is completely negated and (2) the seal between the straw and the crossed slits is so tight that almost no soda will well out, stain car seats and clothing, and cause frustration. And (b) was the ideal solution for them, even leaving aside the attractive price that the straw manufacturers were offering as they switched their plant over from paper-spiraling equipment to high-speed extrusion machines—so they adopted it, not thinking that their decision had important consequences for all restaurants and pizza places (especially) that served cans of soda. Suddenly the paper-goods distributor was offering the small restaurants floating plastic straws and only floating plastic straws, and was saying that this was the way all the big chains were going; and the smaller sub shops did no independent testing using cans of soda instead of cups with crossed-slit slosh caps. In this way the quality of life, through nobody's fault, went down an eighth of a notch, until just last year, I think, when one day I noticed a plastic straw, made of some subtler polymer, with a colored stripe in it, stood anchored to the bottom of my can!

[1] When I was little I had thought a fair amount about the finger-joint effect; I assumed that when you softly crunched over those temporary barriers you were leveling actual "cell walls" that the joint had built to define what it believed from your motionlessness was going to be the final, stable geography for that microscopic region.

half-pint of milk, I smiled at her and said, "No thanks. But maybe I'd like a little bag." She said, "Oh! Sorry," and hurriedly reached under the counter for it, touchingly flustered, thinking she had goofed. She was quite new; you could tell by the way she opened the bag: three anemone splayings of her fingers inside it, the slowest way. I thanked her and left, and then I began to wonder: Why had I requested a bag to hold a simple half-pint of milk? It wasn't simply out of some abstract need for propriety, a wish to shield the nature of my purchase from the public eye— although this was often a powerful motive, and not to be ridiculed. Small mom and pop shopkeepers, who understood these things, instinctively shrouded whatever solo item you bought—a box of pasta shells, a quart of milk, a pan of Jiffy Pop, a loaf of bread—in a bag: food meant to be eaten indoors, they felt, should be seen only indoors. But even after ringing up things like cigarettes or ice cream bars, obviously meant for ambulatory consumption, they often prompted, "Little bag?" "Small bag?" "Little bag for that?" Bagging evidently was used to mark the exact point at which title to the ice cream bar passed to the buyer. When I was in high school I used to unsettle these proprietors, as they automatically reached for a bag for my quart of milk, by raising a palm and saying officiously, "I don't need a bag, thanks." I would leave holding the quart coolly in one hand, as if it were a big reference book I had to consult so often that it bored me.

Why had I intentionally snubbed their convention, when I had loved bags since I was very little and had learned how to refold the large thick ones from the supermarket by pulling the creases taut and then tapping along the infolding center of each side until the bag began to hunch forward on itself, as if wounded, until it lay flat again? I might have defended my snub at the time by saying something about unnecessary waste, landfills, etc. But the real reason was that by then I had become a steady consumer of magazines featuring color shots of naked women, which I bought for the most part not at the mom-and-pop stores but at the newer and more anonymous convenience stores, distributing my purchases among several in the area. And at these stores, the guy at the register would sometimes cruelly, mock-innocently warp the "Little bag?" convention by asking, "You need a bag for that?"— forcing me either to concede this need with a nod, or to be tough and say no and roll up the unbagged nude magazine and clamp it in my bicycle rack so that only the giveaway cigarette ad on the back cover showed—"Carlton Is Lowest."[1]

Hence the fact that I often said no to a bag for a quart of milk at the mom-and-pop store during that period was a way of demonstrating to anyone who might have been following my movements that at least at that moment, exiting that store, I had nothing to hide; that I did make typical, vice-free family purchases from time to time. And now I was asking for a little bag for my half-pint of milk from Donna in order, finally, to clean away the bewilderment I had caused those moms and pops, to submit happily to the convention, even to pass it on to someone who had not yet quite learned it at Papa Gino's.

But there was a simpler, less anthropological reason I had specifically asked Donna for the bag, a reason I hadn't quite iso-

---

[1] For several years it was inconceivable to buy one of those periodicals when a girl was behind the counter; but once, boldly, I tried it—I looked directly at her mascara and asked for a *Penthouse*, even though I preferred the less pretentious *Oui* or *Club*, saying it so softly however that she heard "Powerhouse" and cheerfully pointed out the candy bar until I repeated the name. Breaking all eye contact, she placed the document on the counter between us—it was back when they still showed nipples on their covers—and rang it up along with the small container of Woolite I was buying to divert attention: she was embarrassed and brisk and possibly faintly excited, and she slipped the magazine in a bag without asking whether I "needed" one or not. That afternoon I expanded her brief embarrassment into a helpful vignette in which I became a steady once-a-week buyer of men's magazines from her, always on Tuesday morning, until my very ding-dong entrance into the 7-Eleven was charged with trembly confusion for both of us, and I began finding little handwritten notes placed in the most wide-spread pages of the magazine when I got home that said, "Hi!—the Cashier," and "Last night I posed sort of like this in front of my mirror in my room—the Cashier," and "Sometimes I look at these pictures and think of you looking at them—the Cashier." Turnover is always a problem at those stores, and she had quit the next time I went in.

lated in that first moment of analysis on the sidewalk afterward, but which I now perceived, walking toward the escalator to the mezzanine and looking at the stapled CVS bag I had just transferred from one hand to the other. It seemed that I always liked to have one hand free when I was walking, even when I had several things to carry: I liked to be able to slap my hand fondly down on the top of a green mailmen-only mailbox, or bounce my fist lightly against the steel support for the traffic lights, both because the pleasure of touching these cold, dusty surfaces with the springy muscle on the side of my palm was intrinsically good, and because I liked other people to see me as a guy in a tie yet carefree and casual enough to be doing what kids do when they drag a stick over the black uprights of a cast-iron fence. I especially liked doing one thing: I liked walking past a parking meter so close that it seemed as if my hand would slam into it, and at the last minute lifting my arm out just enough so that the meter passed underneath my armpit. All of these actions depended on a free hand; and at Papa Gino's I already was holding the Penguin paperback, the CVS bag, and the cookie bag. It might have been possible to hold the blocky shape of the half-pint of milk against the paperback, and the tops of the slim cookie bag and the CVS bag against the other side of the paperback, in order to keep one hand free, but my fingers would have had to maintain this awkward grasp, building cell walls in earnest, for several blocks until I got to my building. A bag for the milk allowed for a more graceful solution: I could scroll the tops of the cookie bag, the CVS bag, and the milk bag *as one* into my curled fingers, as if I were taking a small child on a walk. (A straw poking out of the top of the milk bag would have interfered with this scrolling—lucky I had refused it!) Then I could slide the paperback into this space between the scroll of bag paper and my palm. And this is what I had in fact done. At first the Papa Gino's bag was stiff, but very soon my walking softened the paper a little, although I never got it to the state of utter silence and flannel softness that a bag will attain when you carry it around all day, its hand-held curl so finely wrinkled and formed to your fingers by the time you get home that you hesitate to unroll it.

It was only just now, near the base of the escalator, as I watched my left hand automatically take hold of the paperback and the CVS bag together, that I consolidated the tiny understanding I had almost had fifteen minutes before. Then it had not been tagged as knowledge to be held for later retrieval, and I would have forgotten it completely had it not been for the sight of the CVS bag, similar enough to the milk-carton bag to trigger vibratiuncles of comparison. Under microscopy, even insignificant perceptions like this one are almost always revealed to be more incremental than you later are tempted to present them as being. It would have been less cumbersome, in the account I am giving here of a specific lunch hour several years ago, to have pretended that the bag thought had come to me complete and "all at once" at the foot of the up escalator, but the truth was that it was only the latest in a fairly long sequence of partially forgotten, inarticulable experiences, finally now reaching a point that I paid attention to it for the first time.

In the stapled CVS bag was a pair of new shoelaces.

■ Two

MY LEFT SHOELACE had snapped just before lunch. At some earlier point in the morning, my left shoe had become untied, and as I had sat at my desk working on a memo, my foot had sensed its potential freedom and slipped out of the sauna of black cordovan to soothe itself with rhythmic movements over an area of wall-to-wall carpeting under my desk, which, unlike the tamped-down areas of public traffic, was still almost as soft and fibrous as it had been when first installed. Only under the desks and in the little-used conference rooms was the pile still plush enough to hold the beautiful Ms and Vs the night crew left as strokes of their vacuum cleaners' wands made swaths of dustless tufting lean in directions that alternately absorbed and reflected the light. The nearly universal carpeting of offices must have come about in my lifetime, judging from black-and-white movies and Hopper paintings: since the pervasion of carpeting, all you hear when people walk by are their own noises—the flap of their raincoats, the jingle of their change, the squeak of their shoes, the efficient little sniffs they make to signal to us and to themselves that they are busy and walking somewhere for a very good reason, as well as the almost sonic whoosh of receptionists' staggering and misguided perfumes, and the covert chokings and showings of tongues and placing of braceleted hands to windpipes that more tastefully scented secretaries exchange in their wake. One or two individuals in every office (Dave in mine), who have special pounding styles of walking, may still manage to get their footfalls heard; but in general now we all glide at work: a major improvement, as anyone knows who has visited those areas of offices that are still for various reasons linoleum-squared—cafeterias, mailrooms, computer rooms. Linoleum was bearable back when incandescent light was there to counteract it with a softening glow, but the combination of fluorescence and linoleum, which must have been widespread for several years as the two trends overlapped, is not good.

As I had worked, then, my foot had, without any sanction from my conscious will, slipped from the untied shoe and sought out the texture of the carpeting; although now, as I reconstruct the moment, I realize that a more specialized desire was at work as well: when you slide a socked foot over a carpeted surface, the fibers of sock and carpet mesh and lock, so that though you think you are enjoying the texture of the carpeting, you are really enjoying the slippage of the inner surface of the sock against the underside of your foot, something you normally get to experience only in the morning when you first pull the sock on.[1]

At a few minutes before twelve, I stopped working, threw out my earplugs and, more carefully, the remainder of my morning coffee—placing it upright within the converging spinnakers of the trash can liner on the base of the receptacle itself. I stapled a copy of a memo someone had cc:'d me on to a copy of an earlier memo I had written on the same subject, and wrote at the top to my manager, in my best casual scrawl, "Abe—should I keep hammering on these people or drop it?" I put the stapled papers in one of my Eldon trays, not sure whether I would forward them to Abelardo or not. Then I slipped my shoe back on by flipping it on its side, hooking it with my foot, and shaking it into place. I accomplished all this by foot-feel; and when I crouched forward, over the papers on my desk, to reach the untied shoelace, I experienced a faint surge of pride in being able to tie a shoe without looking at it. At that moment, Dave, Sue, and Steve, on their way to lunch, waved as they passed by my office. Right in the middle of tying a shoe as I was, I couldn't wave nonchalantly back, so I called out a startled, overhearty "Have a good one, guys!" They disappeared; I pulled the left shoelace tight, and *bingo*, it broke.

The curve of incredulousness and resignation I rode out at that moment was a kind caused in life by a certain class of events, disruptions of physical routines, such as:

---

[1]When I pull a sock on, I no longer *pre-bunch*, that is, I don't gather the sock up into telescoped folds over my thumbs, and then position the resultant donut over my toes, even though I believed for some years that this was a clever trick, taught by admirable, fresh-faced kindergarten teachers, and that I revealed my laziness and my inability to plan ahead by instead holding the sock by the ankle rim and jamming my foot to its destination, working the ankle a few times to properly seat the heel. Why? The more elegant pre-bunching can leave in place any pieces of grit that have embedded themselves in your sole from the imperfectly swept floor you walked on to get from the shower to your room; while the cruder, more direct method, though it risks tearing an older sock, does detach this grit during the foot's downward passage, so that you seldom later feel irritating particles rolling around under your arch as you depart for the subway.

(a) reaching a top step but thinking there is another step there, and stamping down on the landing;

(b) pulling on the red thread that is supposed to butterfly a Band-Aid and having it wrest free from the wrapper without tearing it;

(c) drawing a piece of Scotch tape from the roll that resides half sunk in its black, weighted Duesenberg of a dispenser, hearing the slightly descending whisper of adhesive-coated plastic detaching itself from the back of the tape to come (descending in pitch because the strip, while amplifying the sound, is also getting longer as you pull on it[1]), and then, just as you are intending to break the piece off over the metal serration, reaching the innermost end of the roll, so that the segment you have been pulling wafts unexpectedly free. Especially now, with the rise of Post-it Notes, which have made the massive black tape-dispensers seem even more grandiose and Biedermeier and tragically defunct, you almost believe that you will never come to the end of a roll of tape; and when you do, there is a feeling, nearly, though very briefly, of shock and grief;

(d) attempting to staple a thick memo, and looking forward, as you begin to lean on the brontosaural head of the stapler arm,[2] to the three phases of the act

---

[1] When I was little I thought it was called Scotch tape because the word "scotch" imitated the descending screech of early cellophane tapes. As incandescence gave way before fluorescence in office lighting, Scotch tape, once yellowish-transparent, became bluish-transparent, as well as superbly quiet.

[2] Staplers have followed, lagging by about ten years, the broad stylistic changes we have witnessed in train locomotives and phonograph tonearms, both of which they resemble. The oldest staplers are cast-ironic and upright, like coal-fired locomotives and Edison wax-cylinder players. Then, in mid-century, as locomotive manufacturers discovered the word "streamlined," and as tonearm designers housed the stylus in aerodynamic ribbed plastic hoods that looked like trains curving around a mountain, the people at Swingline and Bates tagged along, instinctively sensing that staplers were like locomotives in that the two prongs of the staple make contact with a pair of metal hollows, which, like the paired rails under the wheels of the train, forces them to follow a preset path, and that they were like phonograph tonearms in that both machines, roughly the same size, make sharp points of contact with their

first, before the stapler arm makes contact with the paper, the resistance of the spring that keeps the arm held up; then, *second,* the moment when the small independent unit in the stapler arm noses into the paper and begins to force the two points of the staple into and through it; and, *third,* the felt crunch, like the chewing of an ice cube, as the twin tines of the staple emerge from the underside of the paper and are bent by the two troughs of the template in the stapler's base, curving inward in a crab's embrace of your memo, and finally disengaging from the machine completely—

but finding, as you lean on the stapler with your elbow locked and your breath held and it slumps toothlessly to the paper, that it has run out of staples. How could something this consistent, this incremental, betray you? (But then you are consoled: you get to reload it, laying bare the stapler arm and dripping a long zithering row of staples into place; and later, on the phone, you get to toy with the piece of the staples you couldn't fit into the stapler, break-

---

respective media of informational storage. (In the case of the tonearm, the stylus retrieves the information, while in the case of the stapler, the staple binds it together as a unit—the order, the shipping paper, the invoice: *boom,* stapled, a unit; the letter of complaint, the copies of canceled checks and receipts, the letter of apologetic response: *boom,* stapled, a unit; a sequence of memos and telexes holding the history of some interdepartmental controversy: *boom,* stapled, one controversy. In old stapled problems, you can see the TB vaccine marks in the upper left corner where staples have been removed and replaced, removed and replaced, as the problem—even the staple holes of the problem—was copied and sent on to other departments for further action, copying, and stapling.) And then the great era of squareness set in: BART was the ideal for trains, while AR and Bang & Olufsen turntables became angular—no more cream colored bulbs of plastic! The people at Bates and Swingline again were drawn along, ridding their devices of all softening curvatures and offering black rather than the interestingly textured tan. And now, of course, the high-speed trains of France and Japan have reverted to aerodynamic profiles reminiscent of *Popular Science* cities-of-the-future covers of the fifties; and soon the stapler will incorporate a toned-down pompadour swoop as well. Sadly, the tonearm's stylistic progress has slowed, because all the buyers who would appreciate an up-to-date Soviet Realism in the design are buying CD players: its inspirational era is over.

ing it into smaller segments, making them dangle on a hinge of glue.)

In the aftermath of the broken-shoelace disappointment, irrationally, I pictured Dave, Sue, and Steve as I had just seen them and thought, "Cheerful assholes!" because I had probably broken the shoelace by transferring the social energy that I had had to muster to deliver a chummy "Have a good one!" to them from my awkward shoe-tier's crouch into the force I had used in pulling on the shoelace. Of course, it would have worn out sooner or later anyway. It was the original shoelace, and the shoes were the very ones my father had bought me two years earlier, just after I had started this job, my first out of college—so the breakage was a sentimental milestone of sorts. I rolled back in my chair to study the damage, imagining the smiles on my three co-workers' faces suddenly vanishing if I had really called them cheerful assholes, and regretting this burst of ill feeling toward them.

As soon as my gaze fell to my shoes, however, I was reminded of something that should have struck me the instant the shoelace had first snapped. The day before, as I had been getting ready for work, my *other* shoelace, the right one, had snapped, too, as I was yanking it tight to tie it, under very similar circumstances. I repaired it with a knot, just as I was planning to do now with the left. I was surprised—more than surprised—to think that after almost two years my right and left shoelaces could fail less than two days apart. Apparently my shoe-tying routine was so unvarying and robotic that over those hundreds of mornings I had inflicted identical levels of wear on both laces. The near simultaneity was very exciting—it made the variables of private life seem suddenly graspable and law-abiding.

I moistened the splayed threads of the snapped-off piece and twirled them gently into a damp, unwholesome minaret. Breathing steadily and softly through my nose, I was able to guide the saliva-sharpened leader thread through the eyelet without too much trouble. And then I grew uncertain. In order for the shoelaces to have worn to the breaking point on almost the same day, they would have had to be tied almost exactly the same number of times. But when Dave, Sue, and Steve passed my office door, I had been in the middle of tying one shoe—*one shoe only*. And in the course of a normal day it wasn't at all unusual for one shoe to come untied independent of the other. In the morning, of course, you always tied both shoes, but random midday comings-undone would have to have constituted a significant proportion of the total wear on both of these broken laces, I felt—possibly thirty percent. And how could I be positive that this thirty percent was equally distributed—that right and left shoes had come randomly undone over the last two years with the same frequency?

I tried to call up some sample memories of shoe-tying to determine whether one shoe tended to come untied more often than another. What I found was that I did not retain a single specific engram of tying a shoe, or a pair of shoes, that dated from any later than when I was four or five years old, the age at which I had first learned the skill. Over twenty years of empirical data were lost forever, a complete blank. But I suppose this is often true of moments of life that are remembered as major advances: the discovery is the crucial thing, not its repeated later applications. As it happened, the first *three* major advances in my life—and I will list all the advances here—

1. shoe-tying
2. pulling up on Xs
3. steadying hand against sneaker when tying
4. brushing tongue as well as teeth
5. putting on deodorant after I was fully dressed

6. discovering that sweeping was fun
7. ordering a rubber stamp with my address on it to make bill-paying more efficient
8. deciding that brain cells ought to die

—have to do with shoe-tying, but I don't think that this fact is very unusual. Shoes are the first adult machines we are given to master. Being taught to tie them was not like watching some adult fill the dishwasher and then being asked in a kind voice if you would like to clamp the dishwasher door shut and advance the selector knob (with its uncomfortable grinding sound) to Wash. That was artificial, whereas you knew that adults wanted you to learn how to tie your shoes; it was no fun for them to kneel. I made several attempts to learn the skill, but it was not until my mother placed a lamp on the floor so that I could clearly see the dark laces of a pair of new dress shoes that I really mastered it; she explained again how to form the introductory platform knot, which began high in the air as a frail, heart-shaped loop, and shrunk as you pulled the plastic lace-tips down to a short twisted kernel three-eighths of an inch long, and she showed me how to progress from that base to the main cotyledonary string figure, which was, as it turned out, not a true knot but an illusion, a trick that you performed on the lace-string by bending segments of it back on themselves and tightening other temporary bends around them: it looked like a knot and functioned like a knot, but the whole thing was really an amazing interdependent pyramid scheme, which much later I connected with a couplet of Pope's:

> Man, like the gen'rous vine, supported lives;
> The strength he gains is from th'embrace he gives.

Only a few weeks after I learned the basic skill, my father helped me to my second major advance, when he demonstrated thoroughness by showing me how to tighten the rungs of the shoelaces one by one, beginning down at the toe and working up, hooking an index finger under each X, so that by the time you reached the top you were rewarded with surprising lengths of lace to use in tying the knot, and at the same time your foot felt tightly papoosed and alert.

The third advance I made by myself in the middle of a play-ground, when I halted, out of breath, to tie a sneaker,[1] my mouth on my interesting-smelling knee, a close-up view of anthills and the tread marks of other sneakers before me (the best kind, Keds, I think, or Red Ball Flyers, had a perimeter of asymmetrical tri-angles, and a few concavities in the center which printed perfect domes of dust), and found as I retied the shoe that I was doing it automatically, without having to concentrate on it as I had done at first, and, more important, that somewhere over the past year since I had first learned the basic moves, I had evidently evolved two little substeps of my own *that nobody had showed me.* In one I held down a temporarily taut stretch of shoelace with the side of my thumb; in the other I stabilized my hand with a middle finger propped against the side of the sneaker during some final manip-ulations. The advance here was my recognition that I had inde-pendently developed refinements of technique in an area where nobody had indicated there were refinements to be found: I had personalized an already adult procedure.

---

[1] Sneaker knots were quite different from dress knots—when you pulled the two loops tight at the end, the logic of the knot you had just created became untraceable; while in the case of dress-lace knots, you could, even after tightening, follow the path of the knot around with your mind, as if riding a roller coaster. You could imag-ine a sneaker-shoelace knot and a dress-shoelace knot standing side by side saying the Pledge of Allegiance: the dress-shoelace knot would pronounce each word as a grammatical unit, understanding it as more than a sound; the sneaker-shoelace knot would run the words together. The great advantage of sneakers, though, one of the many advantages, was that when you had tied them tightly, without wearing socks, and worn them all day, and gotten them wet, and you took them off before bed, your feet would display the impression of the chrome eyelets in red rows down the sides of your foot, like the portholes in a Jules Verne submarine.

||| BRET EASTON ELLIS

from *American Psycho*

Bret Easton Ellis skillfully captures the allure and despair of the nihilistic and cosmopolitan 1980s in such contemporary classics as Less Than Zero, The Rules of Attraction, American Psycho, *and* The Informers, *all of which are available from Vintage Contemporaries. We first published* American Psycho, *excerpted here, in 1991. Ellis's new novel,* Glamourama, *is forthcoming from Knopf.*

■ LUNCH WITH BETHANY

TODAY I'M MEETING Bethany for lunch at Vanities, the new Evan Kiley bistro in Tribeca, and though I worked out for nearly two hours this morning and even lifted weights in my office before noon, I'm still extremely nervous. The cause is hard to locate but I've narrowed it down to one of two reasons. It's either that I'm afraid of rejection (though I can't understand why: *she* called *me*, she wants to see *me*, she wants to have lunch with *me*, she wants to fuck *me* again) or, on the other hand, it could have something to do with this new Italian mousse I'm wearing, which, though it makes my hair look fuller and smells good, feels very sticky and uncomfortable, and it's something I could easily blame my nervousness on. So we wouldn't run out of things to talk about over lunch, I tried to read a trendy new short-story collection called *Wok* that I bought at Barnes & Noble last night and whose young author was recently profiled in the Fast Track section of *New York* magazine, but every story started off with the line "When the moon hits your eye like a big pizza pie" and I had to put this slim volume back into my bookshelf and drink a J&B on the rocks, followed by two Xanax, to recover from the effort. To make up for this, before I fell asleep I wrote Bethany a poem and it took a long time, which surprised me, since I used to write her poems, long dark ones, quite often when we were both at Harvard, before we broke up. God, I'm thinking to myself as I walk into Vanities, only fifteen minutes late, I hope she hasn't ended up with Robert Hall, that dumb asshole. I pass by a mirror hung over the bar as I'm led to our table and check out my reflection—the mousse looks good. The topic on *The Patty Winters Show* this morning was Has Patrick Swayze Become Cynical or Not?

I have to stop moving as I near the table, following the maître d' (this is all happening in slow motion). She isn't facing me and I can only catch the back of her neck, her brown hair pinned up into a bun, and when she turns to gaze out the window I see only part of her profile, briefly; she looks *just like a model*. Bethany's wearing a silk gazar blouse and a silk satin skirt with crinoline. A Paloma Picasso hunter green suede and wrought-iron handbag sits in front of her on the table, next to a bottle of San Pellegrino water. She checks her watch. The couple next to our table is smoking and after I lean in behind Bethany, surprising her, kissing her cheek, I coolly ask the maître d' to reseat us in the *non*-smoking section. I'm suave but loud enough for the nicotine addicts to hear me and hopefully feel a slight twinge of embarrassment about their filthy habit.

"Well?" I ask, standing there, arms crossed, tapping my foot impatiently.

"I'm afraid there is no nonsmoking section, sir," the maître d' informs me.

I stop tapping my foot and slowly scan the restaurant, the *bistro*, wondering how my hair really looks, and suddenly I wish I *had* switched mousses because since I last saw my hair, seconds ago, it feels different, as if its shape was somehow altered on the walk from bar to table. A pang of nausea that I'm unable to stifle washes warmly over me, but since I'm really dreaming all this

I'm able to ask, "So you say there's *no* nonsmoking section? Is that correct?"

"Yes sir." The maître d', younger than myself, faggy, innocent, an *actor* no doubt, adds, "I'm sorry."

"Well, this is . . . very interesting. I can accept this." I reach into my back pocket for my gazelleskin wallet and press a twenty into the maître d's uncertain fist. He looks at the bill, confused, then murmurs "Thank you" and walks away as if in a daze.

"No. Thank *you*," I call out and take my seat across from Bethany, nodding courteously to the couple next to us, and though I try to ignore her for as long as etiquette allows, I can't. Bethany looks absolutely stunning, *just like a model*. Everything's murky. I'm on edge. Feverish, romantic notions—

"Didn't you smoke at Harvard?" is the first thing she says.

"Cigars," I say. "Only cigars."

"Oh," she says.

"But I quit that," I lie, breathing in hard, squeezing my hands together.

"That's good." She nods.

"Listen, did you have any trouble getting reservations?" I ask, and *I am fucking shaking*. I put my hands on the table like a fool, hoping that under her watchful gaze they will stop trembling.

"You don't need reservations here, Patrick," she says soothingly, reaching out a hand, covering one of mine with hers. "Calm down. You look like a wild man."

"I'm clam, I mean calm," I say, breathing in hard, trying to smile, and then, involuntarily, unable to stop myself, ask, "How's my hair?"

"Your hair is fine," she says. "Shhh. It's okay."

"All right. I am all right." I try to smile again but I'm sure it looks just like a grimace.

After a short pause she comments, "That's a nice suit. Henry Stuart?"

"No," I say, insulted, touching its lapel. "Garrick Anderson."

"It's very nice," she says and then, genuinely concerned, "Are you okay, Patrick? You just . . . twitched."

"Listen. I'm frazzled. I just got back from Washington. I took the Trump shuttle this morning," I tell her, unable to make eye contact, all in a rush. "It was delightful. The service—really fabulous. I need a drink."

She smiles, amused, studying me in a shrewd way. "Was it?" she asks, not totally, I sense, without smugness.

"Yes." I can't really look at her and it takes immense effort to unfold the napkin, lay it across my lap, reposition it correctly, busy myself with the wineglass, praying for a waiter, the ensuing silence causing the loudest possible sound. "So did you watch *The Patty Winters Show* this morning?"

"No, I was out jogging," she says, leaning in. "It was about Michael J. Fox, right?"

"No," I correct her. "It was about Patrick Swayze."

"Oh really?" she asks, then, "It's hard to keep track. You're sure?"

"Yes. Patrick Swayze. I'm positive."

"How was it?"

"Well, it was very interesting," I tell her, breathing in air. "It was almost like a debate, about whether he's gotten cynical or not."

"Do you think he has?" she asks, still smiling.

"Well, no, I'm not sure," I start nervously. "It's an interesting question. It wasn't explored fully enough. I mean after *Dirty Dancing* I wouldn't think so, but with *Tiger Warsaw* I don't know. I might be crazy, but I thought I detected *some* bitterness. I'm not sure."

She stares at me, her expression unchanged.

"Oh, I almost forgot," I say, reaching into my pocket. "I wrote you a poem." I hand her the slip of paper. "Here." I feel sick and broken, tortured, really on the brink.

"Oh Patrick." She smiles. "How sweet."

"Well, you know," I say, looking down shyly.

Bethany takes the slip of paper and unfolds it.

"Read it," I urge enthusiastically.

She looks it over quizzically, puzzled, squinting, then she turns the page over to see if there's anything on the back. Something in her understands it's short and she looks back at the words written, scrawled in red, on the front of the page.

"It's like haiku, you know?" I say. "Read it. Go on."

She clears her throat and hesitantly begins reading, slowly, stopping often. "'The poor nigger on the wall. Look at him.'" She pauses and squints again at the paper, then hesitantly resumes. "'Look at the poor nigger. Look at the poor nigger . . . on . . . the . . . wall.'" She stops again, faltering, looks at me, confused, then back at the paper.

"Go on," I say, looking around for a waiter. "Finish it."

She clears her throat and staring steadily at the paper tries to read the rest of it in a voice below a whisper. "'Fuck him . . . Fuck the nigger on the wall . . .'" She falters again, then reads the last sentence, sighing. "'Black man . . . is . . . de . . . debil?'"

The couple at the next table have slowly turned to gaze over at us. The man looks aghast, the woman has an equally horrified expression on her face. I stare her down, glaring, until she looks back at her fucking salad.

"Well, Patrick," Bethany says, clearing her throat, trying to smile, handing the paper back to me.

"Yes?" I ask. "Well?"

"I can see that"—she stops, thinking—"that your sense of . . . social injustice is"—she clears her throat again and looks down—"still intact."

I take the paper back from her and slip it in my pocket and smile, still trying to keep a straight face, holding my body upright so she won't suspect me of cringing. Our waiter comes over to the table and I ask him what kinds of beer they serve.

"Heineken, Budweiser, Amstel Light," he recites.

"Yes?" I ask, staring at Bethany, gesturing for him to continue.

"That's, um, all, sir," he says.

"No Corona? No Kirin? No Grolsch? No Morretti?" I ask, confused, irate.

"I'm sorry, sir, but no," he says cautiously. "Only Heineken, Budweiser, Amstel Light."

"That's crazy," I sigh. "I'll have a J&B on the rocks. No, an Absolut martini. No, a J&B straight up."

"And I'll have another San Pellegrino," Bethany says.

"I'll have the same thing," I quickly add, my leg jerking up then down uncontrollably beneath the table.

"Okay. Would you like to hear the specials?" he asks.

"By all means," I spit out, then, calming down, smile reassuringly at Bethany.

"You're sure?" He laughs.

"*Please*," I say, unamused, studying the menu.

"For appetizers I have the sun-dried tomatoes and golden caviar with poblano chilies and I also have a fresh endive soup—"

"Wait a minute, wait a minute," I say, holding up a hand, stopping him. "Hold on a minute."

"Yes sir?" the waiter asks, confused.

"*You* have? You mean the *restaurant* has," I correct him. "*You* don't have any sun-dried tomatoes. The restaurant does. *You* don't have the poblano chilies. The restaurant does. Just, you know, clarify."

The waiter, stunned, looks at Bethany, who handles the situation deftly by asking him, "So how is the endive soup served?"

"Er . . . cold," the waiter says, not fully recovered from my outburst, sensing he's dealing with someone very, very on edge. He stops again, uncertain.

"Go on," I urge. "Please go on."

"It's served cold," he starts again. "And for entrées we have monkfish with mango slices and red snapper sandwich on brioche with maple syrup and"—he checks his pad again—"cotton."

"Mmmm, sounds delicious. Cotton, mmmm," I say, rubbing my hands together eagerly. "Bethany?"

"I'll have the ceviche with leeks and sorrel," Bethany says. "And the endive with . . . walnut dressing."

"Sir?" the waiter asks tentatively.

"I'll have . . ." I stop, scan the menu quickly. "I'll have the squid with pine nuts and can I have a slice of goat cheese, of *chèvre*"—I glance over at Bethany to see if she flinches at my mispronunciation—"with that and some . . . oh, some salsa on the side."

The waiter nods, leaves, we're left alone.

"Well." She smiles, then notices the table slightly shaking. "What's . . . wrong with your leg?"

"My leg? Oh." I look down at it, then back at her. "It's . . . the music. I like the music a lot. The music that's playing."

"What is it?" she asks, tilting her head, trying to catch a refrain of the New Age Muzak coming from the speakers hooked to the ceiling over the bar.

"It's . . . I think it's Belinda Carlisle," I guess. "I'm not sure."

"But . . ." she starts, then stops. "Oh, forget it."

"But what?"

"But I don't hear any singing." She smiles, looks down demurely.

I hold my leg still and pretend to listen. "But it's one of her songs," I say, then lamely add, "I think it's called 'Heaven Is a Place on Earth.' You know it."

"Listen," she says, "have you gone to any concerts lately?"

"No," I say, wishing she hadn't brought this, of all topics, up. "I don't like live music."

"*Live* music?" she asks, intrigued, sipping San Pellegrino water.

"Yeah. You know. Like a band," I explain, sensing from her expression that I'm saying totally the wrong things. "Oh, I forgot. I did see U2."

"How were they?" she asks. "I liked the new CD a lot."

"They were great, just totally great. Just totally . . ." I pause, unsure of what to say. Bethany raises her eyebrows quizzically, wanting to know more. "Just totally . . . Irish."

"I've heard they're quite good live," she says, and her own voice has a light, musical lilt to it. "Who else do you like?"

"Oh you know," I say, completely stuck. "The Kingsmen. 'Louie, Louie.' That sort of stuff."

"Gosh, Patrick," she says, looking at every part of my face.

"What?" I panic, immediately touching my hair. "Too much mousse? You don't like the Kingsmen?"

"No." She laughs. "I just don't remember you being so tan back at school."

"I had a tan then, didn't I?" I ask. "I mean I wasn't Casper the Ghost or anything, was I?" I put my elbow on the table and flex my biceps, asking her to squeeze the muscle. After she touches it, reluctantly, I resume my questions. "Was I really not that tan at Harvard?" I ask mock-worriedly, but worriedly.

"No, no." She laughs. "You were definitely the George Hamilton of the class of eighty-four."

"Thanks," I say, pleased.

The waiter brings our drinks—two bottles of San Pellegrino water. Scene Two.

"So you're at Mill . . . on the water? Taffeta? What is it?" I ask. Her body, her skin tone, seem firm and rosy.

"Milbank Tweed," she says. "That's where I am."

"Well," I say, squeezing a lime into my glass. "That's just wonderful. Law school really paid off."

"And you're at . . . P & P?" she asks.

"Yes," I say.

She nods, pauses, wants to say something, debates whether she should, then asks, all in a matter of seconds: "But doesn't your family own—"

"I don't want to talk about this," I say, cutting her off. "But yes, Bethany. Yes."

"And you still work at P & P?" she asks. Each syllable is spaced so that it bursts, booming sonically, into my head.

"Yes," I say, looking furtively around the room.

"But—" She's confused. "Didn't your father—"

"Yes, of course," I say, interrupting. "Have you had the focaccia at Pooncakes?"

"*Patrick.*"

"Yes?"

"What's wrong?"

"I just don't want to talk about . . ." I stop. "About work."

"Why not?"

"Because I hate it," I say. "Now listen, have you tried Pooncakes yet? I think Miller underrated it."

"Patrick," she says slowly. "If you're so uptight about work, why don't you just quit? You don't have to work."

"Because," I say, staring directly at her, "I . . . want . . . to . . . fit . . . in."

After a long pause, she smiles. "I see." There's another pause. This one I break. "Just look at it as, well, a new approach to business," I say.

"How"—she stalls—"sensible." She stalls again. "How, um, practical."

Lunch is alternately a burden, a puzzle that needs to be solved, an obstacle, and then it floats effortlessly into the realm of relief and I'm able to give a skillful performance—my overriding intelligence tunes in and lets me know that it can sense how much she wants me, but I hold back, uncommitted. She's also holding back, but flirting nonetheless. She has made a promise by asking me to lunch and I panic, once the squid is served, certain that I will never recover unless it's fulfilled. Other men notice her as they pass by our table. Sometimes I coolly bring my voice down to a whisper. I'm hearing things—noise, mysterious sounds, inside my head; her mouth opens, closes, swallows liquid, smiles, takes me in like a magnet covered with lipstick, mentions something involving fax machines, twice. I finally order a J&B on the rocks, then a cognac. She has mint-coconut sorbet. I touch, hold her hand across the table, more than a friend. Sun pours into Vanities, the restaurant empties out, it nears three. She orders a glass of chardonnay, then another, then the check. She has relaxed but something happens. My heartbeat rises and falls, momentarily stabilizes. I listen carefully. Possibilities once imagined plummet. She lowers her eyes and when she looks back at me I lower mine.

"So," she asks. "Are you seeing anyone?"

"My life is essentially uncomplicated," I say thoughtfully, caught off guard.

"What does *that* mean?" she asks.

I take a sip of cognac and smile secretly to myself, teasing her, dashing her hopes, her dreams of being reunited.

"Are you seeing anyone, Patrick?" she asks. "Come on, tell me."

Thinking of Evelyn, I murmur to myself, "Yes."

"Who?" I hear her ask.

"A very large bottle of Desyrel," I say in a faraway voice, suddenly very sad.

"What?" she asks, smiling, but then she realizes something and shakes her head. "I shouldn't be drinking."

"No, I'm not really," I say, snapping out of it, then, not of my own accord, "I mean, does anyone really *see* anyone? Does anyone really *see* anyone else? Did *you* ever see *me? See?* What does that mean? Ha! *See?* Ha! I just don't get it. Ha!" I laugh.

After taking this in, she says, nodding, "That has a certain kind of tangled logic to it, I suppose."

Another long pause and I fearfully ask the next question. "Well, are *you* seeing anyone?"

She smiles, pleased with herself, and still looking down, admits, with incomparable clarity, "Well, yes, I have a boyfriend and—"

"Who?"

"What?" She looks up.

"Who is he? What's his name?"

"Robert Hall. Why?"

"With Salomon Brothers?"

"No, he's a chef."

"With Salomon Brothers?"

"Patrick, he's a *chef.* And co-owner of a restaurant."

"Which one?"

"Does it matter?"

"No, really, which one?" I ask, then under my breath, "I want to cross it out of my Zagat guide."

"It's called Dorsia," she says, then, "Patrick, are you okay?"

Yes, my brain does explode and my stomach bursts open inwardly—a spastic, acidic, gastric reaction; stars and planets, whole galaxies made up entirely of little white chef hats, race over the film of my vision. I choke out another question.

"Why Robert Hall?" I ask. "Why him?"

"Well, I don't know," she says, sounding a little tipsy. "I guess it has to do with being twenty-seven and—"

"Yeah? So am I. So is half of Manhattan. So what? That's no excuse to marry Robert Hall."

"Marry?" she asks, wide-eyed, defensive. "Did I say that?"

"Didn't you say marry?"

"No, I didn't, but who knows." She shrugs. "We might."

"Ter-rific."

"As I was saying, Patrick"—she glares at me, but in a playful way that makes me sick—"I think you know that, well, time is running out. That biological clock just won't stop ticking," she says, and I'm thinking: My god, it took only *two* glasses of chardonnay to get her to admit this? Christ, what a lightweight. "I want to have children."

"With Robert Hall?" I ask, incredulous. "You might as well do it with Captain Lou Albano, for Christ sakes. I just don't get you, Bethany."

She touches her napkin, looking down and then out onto the sidewalk, where waiters are setting up tables for dinner. I watch them too. "Why do I sense hostility on your part, Patrick?" she asks softly, then sips her wine.

"Maybe because I'm hostile," I spit out. "Maybe because you sense this."

"Jesus, Patrick," she says, searching my face, genuinely upset. "I thought you and Robert were friends."

"What?" I ask. "I'm confused."

"Weren't you and Robert friends?"

I pause, doubtful. "Were we?"

"Yes, Patrick, you *were*."

"Robert Hall, Robert Hall, Robert Hall," I mutter to myself, trying to remember. "Scholarship student? President of our senior class?" I think about it a second longer, then add, "Weak chin?"

"No, Patrick," she says. "The *other* Robert Hall."

"I'm confusing him with the *other* Robert Hall?" I ask.

"Yes, Patrick," she says, exasperated.

Inwardly cringing, I close my eyes and sigh. "Robert Hall. Not the one whose parents own half of, like, Washington? Not the one who was"—I gulp—"captain of the crew team? Six feet?"

"Yes," she says. "*That* Robert Hall."

"But . . ." I stop.

"Yes? But *what?*" She seems prepared to wait for an answer.

"But he was a *fag*," I blurt out.

"No, he was *not*, Patrick," she says, clearly offended.

"I'm positive he was a fag." I start nodding my head.

"Why are you so positive?" she asks, not amused.

"Because he used to let frat guys—not the ones in my house—like, you know, gang bang him at parties and tie him up and stuff. At least, you know, that's what I've heard," I say sincerely, and then, more humiliated than I have ever been in my entire life, I confess, "Listen, Bethany, he offered me a . . . you know, a blow-job once. In the, um, civics section of the library."

"Oh my god," she gasps, disgusted. "Where's the check?"

"Didn't Robert Hall get kicked out for doing his thesis on Babar? Or something like Babar?" I ask. "Babar the elephant? The, oh Jesus, *French* elephant?"

"What are you *talking* about?"

"Listen to me," I say. "Didn't he go to business school at Kellogg? At Northwestern, right?"

"He dropped out," she says without looking at me.

"Listen." I touch her hand.

She flinches and pulls back.

I try to smile. "Robert Hall's not a fag—"

"I can assure you of that," she says a tad too smugly. How can anyone get indignant over Robert Hall? Instead of saying "Oh yeah, you dumb sorry bitch" I say soothingly, "I'm sure you can," then, "Tell me about him. I want to know how things stand with the two of you," and then, smiling, furious, full of rage, I apologize. "I'm sorry."

It takes some time but she finally relents and smiles back at me and I ask her, once again, "Tell me more," and then, under my breath, smiling a rictus at her, "I'd like to slice open your beaver." The chardonnay has mellowed her, so she softens and talks freely.

I think about other things while she describes her recent past: air, water, sky, time, a moment, a point somewhere when I wanted to show her everything beautiful in the world. I have no patience for revelations, for new beginnings, for events that take place beyond the realm of my immediate vision. A young girl, a freshman, I met in a bar in Cambridge my junior year at Harvard told me early one fall that "Life is full of endless possibilities." I tried valiantly not to choke on the beer nuts I was chewing while she gushed this kidney stone of wisdom, and I calmly washed them down with the rest of a Heineken, smiled and concentrated on the dart game that was going on in the corner. Needless to say, she did not live to see her sophomore year. That winter, her body was found floating in the Charles River, decapitated, her head hung from a tree on the bank, her hair knotted around a low-hanging branch, three miles away. My rages at Harvard were less violent than the ones now and it's useless to hope that my disgust will vanish—there is just *no way.*

"Oh, Patrick," she's saying. "You're still the same. I don't know if that's good or bad."

"Say it's good."

"Why? Is it?" she asks, frowning. "Was it? Then?"

"You only knew one facet of my personality," I say. "Student."

"Lover?" she asks, her voice reminding me of someone human.

My eyes fall on her coldly, untouched. Out on the street, music that sounds like salsa blares. The waiter finally brings the check.

"I'll pay for it," I sigh.

"No," she says, opening her handbag. "*I* invited *you.*"

"But I have a platinum American Express card," I tell her.

"But so do I," she says, smiling.

I pause, then watch her place the card on the tray the check came on. Violent convulsions seem close at hand if I do not get up. "The women's movement. Wow." I smile, unimpressed.

Outside, she waits on the sidewalk while I'm in the men's room throwing up my lunch, spitting out the squid, undigested and less purple than it was on my plate. When I come out of Vanities onto the street, putting on my Wayfarers, chewing a Cert, I murmur something to myself, and then I kiss her on the cheek and make up something else. "Sorry it took so long. Had to call my lawyer."

"Oh?" She acts concerned—the dumb bitch.

"Just a friend of mine." I shrug. "Bobby Chambers. He's in prison. Some friends of his, well, mainly *me*, are trying to remount his defense," I say with another shrug, then, changing the subject, "Listen."

"Yes?" she asks, smiling.

"It's late. I don't want to go back to the office," I say, checking my Rolex. The sun, setting, glints off it, momentarily blinding her. "Why don't you come up to my place?"

"What?" She laughs.

"Why don't you come up to my place?" I suggest again.

"Patrick." She laughs suggestively. "Are you serious?"

"I have a bottle of Pouilly-Fuissé, *chilled,* huh?" I say, arching my eyebrows.

"Listen, that line might've worked at Harvard but"—she laughs, then continues—"um, we're older now and . . ." She stops.

"And . . . what?" I ask.

"I shouldn't have had that wine at lunch," she says again.

We start walking. It's a hundred degrees outside, impossible to breathe. It's not day, it's not night. The sky seems yellow. I hand a beggar on the corner of Duane and Greenwich a dollar just to impress her.

"Listen, come over," I say again, almost whining. "Come on over."

"I can't," she says. "The air-conditioning in my office is broken but I can't. I'd like to but I can't."

"Aw come on," I say, grabbing her shoulders, giving them a good-natured squeeze.

"Patrick, I have to be back at the office," she groans, protesting weakly.

"But you'll be *swelt*ering in there," I point out.

"I have no choice."

"Come on." Then, trying to entice her, "I have a 1940s Durgin Gorham four-piece sterling silver tea and coffee set I'd like to show you."

"I can't." She laughs, putting on her sunglasses.

"Beth*any*," I say, warning her.

"Listen," she says, relenting. "I'll buy you a Dove Bar. Have a Dove Bar instead."

"I'm appalled. Do you know how many grams of fat, of *sodium*, are in the chocolate covering alone?" I gasp, mock horrified.

"Come on," she says. "You don't need to worry about that."

"No, *you* come on," I say, walking in front of her for a little while so she won't sense any aggressiveness on my part. "Listen, come by for a drink and then we'll walk over to Dorsia and I'll meet Robert, okay?" I turn around, still walking, but backward now. *"Please?"*

"Patrick," she says. "You're begging."

"I really want to show you that Durgin Gorham tea set." I pause. "Please?" I pause again. "It cost me three and a half thousand dollars."

She stops walking because I stop, looks down, and when she looks back up her brow, both cheeks, are damp with a layer of perspiration, a fine sheen. She's hot. She sighs, smiling to herself. She looks at her watch.

"Well?" I ask.

"If I did . . . ," she starts.

"Ye-e-es?" I ask, stretching the word out.

"If I did, I have to make a phone call."

"No, negative," I say, waving down a cab. "Call from my place."

"*Patrick,*" she protests. "There's a phone right over there."

"Let's go now," I say. "There's a taxi."

In the cab heading toward the Upper West Side, she says, "I shouldn't have had that wine."

"Are you drunk?"

"No," she says, fanning herself with a playbill from *Les Misérables* someone left in the backseat of the cab, which isn't air-conditioned and even with both windows open she keeps fanning herself. "Just slightly . . . tipsy."

We both laugh for no reason and she leans into me, then realizes something and pulls back. "You have a doorman, right?" she asks suspiciously.

"Yes." I smile, turned on by her unawareness of just how close to peril she really is.

from *Spider*

Master of the contemporary psychological thriller, Patrick McGrath first published his hypnotic novel Spider *with Vintage Contemporaries in 1991. Born in London, McGrath grew up near Broadmoor Hospital, where his father served as medical superintendent for many years. He is the author of a collection of short stories and three other novels,* The Grotesque, Dr. Haggard's Disease, *and* Asylum, *all available from Vintage Contemporaries.*

I'VE ALWAYS FOUND it odd that I can recall incidents from my boyhood with clarity and precision, and yet events that happened yesterday are blurred, and I have no confidence in my ability to remember them accurately at all. Is there some process of fixing, I wonder, whereby time, rather than causing memories to decay (as you would expect) instead does the opposite—it sets them hard, like concrete, the very reverse of the sort of fluid mush I seem to get when I try to talk about yesterday? All I can tell you for certain—about yesterday, that is—is that there were people in the attic again, Mrs. Wilkinson's people—and here *is* a curious thing, something that escaped me until this moment: the woman who runs the boarding house I'm living in (just temporarily) has the same last name as the woman responsible for the tragedy that befell my family twenty years ago. Beyond the name there is no resemblance. My Mrs. Wilkinson is an altogether different creature from Hilda Wilkinson, she's a sour, vindictive woman, big, it's true, as Hilda was big, but with none of Hilda's sauce and vitality, far more interested in questions of control—which brings me back to the people in the attic last night; but of them, on reflection, I think I will speak at another time.

It takes me about ten minutes to walk from the canal back to Mrs. Wilkinson's. I am not a fast walker; I shuffle, rather than walk, and often I am forced to stop dead in the middle of the pavement. I forget how to do it, you see, for nothing is automatic with me anymore, not since I came back from Canada. The simplest actions—eating, dressing, going to the lavatory—can sometimes pose near-insurmountable problems, not because I am physically handicapped in any way, but rather because I lose the easy, fluid sense of being-in-the-body that I once had; the linkage of brain and limb is a delicate mechanism, and often, now, for me, it becomes uncoupled. To the annoyance of those around me I must then stop and make decisions about what it is that I am attempting to do, and slowly the basic rhythms are reestablished. The more involved I am in memories of my father the more frequently it seems to happen, so I suppose I must look forward to a difficult few weeks. Mrs. Wilkinson gets impatient with me at such times, and this is one of the reasons why I intend to leave her house, probably at the beginning of next week.

There are five others living here, but I pay no attention to them. They never go out, they are passive, apathetic creatures, dead souls such as I encountered frequently overseas. No, I prefer the streets, for I grew up in this part of London, in the East End, and while in one sense the changes are total, and I am a stranger, in another sense nothing has changed: there are ghosts, and there are memories, and they rise in clusters as I catch a glimpse of the underside of a familiar railway bridge, a familiar view of the river at dusk, the gasworks—they haven't changed at all—and my memories have a way of crowding in upon the scene and collapsing the block of time that separates then from now, producing a sort of identity, a sort of running together of past and present such that I am confused, and I forget, so rich and immediate are the memories, that I am what I am, a shuffling, spidery figure in a worn-out suit, and not a dreamy boy of twelve or so. It is for this reason that I have decided to keep a journal.

This is actually a most peculiar house. My room is at the very top, immediately beneath the attic. The trunks and suitcases of Mrs. Wilkinson's tenants are all stored up there, so quite how they manage to make as much noise as they do I cannot imagine, unless they are very small. Before I leave I intend to go up and have it out with them, for I have not had a good night's sleep since I got here—though of course there's no point in telling Mrs. Wilkinson this, she doesn't care, why else would she have put me up here? There's a small, rather wobbly table under the window, which is where I sit when I write. I am sitting there now, in fact; in front of me lies my exercise book, all its pages neatly lined, and in my long slender fingers I hold a blunt pencil. I'm wondering where I should hide the book when I'm not using it, and I think for the time being I will simply slide it under the sheet of newspaper lining the bottom drawer of my chest of drawers; later I can find a more secure place.

Not that there are so many possibilities! I have a narrow bed with a cast-iron frame and a thin, tired mattress that lies as uncomfortably upon its few functional springs as I do upon it; this bed is too short for me by about six inches, so my feet stick out the end. There is a small threadbare rug on the cracked green linoleum, and a hook on the back of the door from which a pair of wire hangers dangle, jangling tinnily when I open the door. The window is dirty, and though I have a view of the small park across the road I can never be sure that I see what I think I see down there, so poor is the visibility. The wallpaper is a dingy yellowy-green color with a very faint floral pattern, worn away in places to reveal the older paper and plaster beneath, and from the ceiling hangs a bulb in a hat-shaped shade of some parchmentlike material, the switch being by the door so that I must cross the room in the darkness after turning off the light, a thing I hate. And this, for now, is where I live.

But at least I'm not far from the canal. I've found a bench by the water, in a secluded spot that I can call my own, and there I like to while away an afternoon with no one disturbing me. From this bench I have a clear view of the gasworks, and the sight always reminds me of my father, I don't know why, perhaps because he was a plumber, and a familiar figure in this neighborhood as he pedaled along on his bicycle with his canvas toolbag slung over his shoulder like a quiver of arrows. The streets were narrow in those days, dark poky little slum houses all crammed together with narrow yards behind—there was outside plumbing, and washing lines stretched from wall to wall, and the yards backed onto narrow alleys where thin stray cats scavenged among the dustbins. London seems so wide and empty now, and this is another thing I find odd: I would have expected it to work the other way round, for the scenes of one's childhood tend to loom huge and vast in the memory, as they were experienced at the time. But for me it's all backwards, I remember everything narrow: rooms, houses, yards, alleys, streets—narrow and dark and constricted, and all pushed together beneath an oppressive sky in which the smoke from the chimneypots trailed off in vague, stringy wisps and strands, a sky filled with rainclouds—it always seemed to be raining, and if it wasn't raining it was always about to rain. There was blackened brickwork, and grimy walls, and against them gray figures in raincoats scurried home like phantoms through late winter afternoons before the lamps were lit.

This is how it works, you see. I sit on my bench with my back to the wall. The sky is gray and overcast; there is perhaps a spot or two of rain. An air of desolation pervades the scene; no one is about. Directly in front of me, a scrubby strip of weeds and grass. Then the canal, narrow and murky, green slime creeping up the stones. On the far side, another patch of weeds, another brick wall, beyond the wall the blotchy brickwork of an abandoned factory with shattered windows, and beyond that the great rust-red domes of the gasworks hulking against the gloomy sky, three of the things, each one a dozen towering uprights arranged in a circle and girdled at the top with a hoop of steel. Within those slender, circling masts of steel sit the wide-domed cylinders of gas, paintwork flaking off them, wheel attachments on their rims to run in the rails of the uprights and permit them to rise and fall with fluctuations in volume and demand. But I try not to look at them, for reasons I will explain later; I gaze south instead, toward a humpbacked bridge a hundred yards away crested with an iron railing and framed on this bank by a dead tree, and beyond it a perspective of gray slate roofs, with ranks of spindly red chimneys drifting smoke. I roll my cigarettes, and somehow time slips by me.

Yes, I roll my endless cigarettes, and as I do I watch my fingers, these long, spidery fingers that seem often not to belong to me at all; they are stained a dark yellow round the tips, and the nails are hard and yellowy and hornlike, and some curving over the ends like hooks, hooks that Mrs. Wilkinson seems now determined to snip off with her kitchen scissors. They are always slightly trembling, these days, these long, yellowing, hooknailed fingers of mine, I really don't know why. But it was a dingy place, the London of my boyhood, a clotted web of dark compartments and narrow passageways, and sometimes when I recognize one of its features I return in my mind to those days without even realizing what I'm doing. This is why I intend to keep a journal, so as to create some order in the jumble of memories that the city constantly arouses in me. Today's date: October 17th, 1957.

from *The House on Mango Street*

An award-winning poet and fiction writer, "the impassioned bard of the Mexican border" (Boston Globe), Sandra Cisneros published her widely acclaimed debut novel The House on Mango Street with Vintage Contemporaries in 1991. She is also the author of the short-story collection Woman Hollering Creek and Other Stories; two volumes of poetry, My Wicked Wicked Ways and Loose Woman; and a children's book, Hairs/Pelitos. Sandra Cisneros is currently working on her new novel, Caramelo, forthcoming from Knopf.

■ THE HOUSE ON MANGO STREET

WE DIDN'T ALWAYS live on Mango Street. Before that we lived on Loomis on the third floor, and before that we lived on Keeler. Before Keeler it was Paulina, and before that I can't remember. But what I remember most is moving a lot. Each time it seemed there'd be one more of us. By the time we got to Mango Street we were six—Mama, Papa, Carlos, Kiki, my sister Nenny and me.

The house on Mango Street is ours, and we don't have to pay rent to anybody, or share the yard with the people downstairs, or be careful not to make too much noise, and there isn't a landlord banging on the ceiling with a broom. But even so, it's not the house we'd thought we'd get.

We had to leave the flat on Loomis quick. The water pipes broke and the landlord wouldn't fix them because the house was too old. We had to leave fast. We were using the washroom next door and carrying water over in empty milk gallons. That's why Mama and Papa looked for a house, and that's why we moved into the house on Mango Street, far away, on the other side of town.

They always told us that one day we would move into a house, a real house that would be ours for always so we wouldn't have to move each year. And our house would have running water and pipes that worked. And inside it would have real stairs, not hallway stairs, but stairs inside like the houses on T.V. And we'd have a basement and at least three washrooms so when we took a bath we wouldn't have to tell everybody. Our house would be white with trees around it, a great big yard and grass growing without a fence. This was the house Papa talked about when he held a lottery ticket and this was the house Mama dreamed up in the stories she told us before we went to bed.

But the house on Mango Street is not the way they told it at all. It's small and red with tight steps in front and windows so small you'd think they were holding their breath. Bricks are crumbling in places, and the front door is so swollen you have to push hard to get in. There is no front yard, only four little elms the city planted by the curb. Out back is a small garage for the car we don't own yet and a small yard that looks smaller between the two buildings on either side. There are stairs in our house, but they're ordinary hallway stairs, and the house has only one washroom. Everybody has to share a bedroom—Mama and Papa, Carlos and Kiki, me and Nenny.

Once when we were living on Loomis, a nun from my school passed by and saw me playing out front. The laundromat downstairs had been boarded up because it had been robbed two days before and the owner had painted on the wood YES WE'RE OPEN so as not to lose business.

Where do you live? she asked.

There, I said pointing up to the third floor.

You live *there?*

There. I had to look to where she pointed—the third floor, the paint peeling, wooden bars Papa had nailed on the windows so we wouldn't fall out. You live *there?* The way she said it made me feel like nothing. *There.* I lived *there.* I nodded.

I knew then I had to have a house. A real house. One I could point to. But this isn't it. The house on Mango Street isn't it. For the time being, Mama says. Temporary, says Papa. But I know how those things go.

■ HAIRS

EVERYBODY IN OUR family has different hair. My Papa's hair is like a broom, all up in the air. And me, my hair is lazy. It never obeys barrettes or bands. Carlos' hair is thick and straight. He doesn't need to comb it. Nenny's hair is slippery—slides out of your hand. And Kiki, who is the youngest, has hair like fur.

But my mother's hair, my mother's hair, like little rosettes, like little candy circles all curly and pretty because she pinned it in pincurls all day, sweet to put your nose into when she is holding you, holding you and you feel safe, is the warm smell of bread before you bake it, is the smell when she makes room for you on her side of the bed still warm with her skin, and you sleep near her, the rain outside falling and Papa snoring. The snoring, the rain, and Mama's hair that smells like bread.

■ BOYS & GIRLS

THE BOYS AND the girls live in separate worlds. The boys in their universe and we in ours. My brothers for example. They've got plenty to say to me and Nenny inside the house. But outside they can't be seen talking to girls. Carlos and Kiki are each other's best friend . . . not ours.

Nenny is too young to be my friend. She's just my sister and that was not my fault. You don't pick your sisters, you just get them and sometimes they come like Nenny.

She can't play with those Vargas kids or she'll turn out just like them. And since she comes right after me, she is my responsibility.

Some day I will have a best friend all my own. One I can tell my secrets to. One who will understand my jokes without my having to explain them. Until then I am a red balloon, a balloon tied to an anchor.

from *Will You Please Be Quiet, Please?*

Master storyteller Raymond Carver's Cathedral *was one of the three books included on Vintage Contemporaries' debut list in 1984. The Oregon native was a Guggenheim Fellow and was twice awarded grants from the National Endowment for the Arts; received Poetry magazine's Levinson Prize, a Brandeis Citation for fiction, a Doctorate of Letters from Hartford University, and the prestigious Mildred and Harold Strauss Living Award; and was elected into the American Academy and Institute of Arts and Letters. Carver was the author of five collections of short stories, five collections of poetry, and two collections of prose and poetry, among them,* Fires; No Heroics Please; Ultramarine; What We Talk About When We Talk About Love; Where I'm Calling From; Where Water Comes Together With Other Water; Will You Please Be Quiet, Please?; *and* Short Cuts: Selected Stories, *all available from Vintage Contemporaries. Raymond Carver died in 1988, at the age of forty-nine.*

■ WHY, HONEY?

DEAR SIR:

I was so surprised to receive your letter asking about my son, how did you know I was here? I moved here years ago right after it started to happen. No one knows who I am here but I'm afraid all the same. Who I am afraid of is him. When I look at the paper I shake my head and wonder. I read what they write about him and I ask myself is that man really my son, is he really doing these things?

He was a good boy except for his outbursts and that he could not tell the truth. I can't give you any reasons. It started one summer over the Fourth of July, he would have been about fifteen. Our cat Trudy disappeared and was gone all night and the next day. Mrs. Cooper who lives behind us came the next evening to tell me Trudy crawled into her backyard that afternoon to die. Trudy was cut up she said but she recognized Trudy. Mr. Cooper buried the remains.

Cut up? I said. What do you mean cut up?

Mr. Cooper saw two boys in the field putting firecrackers in Trudy's ears and in her you know what. He tried to stop them but they ran.

Who, who would do such a thing, did he see who it was?

He didn't know the other boy but one of them ran this way. Mr. Cooper thought it was your son.

I shook my head. No, that's just not so, he wouldn't do a thing like that, he loved Trudy, Trudy has been in the family for years, no, it wasn't my son.

That evening I told him about Trudy and he acted surprised and shocked and said we should offer a reward. He typed something up and promised to post it at school. But just as he was going to his room that night he said don't take it too hard, mom, she was old, in cat years she was 65 or 70, she lived a long time.

He went to work afternoons and Saturdays as a stockboy at Hartley's. A friend of mine who worked there, Betty Wilks, told me about the job and said she would put in a word for him. I mentioned it to him that evening and he said good, jobs for young people are hard to find.

The night he was to draw his first check I cooked his favorite supper and had everything on the table when he walked in. Here's the man of the house, I said, hugging him. I am so proud, how much did you draw, honey? Eighty dollars, he said. I was flabbergasted. That's wonderful, honey, I just cannot believe it. I'm starved, he said, let's eat.

I was happy, but I couldn't understand it, it was more than I was making.

When I did the laundry I found the stub from Hartley's in his pocket, it was for 28 dollars, he said 80. Why didn't he just tell the truth? I couldn't understand.

I would ask him where did you go last night, honey? To the show he would answer. Then I would find out he went to the school dance or spent the evening riding around with somebody in a car. I would think what difference could it make, why doesn't he just be truthful, there is no reason to lie to his mother.

I remember once he was supposed to have gone on a field trip, so I asked him what did you see on the field trip, honey? And he shrugged and said land formations, volcanic rock, ash, they showed us where there used to be a big lake a million years ago, now it's just a desert. He looked me in the eyes and went on talking. Then I got a note from the school the next day saying they wanted permission for a field trip, could he have permission to go.

Near the end of his senior year he bought a car and was always gone. I was concerned about his grades but he only laughed. You know he was an excellent student, you know that about him if you know anything. After that he bought a shotgun and a hunting knife.

I hated to see those things in the house and I told him so. He laughed, he always had a laugh for you. He said he would keep the gun and the knife in the trunk of his car, he said they would be easier to get there anyway.

One Saturday night he did not come home. I worried myself into a terrible state. About ten o'clock the next morning he came in and asked me to cook him breakfast, he said he had worked up an appetite out hunting, he said he was sorry for being gone all night, he said they had driven a long way to get to this place. It sounded strange. He was nervous.

Where did you go?

Up to the Wenas. We got a few shots.

Who did you go with, honey?

Fred.

Fred?

He stared and I didn't say anything else.

On the Sunday right after I tiptoed into his room for his car keys. He had promised to pick up some breakfast items on his way home from work the night before and I thought he might have left the things in his car. I saw his new shoes sitting half under his bed and covered with mud and sand. He opened his eyes.

Honey, what happened to your shoes? Look at your shoes.

I ran out of gas, I had to walk for gas. He sat up. What do you care?

I am your mother.

While he was in the shower I took the keys and went out to his car. I opened the trunk. I didn't find the groceries. I saw the shotgun lying on a quilt and the knife too and I saw a shirt of his rolled in a ball and I shook it out and it was full of blood. It was wet. I dropped it. I closed the trunk and started back for the house and I saw him watching at the window and he opened the door.

I forgot to tell you, he said, I had a bad bloody nose, I don't know if that shirt can be washed, throw it away. He smiled.

A few days later I asked how he was getting along at work. Fine, he said, he said he had gotten a raise. But I met Betty Wilks on the street and she said they were all sorry at Hartley's that he had quit, he was so well liked, she said, Betty Wilks.

Two nights after that I was in bed but I couldn't sleep, I stared at the ceiling. I heard his car pull up out front and I listened as he put the key in the lock and he came through the kitchen and down the hall to his room and he shut the door after him. I got up. I could see light under his door, I knocked and pushed on the door and said would you like a hot cup of tea, honey, I can't sleep. He was bent over by the dresser and slammed a drawer and turned on me, get out he screamed, get out of here, I'm sick of you spying he screamed. I went to my room and cried myself to sleep. He broke my heart that night.

The next morning he was up and out before I could see him, but that was all right with me. From then on I was going to treat him like a lodger unless he wanted to mend his ways, I was at my limit. He would have to apologize if he wanted us to be more than just strangers living together under the same roof.

When I came in that evening he had supper ready. How are you? he said, he took my coat. How was your day?

I said I didn't sleep last night, honey. I promised myself I wouldn't bring it up and I'm not trying to make you feel guilty but I'm not used to being talked to like that by my son.

I want to show you something, he said, and he showed me this essay he was writing for his civics class. I believe it was on relations between the congress and the supreme court. (It was the paper that won a prize for him at graduation!) I tried to read it and then I decided, this was the time. Honey, I'd like to have a talk with you, it's hard to raise a child with things the way they are these days, it's especially hard for us having no father in the house, no man to turn to when we need him. You are nearly grown now but I am still responsible and I feel I am entitled to some respect and consideration and have tried to be fair and honest with you. I want the truth, honey, that's all I've ever asked from you, the truth. Honey, I took a breath, suppose you had a child who when you asked him something, anything, where he's been or where he's going, what he's doing with his time, anything, never, he never once told you the truth? Who if you asked him is it raining outside, would answer no, it is nice and sunny, and I guess laugh to himself and think you were too old or too stupid to see his clothes are wet. Why should he lie, you ask yourself, what does he gain I don't understand. I keep asking myself why but I don't have the answer. Why, honey?

He didn't say anything, he kept staring, then he moved alongside me and said I'll show you. Kneel is what I say, kneel down is what I say, he said, that's the first reason why.

I ran to my room and locked the door. He left that night, he took his things, what he wanted, and he left. Believe it or not I

WILL YOU PLEASE BE QUIET, PLEASE? | 157

never saw him again. I saw him at his graduation but that was with a lot of people around. I sat in the audience and watched him get his diploma and a prize for his essay, then I heard him give the speech and then I clapped right along with the rest.

I went home after that.

I have never seen him again. Oh sure I have seen him on the TV and I have seen his pictures in the paper.

I found out he joined the marines and then I heard from someone he was out of the marines and going to college back east and then he married that girl and got himself in politics. I began to see his name in the paper. I found out his address and wrote to him, I wrote a letter every few months, there never was an answer. He ran for governor and was elected, and was famous now. That's when I began to worry.

I built up all these fears, I became afraid, I stopped writing him of course and then I hoped he would think I was dead. I moved here. I had them give me an unlisted number. And then I had to change my name. If you are a powerful man and want to find somebody, you can find them, it wouldn't be that hard.

I should be so proud but I am afraid. Last week I saw a car on the street with a man inside I know was watching me, I came straight back and locked the door. A few days ago the phone rang and rang, I was lying down. I picked up the receiver but there was nothing there.

I am old. I am his mother. I should be the proudest mother in all the land but I am only afraid.

Thank you for writing. I wanted someone to know. I am very ashamed.

I also wanted to ask how you got my name and knew where to write, I have been praying no one knew. But you did. Why did you? Please tell me why?

Yours truly,

from *What Was Mine*

Ann Beattie has been a Vintage Contemporaries author for over a decade, beginning in 1986 with our publication of her novel Love, Always. Revered as one of America's most beloved fiction writers, Beattie is the author of six novels and five collections of stories, among them, Chilly Scenes of Winter, Secrets and Surprises, Falling in Place, The Burning House, Picturing Will, What Was Mine, Another You, *and* My Life, Starring Dara Falcon. *A collection of her new and selected stories, entitled* Park City, *was just published by Knopf.*

■ WHAT WAS MINE

I DON'T REMEMBER my father. I have only two photographs of him—one of two soldiers standing with their arms around each other's shoulders, their faces even paler than their caps, so that it's difficult to make out their features; the other of my father in profile, peering down at me in my crib. In that photograph, he has no discernible expression, though he does have a rather noble Roman nose and thick hair that would have been very impressive if it hadn't been clipped so short. On the back of the picture in profile is written, unaccountably, "Guam," while the back of the picture of the soldiers says, "Happy with baby: 5/28/49."

Until I was five or six I had no reason to believe that Herb was not my uncle. I might have believed it much longer if my mother had not blurted out the truth one night when I opened her bedroom door and saw Herb, naked from the waist down, crouched at the foot of the bed, holding out a bouquet of roses much the way teasing people shake a biscuit in front of a sleeping dog's nose. They had been to a wedding earlier that day, and my mother had caught the nosegay. Herb was tipsy, but I had no sense of that

then. Because I was a clumsy boy, I didn't wonder about his occasionally knocking into a wall or stepping off a curb a bit too hard.
He was not allowed to drive me anywhere, but I thought only that
my mother was full of arbitrary rules she imposed on everyone:
no more than one hour of TV a day; put Bosco in the glass first,
then the milk.

One of the most distinct memories of my early years is of that
night I opened my mother's door and saw Herb lose his balance
and fall forward on the bouquet like a thief clutching bread under
his shirt.

"Ethan," my mother said, " I don't know what you are doing in
here at a time when you are supposed to be in bed—and without
the manners to knock—but I think the time has come to tell you
that Herbert and I are very close, but not close in the way family
members such as a brother and sister are. Herbert is not your
uncle, but you must go on as if he were. Other people should not
know this."

Herb had rolled onto his side. As he listened, he began laughing. He threw the crushed bouquet free, and I caught it by taking
one step forward and waiting for it to land in my outstretched hand.
It was the way Herb had taught me to catch a ball, because I had a
tendency to overreact and rush too far forward, too fast. By the time
I had caught the bouquet, exactly what my mother said had
become a blur: manners, Herbert, not family, don't say anything.

Herb rolled off the bed, stood, and pulled on his pants. I had
the clear impression that he was in worse trouble than I was. I
think that what he said to me was that his affection for me was
just what it always had been, even though he wasn't actually my
uncle. I know that my mother threw a pillow at him and told him
not to confuse me. Then she looked at me and said, emphatically,
that Herb was not a part of our family. After saying that, she
became quite flustered and got up and stomped out of the bedroom, slamming the door behind her. Herb gave the door a dismissive wave of the hand. Alone with him, I felt much better. I

suppose I had thought that he might vanish—if he was not my uncle, he might suddenly disappear—so that his continued presence was very reassuring.

"Don't worry about it," he said. "The divorce rate is climbing, people are itching to change jobs every five minutes. You wait: Dwight Eisenhower is going to be reevaluated. He won't have the same position in history that he has today." He looked at me. He sat on the side of the bed. "I'm your mother's boyfriend," he said. "She doesn't want to marry me. It doesn't matter. I'm not going anywhere. Just keep it between us that I'm not Uncle Herb."

MY MOTHER WAS tall and blond, the oldest child of a German family that had immigrated to America in the 1920s. Herb was dark-haired, the only child of a Lebanese father and his much younger English bride, who had considered even on the eve of her wedding leaving the Church of England to convert to Catholicism and become a nun. In retrospect, I realize that my mother's shyness about her height and her having been indoctrinated to believe that the hope of the future lay in her accomplishing great things, and Herb's self-consciousness about his kinky hair, along with his attempt as a child to negotiate peace between his mother and father, resulted in an odd bond between Herb and my mother: she was drawn to his conciliatory nature, and he was drawn to her no-nonsense attitude. Or perhaps she was drawn to his unusual amber eyes, and he was taken in by her inadvertently sexy, self-conscious girlishness. Maybe he took great pleasure in shocking her, in playing to her secret, more sophisticated desires, and she was secretly amused and gratified that he took it as a given that she was highly competent and did not have to prove herself to him in any way whatsoever.

She worked in a bank. He worked in the automotive section at Sears, Roebuck, and on the weekend he played piano, harmonica, and sometimes tenor sax at a bar off Pennsylvania Avenue called the Merry Mariner. On Saturday nights my mother and I would sit side by side, dressed in our good clothes, in a booth upholstered in blue Naugahyde, behind which dangled nets that were nailed to the wall, studded with starfish, conch shells, sea horses, and clamshells with small painted scenes or decals inside them. I would have to turn sideways and look above my mother to see them. I had to work out a way of seeming to be looking in front of me and listening appreciatively to Uncle Herb while at the very same time rolling my eyes upward to take in those tiny depictions of sunsets, rainbows, and ships sailing through the moonlight. Uncle Herb played a slowish version of "Let Me Call You Sweetheart" on the harmonica as I sipped my cherry Coke with real cherries in it: three, because the waitress liked me. He played "As Time Goes By" on the piano, singing so quietly it seemed he was humming. My mother and I always split the fisherman's platter: four shrimp, one crab cake, and a lobster tail, or sometimes two if the owner wasn't in the kitchen, though my mother often wrapped up the lobster tails and saved them for our Sunday dinner. She would slice them and dish them up over rice, along with the tomato-and-lettuce salad she served almost every night.

Some of Uncle Herb's songs would go out to couples celebrating an anniversary, or to birthday boys, or to women being courted by men who preferred to let Uncle Herb sing the romantic thoughts they hesitated to speak. Once during the evening Herb would dedicate a song to my mother, always referring to her as "my own special someone" and nodding—but never looking directly—toward our booth.

My mother kept the beat to faster tunes by tapping her fingers on the shiny varnished tabletop. During the slow numbers she would slide one finger back and forth against the edge of the table, moving her hand so delicately she might have been testing the blade of a knife. Above her blond curls I would see miniature versions of what I thought must be the most exotic places on earth—so exotic that any small reference to them would quicken the heart of anyone familiar with the mountains of Hawaii or the seas of Bora-Bora. My mother smoked cigarettes, so that sometimes I would see these places through fog. When the overhead lights were turned from blue to pink as Uncle Herb played the last set, they would be transformed to the most ideal possible versions of paradise. I was hypnotized by what seemed to me their romantic clarity, as Herb sang a bemused version of "Stormy Weather," then picked up the saxophone for "Green Eyes," and finished, always, with a Billie Holiday song he would play very simply on the piano, without singing. Then the lights went to a dusky red and gradually brightened to a golden light that seemed as stupefying to me as the cloud rising at Los Alamos must have seemed to the observers of Trinity. It allowed people enough light to judge their sobriety, pay the bill, or decide to postpone functioning until later and vanish into the darker reaches of the bar at the back. Uncle Herb never patted me on the shoulder or tousled my cowlick. He usually sank down next to my mother—still bowing slightly to acknowledge the applause—then reached over with the same automatic motion my mother used when she withdrew a cigarette from the pack to run his thumb quickly over my knuckles, as if he were testing a keyboard. If a thunderbolt had left his fingertips, it could have not been more clear: he wanted me to be a piano player.

THAT PLAN HAD to be abandoned when I was thirteen. Or perhaps it did not really have to be abandoned, but at the time I found a convenient excuse to let go of the idea. One day, as my mother rounded a curve in the rain, the car skidded into a telephone pole. As the windshield splattered into cubes of glass, my wrist was broken and my shoulder dislocated. My mother was not hurt at all, though when she called Herb at work she became so hysterical that she had to be given an injection in the emergency room before he arrived to take us both away.

I don't think she was ever really the same after the accident. Looking back, I realize that was when everything started to change—though there is every chance that my adolescence and her growing hatred of her job might have changed things anyway. My mother began to seem irrationally angry at Herb and so solicitous of me I felt smothered. I held her responsible, suddenly, for everything, and I had a maniac's ability to transform good things into something awful. The five cherries I began to get in my Cokes seemed an unwanted pollution, and I was sure that my mother had told the waitress to be extra kind. Her cigarette smoke made me cough. Long before the surgeon general warned against the dangers of smoking, I was sure that she meant to poison me. When she drove me to physical therapy, I misconstrued her positive attitude and was sure that she took secret delight in having me tortured. My wrist set wrong, and had to be put in a cast a second time. My mother cried constantly. I turned to Herb to help me with my homework. She relented, and he became the one who drove me everywhere.

When I started being skeptical of my mother, she began to be skeptical of Herb. I heard arguments about the way he arranged his sets. She said that he should end on a more upbeat note. She thought the lighting was too stagy. He began to play—and end—in a nondescript silver glow. I looked at the shells on the netting, not caring that she knew I wasn't concentrating on Herb's playing. She sank lower in the booth, and her attention also drifted: no puffs of smoke carefully exhaled in the pauses between sung phrases; no testing of the edge of the table with her fingertip. One Saturday night we just stopped going.

By that time, she had become a loan officer at Riggs Bank. Herb had moved from Sears to Montgomery Ward, where he was in charge of the lawn and leisure-activities section—everything from picnic tables to electric hedge clippers. She served TV dinners. She complained that there wasn't enough money, though she bought expensive high heels that she wore to work. On Wednesday nights Herb played handball with friends who used to be musicians but who were suddenly working white-collar jobs to support growing families. He would come home and say, either with disbelief or with disorientation, that Sal, who used to play in a Latino band, had just had twins, or that Earl had sold his drums and bought an expensive barbecue grill. She read Perry Mason. He read magazine articles about the Second World War: articles, he said, shaking his head, that were clearly paving the way for a reassessment of the times in which we lived.

I DIDN'T HAVE a friend—a real friend—until I was fourteen. That year my soul mate was a boy named Ryuji Anderson, who shared my passion for soccer and introduced me to *Playboy*. He told me to buy Keds one size too large and stuff a sock in the toe so that I could kick hard and the ball would really fly. We both suffered because we sensed that you had to *look* like John F. Kennedy in order to *be* John F. Kennedy. Ryuji's mother had been a war bride, and my mother had lost her husband six years after the war in a freak accident: a painter on scaffolding had lost his footing high up and tumbled backward to the ground, releasing, as he fell, the can of paint that struck my father on the head and killed him. The painter faithfully sent my mother a Christmas card every year, informing her about his own slow recovery and apologizing for my father's death. Uncle Herb met my mother when his mother, dead of leukemia, lay in the room adjacent to my father's room in the funeral home. They had coffee together one time when they both were exiled to the streets, late at night.

It was not until a year later, when he looked her up in the phone book (the number was still listed under my father's name), that he saw her again. That time I went along, and was bought a paper cone filled with french fries. I played cowboy, circling with an imaginary lasso the bench on which they sat. We had stumbled on a carnival. Since it was downtown Washington, it wasn't really a carnival but a small area of the mall, taken over by dogs who would jump through burning hoops and clowns on roller skates. It became a standing refrain between my mother and Herb that some deliberate merriment had been orchestrated just for them, like the play put on in *A Midsummer Night's Dream.*

I, of course, had no idea what to make of the world on any given day. My constants were that I lived with my mother, who cried every night; that I could watch only two shows each day on TV; and that I would be put to bed earlier than I wanted, with a nightlight left burning. That day my mother and Herb sat on the bench, I'm sure I sensed that things were going to be different, as I inscribed two people destined to be together in an imaginary lassoed magic circle. From then on, we were a threesome.

HE MOVED IN as a boarder. He lived in the room that used to be the dining room, which my mother and I had never used, since we ate off TV trays. I remember his hanging a drapery rod over the arch—nailing the brackets in, then lifting up the bar, pushing onto it the brocade curtain my mother had sewn, then lowering the bar into place. They giggled behind it. Then they slid the curtain back and forth, as if testing to see that it would really work. It was like one of the games I had had as a baby: a board with a piece of wood that slid back and forth, exposing first the sun, then the moon.

Of course, late at night they cheated. He would simply push the curtain aside and go to her bed. Since I would have accepted anything, it's a wonder they didn't just tell me. A father, an uncle, a saint, Howdy Doody, Lassie—I didn't have a very clear idea of how any of them truly behaved. I believed whatever I saw. Looking back, I can only assume that they were afraid not so much of what I would think as of what others might think, and that they were unwilling to draw me into their deception. Until I wandered into her bedroom, they simply were not going to blow their cover. They were just going to wait for me. Eventually, I was sure to stumble into their world.

"The secret about Uncle Herb doesn't go any farther than this house," my mother said that night after I found them together. She was quite ashen. We stood in the kitchen. I had followed her—not because I loved her so much, or because I trusted her, but because I was already sure of Herb. Sure because even if he had winked at me, he could not have been clearer about the silliness of the slammed door. She had on a beige nightgown and was backlit by the counter light. She cast a pondlike shadow on the floor. I would like to say that I asked her why she had lied to me, but I'm sure I wouldn't have dared. Imagine my surprise when she told me anyway: "You don't know what it's like to lose something forever," she said. "It will make you do anything—even lie to people you love—if you think you can reclaim even a fraction of that thing. You don't know what *fraction* means. It means a little bit. It means a thing that's been broken into pieces."

I knew she was talking about loss. All week, I had been worried that the bird at school, with its broken wing, might never fly again and would hop forever in the cardboard box. What my mother was thinking of, though, was that can of paint—a can of paint that she wished had missed my father's head and sailed into infinity.

We looked down at the sepia shadow. It was there in front of her, and in front of me. Of course it was behind us, too.

MANY YEARS LATER, the day Herb took me out for "a talk," we drove aimlessly for quite a while. I could almost feel Herb's moment of inspiration when it finally came, and he went around a traffic circle and headed down Pennsylvania Avenue. It was a Saturday, and on Saturdays the Merry Mariner was open only for dinner, but he had a key, so we parked and went inside and turned on a light. It was not one of those lights that glowed when he played, but a strong, fluorescent light. Herb went to the bar and poured himself a drink. He opened a can of Coke and handed it to me. Then he told me that he was leaving us. He said that he himself found it unbelievable. Then, suddenly, he began to urge me to listen to Billie Holiday's original recordings, to pay close attention to the paintings of Vermeer, to look around me and to listen. To believe that what to some people might seem the silliest sort of place might be, to those truly observant, a temporary substitute for heaven.

I was a teenager, and I was too embarrassed to cry. I sat on a bar stool and simply looked at him. That day, neither of us knew how my life would turn out. Possibly he thought that so many unhappy moments would have damaged me forever. For all either of us knew, he had been the father figure to a potential hoodlum, or even to a drifter—that was what the game of pretense he and my mother had been involved in might have produced. He shook his head sadly when he poured another drink. Later, I found out that my mother had asked him to go, but that day I didn't even think to ask why I was being abandoned.

Before we left the restaurant he told me—as he had the night I found him naked in my mother's room—how much he cared for me. He also gave me practical advice about how to assemble a world.

He had been the one who suggested that the owner string netting on the walls. First he and the owner had painted the ocean: pale blue, more shine than paint at the bottom, everything larger than it appeared on land. Then gradually the color of the paint changed, rays of light streamed in, and things took on a truer size. Herb had added, on one of the walls, phosphorescence. He had touched the paintbrush to the wall delicately, repeatedly, meticulously. He was a very good amateur painter. Those who sat below it would never see it, though. Those who sat adjacent to it might see the glow in their peripheral vision. From across the room, where my mother and I sat, the highlights were too delicate, and too far away to see. The phosphorescence had never caught my eye when my thoughts drifted from the piano music, or when I blinked my eyes to clear them of the smoke.

The starfish had been bought in lots of a dozen from a store in Chinatown. The clamshells had been painted by a woman who lived in Arlington, in the suburbs, who had once strung them together as necklaces for church bazaars, until the demand dried up and macramé was all the rage. Then she sold them to the owner of the restaurant, who carried them away from her yard sale in two aluminum buckets years before he ever imagined he would open a restaurant. Before Herb and I left the Merry Mariner that day, there wasn't anything about how the place had been assembled that I didn't know.

FIFTEEN YEARS AFTER that I drove with my fiancée to Herb's cousin's house to get some things he left with her for safekeeping in case anything happened to him. His cousin was a short, unattractive woman who lifted weights. She had converted what had been her dining room into a training room, complete with Nautilus, rowing machine, and barbells. She lived alone, so there was no one to slide a curtain back for. There was no child, so she was not obliged to play at anything.

She served us iced tea with big slices of lemon. She brought out guacamole and a bowl of tortilla chips. She had called me several days before to say that Herb had had a heart attack and died. Though I would not find out formally until some time later, she also told me that Herb had left me money in his will. He also asked that she pass on to me a large manila envelope. She handed it to me, and I was so curious that I opened it immediately, on the back porch of some muscle-bound woman named Frances in Cold Spring Harbor, New York.

There was sheet music inside: six Billie Holiday songs that I recognized immediately as Herb's favorites for ending the last set of the evening. There were several notes, which I suppose you could call love notes, from my mother. There was a tracing, on a food-stained Merry Mariner place mat, of a cherry, complete with stem, and a fancy pencil-drawn frame around it that I vaguely remembered Herb having drawn one night. There was also a white envelope that contained the two pictures: one of the soldiers on Guam; one of a handsome young man looking impassively at a sleeping young baby. I knew the second I saw it that he was my father.

I was fascinated, but the more I looked at it—the more remote and expressionless the man seemed—the more it began to dawn on me that Herb wanted me to see the picture of my father because he wanted me to see how different he had been from him. When I turned over the picture of my father in profile and read "Guam," I almost smiled. It certainly wasn't my mother's handwriting. It was Herb's, though he had tried to slope the letters so that it would resemble hers. What sweet revenge, he must have thought—to leave me with the impression that my mother had been such a preoccupied, scatterbrained woman that she could not even label two important pictures correctly.

My mother had died years before, of pneumonia. The girl I had been dating at the time had said to me, not unkindly, that although I was very sad about my mother's death, one of the advantages of time passing was sure to be that the past would truly become the past. Words would become suspect. People would seem to be only poor souls struggling to do their best. Images would fade.

NOT THE IMAGE of the wall painted to look like the ocean, though. She was wrong about that. Herb had painted it exactly the way it really looks. I found this out later when I went snorkeling and saw the world underwater for the first time, with all its spooky spots of overexposure and its shimmering irregularities. But how tempting—how reassuring—to offer people the possibility of climbing from deep water to the surface by moving upward on lovely white nets, gigantic ladders from which no one need ever topple.

On Frances's porch, as I stared at the photographs of my father, I saw him as a young man standing on a hot island, his closest friend a tall broomstick of a man whom he would probably never see again once the war was over. He was a hero. He had served his country. When he got off Guam, he would have a life. Things didn't turn out the way he expected, though. The child he left behind was raised by another man, though it is true that his wife missed him forever and remained faithful in her own strange way by never remarrying. As I continued to look at the photograph, though, it was not possible to keep thinking of him as a hero. He was an ordinary man, romantic in context—a sad young soldier on a tropical island that would soon become a forgotten land. When the war was over he would have a life, but a life that was much too brief, and the living would never really recover from that tragedy.

Herb must also have believed that he was not a hero. That must have been what he was thinking when he wrote, in wispy letters, brief, transposed captions for two pictures that did not truly constitute any legacy at all.

In Cold Spring Harbor, as I put the pictures back in the envelope, I realized that no one had spoken for quite some time. Frances tilted her glass, shaking the ice cubes. She hardly knew us. Soon we would be gone. It was just a quick drive to the city, and she would see us off, knowing that she had discharged her responsibility by passing on to me what Herb had said was mine.

from *Et Tu, Babe*

Mark Leyner is the author of such hilarious, morally reprehensible, post-modern Vintage Contemporaries novels as Et Tu, Babe, *and* The Tetherballs of Bougainville, *forthcoming in the fall of 1998; two collections of stories,* I Smell Esther Williams *and* My Cousin, My Gastroenterologist; *and a collection of fiction, plays, and journalism,* Tooth Imprints on a Corn Dog. *A monthly columnist for* Esquire *magazine, he has also published work in* The New Yorker, The New Republic, George, *and* Harper's.

IT WAS DETERMINED at an October 17th meeting—attended by my literary agent Binky Urban, editor Marty Asher, publicist Katy Barrett, and lecture agent George Greenfield—that I disguise my appearance before entering the Hyatt Self-Surgery Clinic in New Brunswick, New Jersey. Although the dimpled, clean-shaven face framed by blond-flecked chestnut tresses combed back into an undulating pompadour had become an instant icon to millions of fans who clipped photos from the pages of *Rolling Stone, Creem,* the *New York Times,* and the *Asbury Park Press* and pasted them to dormitory walls and three-ring binders, sometime in early November, a makeup artist was summoned to Team Leyner headquarters and instructed to execute a temporary new Look. The Look was Hezbollah—Party of God—closely cropped black hair, black beard, white button-down shirt, black pants.

The Hyatt Self-Surgery clinic? Self-surgery clinics were the medical equivalent of U-Hauls or rental rug shampooers. Clinics provided a private operating room, instruments, monitoring devices, drugs, and instructional videocassettes for any procedure that could be performed solo, under local anesthetic, on any part of your anatomy that you could reach easily with *both* hands.

As I pulled into the parking lot of the recently renovated Hyatt, I realized that I'd left my copy of Edmund Spenser's *The Faerie Queene* in the Mercury Capri XR2 that I'd test-driven for *Gentleman's Quarterly*. All my notes on the 132-hp turbocharged roadster were scrawled in the margins of the Elizabethan poet's magnum opus. I called Casale Lincoln Mercury on my cellular car phone and asked for Joe Casale, showroom manager. My heart went out to Joe—tiny misshapen "pinhead," flipper-like forearms.

"Joe Casale."

"Joe, this is Mark Leyner. I was in about an hour ago to test-drive the new Capri and I think I left a book on the passenger seat. Can you have someone check and see if it's there?"

"No problem, Mr. Leyner. Just hold for a couple of seconds."

"Thanks, babe."

A minute or two passed and Casale returned to the line.

"Mr. Leyner, I'm sorry but the Capri you drove is out on the road again. Where are you now?"

"I'm at the Hyatt Self-Surgery Clinic in New Brunswick."

"I'll tell you what, Mr. Leyner, why don't I drop the book off at the clinic later this evening."

"It's not out of your way?"

"It's no problem, Mr. Leyner."

"Thanks, babe."

I parked, slung my overnight bag over my shoulder, and went in to register. The clerk at the front desk keyed my name and American Express number into the computer.

"Mr. Leyner, what procedure will you be performing on yourself?"

I hesitated for a moment before responding. It seemed injudicious to divulge to this woman that a deceased rodent was impacted between my prostate gland and urethra and that the surgical procedure I intended to perform was a radical gerbilectomy.

"Appendectomy," I lied.

"Mr. Leyner, do you have a preference with regard to O.R. accommodations?"

"Well, where do the real players stay?"

"The 'real players,' sir?"

I pushed my sunglasses down the bridge of my nose and superciliously eyeballed the desk clerk over the blue mirrored lenses.

"The players . . . the Stephen Kings, the Louis L'Amours, the Jeffrey Archers, and Ken Folletts and James Clavells."

"Mr. L'Amour was in last month to perform his own cold-fusion blepharoplasty and he stayed in . . . let me check . . . ah yes, the Tivoli Suite."

"I would like the Tivoli Suite, then."

"Very good, sir."

IT'S 10:30 P.M. I'm in the Tivoli Suite and I've just self-administered a spinal block leaving my lower torso insensible to pain. I'm about to make my first incision when I hear the door-knob turn.

"¿Quién es?" I ask. "Who is it?"

With the exception of my instrument tray and my lower abdomen, which are illuminated by high-powered halogen lamps, the room is pitch dark. I tilt a lamp toward the door and discern a figure with a tiny head and a copy of Edmund Spenser's The Faerie Queene tucked under his flipper.

"Joe?" I inquire.

"It was right on the passenger seat where you left it, Mr. Leyner!"

"Thanks, babe."

Joe turns to leave.

"Joe, wait a minute. How'd you like to come to work for me?"

"Work for you, Mr. Leyner?"

"Yeah. Move into headquarters, coordinate the staff, oversee the bodyguards, y'know, do a little of this, a little of that—you'd be my adjutant, my aide-de-camp. It's a great group of people, you get free medical treatment from Dr. Larry Werther—my cousin, my gastroenterologist—and basically I think you'd do a great job and I think you'd have a ball. What do you say?"

"Mr. Leyner . . . I think you have yourself an aide-de-camp," Joe says, extending a flipper.

"Welcome aboard, babe."

YOU ENTER THE pink-and-yellow-splashed foyer and you're swept quickly toward the inner sanctum. Flashbulbs pop as svelte spokesmodel and media liaison Baby Lago pours the Moët. Out of the corner of your eye, you see Arleen ravaging a french-fried yam. She's wearing a short, provocative strapless dress by Emanuel Ungaro that's candy-box pink and pale green. The dress is so provocative that you want to approach Arleen and perhaps caress the nape of her neck. But you dare not. Because there I am. Even more heavily muscled than you'd expected. More frightening and yet somehow more alluring than you'd imagined. My crisp white shirt is by Georges Marciano and costs about $88. My suede jeans—Ender Murat, $550—are rolled up, exposing calves that make you realize for perhaps the first time in your life how beautiful the human calf can actually be—when it's pumped up almost beyond recognition. I'm being interviewed by a reporter from *Allure,* the new Condé Nast beauty magazine.

"I have a way of being noticed and being mysterious at once," I'm saying, "like a gazelle that is there one second and then disappears."

Joe Casale comes running in. "Mr. Leyner, Mr. Leyner— Marla's on '20/20.' You said I should let you know."

"OK, babe, thanks. Everybody quiet down! Joe, turn it up."

"Today Marla Maples, the twenty-six-year-old model-actress who first achieved notoriety as the 'other woman' in the Donald and Ivana Trump divorce, sits on death row at San Quentin as her attorneys exhaust their final appeals in an apparently futile attempt to save the blond serial killer from the gas chamber. Implicated in the deaths of Leonard Bernstein, Malcolm Forbes, Grace Kelly, Billy Martin, Muppet-creator Jim Henson, and reggae singer Peter Tosh, Maples has devoted her final weeks to a letter-writing campaign in support of a congressional bill that will require television sets manufactured after July 1997 to be equipped with a computer chip that provides caption service for the deaf.

"Marla, you're young, you're leggy, you're busty— yet in a matter of days, the State of California is going to put you in a metal room and fill it with sodium cyanide gas. Do you have any advice for other leggy, busty, young women who might be experiencing peer pressure to experiment with serial killing and who might be watching tonight?"

"That's enough, Joe. Turn the TV off, OK? Thanks, babe."

I apologize to the *Allure* reporter.

"Now . . . where were we?"

"I was asking you how you got started as a writer, and, more specifically, how you got started writing liner notes for albums."

"When I was six, I came home from school one day and I went down into the basement to look for a bicycle pump and I found the dead bodies of my parents. They were each hanging from a noose, naked. All their fingers had been cut off and arranged in a pentagram under their dangling feet and in the center of this pentagram of bloody fingers was a note and the note said: 'Dear Mark, You did this to us.'

"A year later, I took a job as a bookkeeper at an insurance agency that was located in an old two-story brick building not far from here. And on my first day of work, a few of my colleagues took me out to lunch. After a long silence, one of them finally said that there was something very important that they needed to tell me. He said that about thirty or forty years ago, our office building had been owned by a very wealthy man. And this man was a chronic philanderer. And his wife knew about his affairs. And she decided that the only way to end his infidelity and to preserve their marriage was to get pregnant again, to have a 'change-of-life baby.' So she stopped using contraceptives and, sure enough, she got pregnant. The baby was born, a boy. And he was horribly deformed. He had neurofibromatosis—Elephant Man's disease. The couple kept the child shackled in a storeroom in the husband's commercial property. He was never brought to the couple's home, but kept for his entire childhood in a dark, windowless storage room in the very building that this insurance company now occupies. The child, the monster child, did nothing to stop the husband's philandering. In fact, if anything, the tragedy of this birth, of having to go every day to the storage room and find this chained horror writhing in its own excrement, simply deepened the husband's despair and inflamed his bitter compulsion to betray his wife. All of this finally drove the wife over the edge and one night, while the husband was working in the office building, she set it on fire. The husband's charred body was found, but somehow the deformity escaped. And although he's never been seen, it's rumored that on his birthday he goes foraging for a special meal of human flesh.

"At this point, my colleagues looked at me beseechingly and confided their suspicion that the monster child returns at night to the building. 'We're begging you,' they said, 'don't stay late. If there's extra work to be done, take it home. But there's danger— we feel it, we feel that he comes back.'

"It was soon Christmas season. And one of my responsibilities was to close out the books for the year. It was a very hectic time for us and one night I was asked by the president of the company to stay late, finish some work, and then lock up. That night I worked on the books until almost two in the morning—the building, of course, completely empty except for me. I finished up, turned out the lights, armed the building's security system, locked the door, and exited. I walked through the parking lot to my car, opened the front door, and got in. There was a smell . . . a smell of rotting flowers, of putrid water from a neglected vase . . . and the stench of decaying flesh. I felt something on my neck . . . not fingers, but stumps . . . finger stumps caressing my neck. I turned around and there were the corpses of my parents seated in the back, and they were gazing at me with wide eyes and horrible grins on their faces. I was ice-cold and nauseous with terror. I opened the car door, rolled to the ground, and ran back to the building. Fumbling frantically with the keys, I finally got the door open. I took a few trembling steps into the dark hallway, when I felt something brush against my leg and then do a series of . . . are you familiar with classical ballet steps?"

The *Allure* reporter nods. "Somewhat."

"Well, it did a series of *brisés volés*. This is a flying *brisé* where you finish on one foot after the beat and the other is crossed in back . . . it's basically a *fouetté* movement with a *jeté battu*. And then it landed in the middle of the reception area in an *arabesque à la hauteur*—that's an *arabesque* where the working leg is raised at a right angle to the hip, one arm curved over the head, the other extended to the side. It was the monster child! And he had a birthday hat on his head! To my astonishment—especially after everything I'd heard—he wasn't such a malevolent creature after all. We talked for quite a while—touching on a wide range of issues—and then he said that he had a friend who was in trouble and he asked me if I could help her. I said I'd try. I followed him deep into the woods, maybe two or three miles until we stopped. And there seated against a tree, sobbing inconsolably, was Julianne Phillips.

"'What's wrong?' I asked her.

"She said that Bruce Springsteen had just left her for Patti Scialfa.

"'Listen, I've got a car,' I said. 'Is there somewhere I could take you?'

"'P-P-Paula's.'

"Well, it turned out that Paula was Paula Abdul. And we became very close. And it was through Paula that I met Elton and then Axl and Queen Latifah. And that's basically how I got started writing liner notes."

"Thank you very much, Mr. Leyner, that was absolutely fascinating!" the *Allure* reporter gushes. "And good luck on your new book."

"Thanks, it was a pleasure chatting."

from *Nothing But Blue Skies*

Michigan native Thomas McGuane has been one of the mainstay writers of the Vintage Contemporaries series for more than a decade. He is the author of several highly acclaimed novels, including The Sporting Club, The Bushwacked Piano, Ninety-two in the Shade *(a National Book Award finalist),* Panama, Nobody's Angel, Something to Be Desired, Keep the Change, *and* Nothing But Blue Skies.

FRANK COPENHAVER PUT his wife Gracie's suitcases in the back of the Electra and held the door for her. She got in. He walked around the front of the car gravely and he got in. He leaned forward over the steering wheel to look up at their house as though it were he, rather than Gracie, who was looking at it for the last time. A magpie flew across his view. It was a clue for Gracie in the event she didn't realize that this was her chance. He didn't want her, halfway to Arizona, to realize she had, in her sadness, forgotten to do this very important thing.

Once they were under way, he said, "We've got a few extra minutes, let me take the scenic route."

"Oh, Frank, oh, please God no, not the scenic route," said Gracie.

He was undeterred. As he drove, he chatted easily about the clash between Kellogg and General Mills over the seven-and-a-half-billion-dollar cereal business, realizing too late that it might seem to be an attempt to prefigure their own impending divorce and settlement. He tried to be almost too specific in fending off this parallel, running on about Cheerios and Wheaties and Rice Krispies and Raisin Bran; and, considering the state of their own

lives, making far too much of Tony the Tiger autographing base-
balls at Safeway stores.

Gracie was dressed for travel, jeans, a cotton sweater tied
around her waist, tennis shoes; her long black hair was braided
and wound atop her head. She was at once weathered and pretty,
remarkably girlish for the mother of a college student. She was
wearing mountaineering glasses with leather side pieces. She
didn't seem to see much of the ordinary suburb and barely tightened her focus when Frank stopped in front of his—their—medical clinic on Alder Street and watched in apparent satisfaction
as patients wandered in and out of its breezy, modern entryway.
They had not owned the clinic long, and the many nursery aspens
were still held up by stakes and wires; the beds of annuals had an
uncanny uniformity. Frank took one more turn so that he could
see the building from the side, then went on to the Kid Royale,
his pet project.

The Kid Royale Hotel was a short walk from Deadrock's old
Territorial railroad station and was one of the monuments of the
Montana frontier. Frank was going to restore it to its original
glory, with its carriage bays and hitching racks and vaulted
lobby. It was in poor shape now and stood with faded tobacco and
soft drink advertisements painted on its side in a neighborhood
that was giving way to transience and light industry. The success
of this project would probably do more to endear Frank to this
small city than anything. And it was only with the mildest of
irony that he looked forward to his acceptance.

"Can we skip the mini-storage?" Gracie asked. "It's getting
late." Fank was able to include the mini-storage facility in the
scenic tour despite Gracie leaning disconsolately against the
side of the car.

"You know," he said, "it's hard to believe, but there's some five
percent adjustable mortgages out there. Sometimes I think my
bank is trying to put me out of business. You can't always absorb

these little things just to be courteous, let people nick you when they want. Like today, the Nikkei stock index plunged under the effect of arbitrage-related selling. This crap skids around the Pacific Rim in about four nanoseconds and scares hell out of little guys in Montana like me. Gracie, I hate to see you go. It's been what, exactly?"

"A long time."

"A long time. But Grace, you should have never done what you did. People don't rise above things like that. Their marriages don't."

"I know, Frank." As they reached the airport behind a stream of cars looking for short-term parking, Frank suddenly felt wild and unacknowledged conflicts in his breast. He had not spent enough time thinking about what this moment could mean. There was something spinning loose.

"Gracie, I just know you're going to hit the ground running." The thought that that might actually be true renewed his malice. "I'm going to focus on my business. Our situation has been so anti-synergistic that, to be completely honest, I expect to take off like a rocket as soon as you're gone."

"I bet you're right."

"If you get a chance, I'd like to see you salt a few bucks away in tax-deferred variable annuities, but that's between you and whoever." "Whoever" was like a drooling new face at Mount Rushmore.

"Thanks."

Frank manged to catch a skycap's eye. The skycap, a boy of about eighteen with long hair falling out of his cap, came to the driver's side window where Frank gave him several bills. "Give the lady a hand with her luggage if you would." Then he turned to Gracie, who was getting out of the car. "Goodbye, Grace. Give my regards to a town of your choice."

"Goodbye, Frank." Her cheeks were wet with tears.

He pulled away with a bizarre, all-knowing expression on his face, his hands parallel on the wheel and feeling, as he glanced in the rearview mirror too late to see Gracie enter the airport, that something inside had come completely undone. There was no chance to analyze her gait and try to determine if she was eager to get on the plane. There was no chance to collapse with grief and, perhaps, start all over again.

He had really thought he was adjusting to a changed Gracie but not an entirely new one. They had two cars but they never went anywhere in two cars before. They picked one and both went in it together, either Gracie's unkillable Plymouth Valiant with its smooth-ticking little slant six or his low, domineering blue-black Electra with the insouciant lag shifts of its fluid-swilling transmission. Often Gracie slid over near him like in high school, elevating slightly on the spheres of her buttocks to touch her hair into place in the rearview mirror or put her hand high on his thigh. The Buick seemed like an old-time sex car, and unlike the light-spirited Japanese cars that had come to dominate things, the Electra still seemed to say, You're going with me and you're going to put out, period. The wanton deep pleats of its velvety upholstery invited stains. Recently, however, Gracie had begun to take the Plymouth for "time to think" on her way to her restaurant, Amazing Grease—sometimes, it seemed to Frank, with plenty of time to think. She had promised she would learn how to fish so that they would have more time together, but that plan went sour. He was quick to notice that things had changed but slow to realize what should be done about it. He reminded himself that he still had his health.

Frank buried himself not in his work but in fantasies of escape. He became a connoisseur of maps. He loved the history of maps and he felt drawn to the theory of the flat earth as the only one that adequately explained the disappearances common to everyone, especially death. He saw a kind of poetry in the spherical projections of the world as devised by Ptolemy. The more insistently the mystery of Gracie's changed patterns intruded upon his thoughts, the more interested he was in the shrinking *terrae incognitae* of the old world; flat or round, what was the difference? Really, he often thought, what is the damn difference? It just seems likely that my parents, like other generations, milled around for sixty-eighty years and fell off the end.

He bought a scale model of a nineteenth-century surveyor's carriage and had booked a trip with Gracie's travel agent friend, Lucy, to visit the Royal Observatory at Greenwich, home of the Greenwich meridian, about the time Gracie hit the road without a map of any kind. By this time, the impending change had elaborated into a full-fledged human by the name of Edward Ballantine, a traveler and breeder of race horses, a resident of Sedona, Arizona, spiritual headquarters for Shirley MacLaine's crystal people. Suddenly, Galileo's discovery of the satellites of Jupiter, Newton's announcement that the earth was flattened at the poles, even his simple pleasure at reading the mileage tables in his gas station, were out the window. He had never really thought about his wife leaving him. She was gone and he would never be the same again. He would never have a single second of time that was in any way continuous with his previous life, even if she came back, which was not likely. What good was his map collection now?

IN 1968, A now ancient time full of scathing situations, trying love but preferring lust and, for many, one meretricious *scène à faire*, the flushing of narcotics down the toilet, Frank was banished from the family business by his father. This involved a long autobiographical recitation in which his father told about his early years on the ranch, the formulaic (in Frank's eyes) long walk to a poorly heated country school, the pain of being Catholic in a community of Norwegian Lutherans, the early success in getting calf weights up, the malt barley successes, the highest certifications and the prize ribbons, the sod farm successes, the nursery, the Ford dealership, the implement dealership and the four apartment buildings, including the one regularly demolished by the fraternity boys "and their concubines." Frank's father was a self-taught, almost bookish individual, and he wore his education on his sleeve.

Among the fraternity boys was Frank, the son of the landlord, who had graduated a year earlier but who was now "managing the building" for his family, hoping to make it another of the family's successes. The occasion of his banishment was a theme party, the theme being Farm Life, a kind of witticism on Frank's part involving hauling three tons of straw into the building and piling it higher than not only the furniture but the heads of the occupants. Barnyard animals, chiefly pigs, were turned loose in this lightless wilderness and the party began. It lasted two days. Tunnels quickly formed that led to the beer kegs and to small clearings where people could gather. There was a proscribed area for bodily functions, a circular clearing in the hay with dove gray shag carpet for a floor, and another for the operations of the stereo and its seemingly endless loop of the beloved Neil Young's "Are you ready for the country, 'cause it's time to go!"

The world of straw became damp and odorous with beer, marijuana, sperm, perfume and pig droppings. Frank would remember ever afterward the terror of crawling stoned, in his underwear, down a small side tunnel to meet headlong in the semi-darkness a bristling, frightened three-hundred-pound pig. Right after that, clutching a beer and a joint and hearing the approach of another pig, he withdrew into the straw alongside the tunnel to let the pig pass, watched it go by ridden by the most beautiful naked sorority girl he had ever seen, Janet Otergaard from Wolf Point, now vice president of the First National Bank. Frank crawled after her but fell behind a bit, and when he caught up she was already going off into the straw with Barry Danzig, who was home from Northwestern Law School. This disappointment had the effect of making Frank long for fresh air. He made his way toward the entrance, and crawling out of the straw in his underwear, a bleak and tarry roach hanging from one of his slack lips, he met his father.

Mr. Copenhaver continued to wear suspenders long after they had gone out of fashion. He wore wide ones with conspicuous brass hardware to remind people of his agricultural origins. Most people hadn't gotten the news that farmers were as liable to be envy-driven crooks as anybody else, the stream of information having been interrupted by the Civil War; so, wearing wide suspenders was like wearing an "I Am Sincere" sign. Today, curving over the powerful chest of his father, they stood for all the nonsense he was not brooking. A bleary girl in a straw-flecked blue sweater emerged pulling the sweater down at the sides over her bare hips. She peered unwelcomingly at Frank's father and said, "Who's this one?"

"The owner of the building!" boomed Mr. Copenhaver. She dove back into the straw. Frank was now overpowered by fear of his father. He felt his drugged and drunken vagueness in muzzy contrast to his father's forceful clarity next to him, a presence formed by a lifetime of unstinting forward movement, of farming, warfare and free-market capitalism as found in a small Montana city. Next to his father, Frank felt like a pudding. As against making a world, he was prepared to offer the quest for pussy and altered states—an edgeless generation, dedicated to escaping the self and inconsequential fornicating, dedicated to the idea of the Relationship and all-terrain shoes that didn't lie to your feet. Frank's fear was that his father would strike him. Worse, he said to get the people out, clean up the building and appear at his office in the morning.

That didn't start out well either. He was exhausted from cleaning up the mess himself. His companions were unwilling to help until they had had a night's sleep. He found himself shouting, on the verge of tears: "Is this friendship? You know my back is against the wall? I'm about to get my ass handed to me. I need you to help me!" We need sleep, they said. So, he cleaned the mess up himself, hauling twenty-seven loads in the back of his car out to the landfill and simply, hopelessly, releasing the pigs into the neighborhood. They belonged to the family of one of the fellows who hadn't stayed to help. Frank found the most awful things on the floor: false teeth taped to the end of a stick, hot dogs and half-finished bags of miniature doughnuts dusted with powdered sugar, rotten panties, a Bible, a catcher's chest protector. He showered, changed into a clean shirt, clean jeans and a corduroy sport jacket. Then, having been up all night, he headed for his father's office. He drove up Assiniboine Avenue and then turned at College Street. His nerves were shattered by the sight of three pigs jogging up the center of Third Street, loosely glancing over their shoulders. Here and there, people stopped to watch these out-of-place animals.

He parked his car, an old blue Mercury with sarcastic tail fins and speckled bumpers, in front of his father's office, a handsomely remodeled farmhouse on West Deadrock, and went in. He presented himself shakily to the secretary, the very Eileen who now worked for him, who waved him on with a gesture that suggested she knew all about people like Frank and his friends. And perhaps she did, he thought. It's easy to detect motion when you're frozen in position, an old hunter's trick.

"Come in, Frank," his father said evenly.

"Hi, Dad."

His father stayed at his desk while Frank sank subdued into an upholstered chair placed in front of the desk, a chair so ill sprung that Frank, at six-one, was barely able to see over the front of his father's desk. The view of his father's head and neck rising from the horizontal line in front was reminiscent of a poorly lit documentary shot of a sea serpent and added to the state begun by Frank's shattered condition.

Mr. Copenhaver made a steeple with his fingertips. The high color in his cheeks, the silver-and-sand hair combed straight across his forehead and the blue suit gave him an ecclesiastical look, and Frank felt a fleeting hope that this was no accident and Christian forgiveness lay just around the corner.

"Frank, you're interested in so many things." His father glanced down; Frank could see he had the desk drawer slightly open so that he could make out some notes he had made for this conversation.

"Yes, sir."

"You like to hunt and fish."

"Yes, sir."

"You like the ladies. You like a high old time. You like to meet your buddies for a drink in the evening and you read our daily newspaper, indicating, I might have hoped, an interest in current events but probably only the ball scores. I rarely see you with anything uplifting in your hand bookwise and the few you've left around the place are the absolute utmost in prurience, illustrated with photographs for those who are unable to follow the very descriptive text. So far so good: at least it was confined between the covers of a book. There was a day in time when I had my own Tillie the Toiler comics and I am not here setting myself up to moralize about your condition. I have for a long time now, heaving a great sigh, accepted that I was the father of a drunken sports lecher and let it go at that. But when I gave you the opportunity to find some footing in the day-to-day world that would have implications for your livelihood many years down the road, you gave it the kind of disrespect I have to assume was directed at me. Last night, I felt personally smothered in straw and pig manure. That was your valentine to your father, Frank, thank you. And Frank, see how this flies: I'm not going to put up with it anymore. You're not going to run that building anymore and my hope that you would one day manage the old home place is dead. I think your brother Mike is the man for that job."

Mr. Copenhaver tipped back in his chair and began to talk about growing up on the old home place, the long walk to school, the cold, some parenthetical remarks about rural electrification and rural values. Frank tried to stare out the window but his eyes were too weak to get past the glass. He was cottonmouthed with exhaustion and prepared to endorse any negative view of his character. At the same time, he'd had enough. He got to his feet on his leaden legs and raised his hand, palm outward, to his father.

"Goodbye," Frank said. He went out the door and rarely saw his father again. Mike saw him frequently, even driving down from the school of dentistry. They had a nice, even relationship that Frank envied. Mike never made an attempt to be a business-man like his father. That, much later, would be Frank's job, seeking approval from someone who had departed this world for the refrigerated shadows of death.

from *The Country Ahead of Us,*
the Country Behind

Winner of the 1995 PEN/Faulkner Award and the Pacific Northwest Booksellers Association Award for his nationally bestselling novel, Snow Falling on Cedars, *Harper's contributing editor David Guterson originally published his short-story collection,* The Country Ahead of Us, the Country Behind, *in 1989. His new novel,* East of the Mountains, *is forthcoming from Harcourt Brace in Fall 1998.*

■ PIRANHAS

THE DOOR OF Paul's bedroom opened one evening and his parents and their dinner guests came in.

"Paul's room," his mother announced. "And Paul."

"And is this connected to the intercom system?"

"Certainly it is. The whole house is."

"So you can call him for dinner. How convenient."

"If there were such a thing as dinner," said Paul's mother. "If dinner existed, yes."

She laughed, airily, at her own words.

The guests fanned out, looking at things with calm detachment, absorbed by the walls, the floor. Paul, his hands in his lap, sat on the edge of his bed and watched them silently.

"He has his own television," someone pointed out.

"He has his own television, yes," said Paul's mother.

"Strictly regulated," added his father. "The homework has to get done right before the television comes on at night."

The guests eyed Paul with curiosity now. He thought he knew

what they were thinking, though—was he the sort of boy who had trouble at school? Was his homework a family problem?

"What grade are you in, Paul?" somebody asked.

"Seventh," his mother said. "We started him early."

"Look at this," one of the guests insisted. "The dial on this intercom's turned all the way down. How can he hear anything?"

"He can't," said Paul's mother. "We never use that, really. It's just there."

"I've always thought that about intercoms. You can't justify the expense."

"Oh, come on," answered Paul's mother. "Let me tell you something. It came in handy when Paul was a baby. We could monitor his crying from upstairs."

"Well how much is an intercom system? Let's hear some figures on this."

"I don't remember," Paul's mother answered.

"It came with the house," said Paul's father.

"Well, what good is it if you don't use it?" said the guest. "It's just a lot of useless wires running through the walls."

"That's it," said Paul's mother. "Useless wires."

For some reason everybody laughed at these words. Then, as if by some unspoken agreement, it was time for the house tour to move on.

"Hey, Paul," somebody said. "You're one lucky guy living in a place like this. And I bet you don't even appreciate it."

Once again, everybody stared at Paul. They stood together in a group near the doorway, drinks in their hands, bored.

"He's the silent type," explained Paul's mother. "Say good-bye to everybody, Paul."

"Good-bye," Paul said. "See you."

They went out. He could hear them in the hall. "Let me show you my new hot tub," his mother was saying. "It's *wonderful*."

—

WALKING HOME IN the rain on Monday afternoon, Paul slipped into the pet shop on Sixty-fifth Street.

"Wet out," the man at the counter said in greeting. "You know what I'm saying? *Wet.*"

The man wore a square mustache and black plastic glasses. He stood at the cash register with a pencil behind his ear eating popcorn from a brown paper bag, and looking, to Paul, a little sinister for some reason. His shop had the vaguely menacing aura of a laboratory set up in a cave. Four rows of aquariums stretched away into the darkness. Only they were lit—nothing else. The fish hovered as if in a dream, secure in their lit glass houses. The place smelled of jungle; vapor fogged all its windows. In another room caged birds sang.

"Wow," Paul said. "It's neat in here."

"Look around," the man advised. "Go ahead. Dry off. Put your books down and look some."

"Okay," Paul said. "Thanks."

He wandered between the rows, peering into each tank with his hands on his knees, feeling immense suddenly. The man had hung a placard over each aquarium: PARADISEFISH—FROM TAIWAN; CHOCOLATE GOURAMI—THE MALAY PENINSULA; BANDED CLIMBING PERCH—THE ZAIRE BASIN. The imprisoned fish appeared to lead effortless and aimless lives. They hung suspended in corners, one eye to the glass, or tipped themselves toward the membrane of the surface. Some swam diligently, but most seemed to understand there was no point to that. They went wherever the water took them as it bubbled up from the filters.

Paul watched them for some time. He decided—though he had no words for it—that they lived in a private and trivial universe, subject to currents of thought so removed from their lives that their identities as individual fish had been submerged. Perhaps they had known all the miseries of capture; perhaps in transport from some exotic home the unassailable loneliness of the world had been revealed to them. Now they swung about in watery cages, forgetting or remembering, uncertain if what occurred in the course of their hours constituted an actual existence. Paul, with a conscious exertion of the imagination, thought of them as they might have been in their other lives— free, inhabiting a warm and boundless ocean, darting joyfully, their hearts light, feeding, in conquest, at liberty to live. He thought of them as cultivating a preordained singularity, nurtured by forces that were rightfully in effect, according to the universe's grand plan.

When he looked up the man at the counter was watching him suspiciously. He still stood behind his cash register stuffing his mouth with popcorn.

"You're interested," he said to Paul. "I can tell."

Paul nodded.

"Start small," the man advised. "Ten gallons, max. Decide if you like it, then move up gradual. You've got all kinds of time."

"I already know I like it," Paul said.

The man crammed more popcorn between his lips. "Oh, yeah?" he said. "How can you tell?"

"I just can," Paul said. "I'm like that."

"Well," said the man. "Fine then. If you know yourself that well, *fine.*"

PAUL CAME UPSTAIRS at six-thirty. His parents were in their living room now—he'd heard them turn the lock fifteen minutes before, he'd given them time to get settled. The television was on: news. His father sat in the wing chair with his feet across an ottoman, listening through headphones to the CD player, pieces of the mail scattered on the floor beside him. His mother—her feet pulled up beneath her on the sofa—leafed through a mail-order catalog.

"Hello," Paul said to them. "You're home."

His father pried off the headphones. "Hello," he said. "Did you use the VCR after school, Paul? I noticed someone left the power on."

"No," Paul said. "I didn't."

"You're wasting electricity," his mother said.

"I didn't use it," Paul repeated.

They stopped talking in order to watch a television advertisement. A car rose up from the surface of the road and flew off into the glitter of deep space. Then it returned, a woman got into it. A man in jeans, leaning jauntily against the side of a barn, watched her flash by. She went around a corner, got out in front of a nightclub. A man played a saxophone beside a water fountain, sweating. The woman was driving again, her lavender fingernails trailing across the upholstery. A man sitting in front of a gas station, the sun setting in the mountains behind him, scratched his head as she blew past.

"Boring," announced Paul's mother, and turned a page in her mail-order catalog.

Paul wandered into the kitchen. For a while he opened cabinets, looking at things—noodles, canned olives, bottled salad dressing. His father came in and went to the refrigerator, pulled out a beer, snapped it open and drank leaning against the counter.

"We can microwave," he said, loosening his tie. "Sound okay to you, Paul?"

Paul nodded.

His father opened the freezer door. "Beef stroganoff," he announced. "Halibut in cream sauce, pasta marinara, shrimp gumbo—what'll it be?"

"Beef stroganoff," Paul said.

"I'm for halibut," said his father.

His father opened the microwave oven. "Can I get an aquarium?" Paul asked.

"What?"

"I want to buy an aquarium," said Paul.

"An aquarium?" said his father. "What for?"

"I just want one, that's all. Can I?"

"I don't know," said his father. "You'd better ask your mother, Paul."

They went into the living room together.

"An aquarium," said his mother. "Where do you want to keep it?"

"In my room," Paul answered. "Please?"

"Is it messy?"

"No."

"Who's going to clean it when it needs to be cleaned?"

"I will. I promise, Mom."

"I don't know," said his mother.

She turned the pages of her catalog.

"It's not like a dog or a cat," said his father. "Personally, I'm for it, Kim."

"Why do you want fish?" said his mother.

"I don't know," answered Paul.

"All you can do is *look* at them," said his mother.

"I know that," said Paul.

"How much money are we talking about?"

"I don't know," Paul told her. "I could use my Christmas money, though."

His mother tossed her catalog on the coffee table. She stood, tossed her bangs from her eyes, brushed a wrinkle from the front of her skirt and—stretching toward the ceiling, only her toes still touching the carpet, her hands balled into fists above her head—she yawned.

"No," she said. "You leave your Christmas money in the bank, all right? *I'll* pay for the aquarium."

"*I* want to pay for it," Paul said.

"You can't," said his mother. "*I* want to."

KEN, A FRIEND from school, a boy who wore a ski parka and who put gel in his blond hair, came to look at the new aquarium one afternoon.

"Weird," he said. "That one with the thing on his nose."

"That's an elephant fish," Paul said.

"What's with this one?"

"That's a severum. He got his tail chewed. That guy there— the Jack Dempsey?—he does it. He's *rude*."

"Cool," said Ken. "Do they fight?"

"No."

"You ever see a Siamese fighting fish?"

"No."

"I saw it on television," Ken explained. "It's so cool. They kill each other. You throw them in a tank together and watch them *brawl*."

"Really?"

"People bet on them, I think in China."

"Really?"

"It's so cool," Ken said.

"You ever see two cats wrestle?" Paul asked. "It's so cool. They—"

"They're *screwing*," Ken said. "That's different."

Paul fell silent.

"What're the ones with the stripes?" Ken asked.

"Those are tiger barbs."

"They're kind of small."

"Yeah. Sort of."

"Maybe the Jack Dempsey fish could eat those guys. How come they're not all chewed up?"

"They're fast," Paul said. "They get away."

"Well, what about the blue ones? They don't look so fast."

"I don't know," Paul said. "Those are gouramis. The Dempsey leaves those guys alone."

"What's this?" Ken said, tapping the glass of the tank. "This one? Right over here?"

"That's a red-tailed shark."

"Cool," said Ken. "What does he eat?"

"They all eat the same stuff," Paul explained. "This."

He held up the can of Tetramin. "It's like leaves and stuff," he said to Ken.

"Maybe you ought to throw in some *meat*," Ken advised. "So they can get bigger—they're pretty dinky looking."

"They don't get big," explained Paul. "You want them to get big, you put them in a bigger tank."

"You ever see that movie?" Ken asked. "This girl goes down to South America with her dad. He's a scientist or something. She takes her clothes off to go swimming and these *piranhas* eat her. It's so *cool*," he added.

"I saw that," Paul said. "Gross."

"It grossed my friend out," Ken said. "*I* didn't get grossed out, though. You remember when that scientist guy gets it?"

"*That* was gross. That was *really* gross."

"Yeah," said Ken. "You want to go to the arcade with me?"

"I can't," said Paul. "My parents won't let me."

"Neither will mine," Ken said.

AT NIGHT, EVERY light turned off but the one in the aquarium, Paul watched his fish from the safety of his comforter. Their eternal passivity struck him as offensive: their hearts should boil over, they ought to dash their brains against the glass. But they were only fish and so they hovered, ghosts of themselves, unrealized souls. They could not concoct a plan of escape or rail against their condition. There was no identifiable question for them to ask, and anyway their world was warm and luminous and food appeared in it at regular intervals. What would it mean to be a fish and did they hear him when he spoke out loud? And when his face was pressed against the glass was he there for them, or was he nothing? And what did they make of the formality of their world, its lines and corners, its cramped geometry? Were their brains pitched to the proper degree of uselessness, in order that contented lives might be lived in such conditions as these? Even a fish must experience captivity as some agonizing, ceaseless form of suffering. There together, living out entire lives in maddening, langorous comfort, they must gently become unhinged in the head; either that or die. And so they circled, or hung in the void, or sulked, inert, above the gravel. They hated and ignored one another endlessly, and when the light in their home went off at night they slept with thankfulness that their world had been erased until morning returned it to them. And this they lived through—Paul decided—with thoughts commensurate to their station in the order of being, as it had been explained to him at school recently: these fish, because they were not anything but fish, were condemned to only the faintest understanding of matters, perhaps to none at all; no one knew.

Paul, on the other hand, would grow older and understand. In fact he was beginning to understand already; he was twelve.

"PIRANHAS?" THE MAN at the pet shop said, cleaning his glasses on his shirttail. "Piranhas are vicious, all right? They'll mess up your other fish in no time."

"I saw this movie," said Paul. "They eat you."

"Only if you go in the water," said the man with a wink. "Come here and have a look."

They went down between the rows of aquariums. They came to a tank with rust-red gravel, algae mottling its sides. The man stopped by it, grave-faced. Then, strangely, he began to hum the theme from *Jaws*.

"Piranhas," he announced. "There."

Paul looked in. A dozen fish traveled in a group restlessly, silver, deep-bodied, blunt-headed animals, no bigger than fifty-cent pieces.

"A lot of people buy them," the man explained. "Basically you've got two choices. You start a separate piranha tank—nothing but, just piranhas, that's all. Or you throw them in with your other fish and raise them vegetarian-like. Never let them get the taste of meat, pretty soon they're docile like the rest. You have to figure there's an instinct, though. They start in chewing on someone's fins or tail, pull them quick—they're trouble."

"Pull them?" Paul said. "Where?"

"You can flush them down your toilet," the man explained. "They won't live up around here—too cold."

He leaned down and tapped on the aquarium glass. The piranhas flashed away for a half-second, a wave of movement, undulant, then fell back into their silent weaving.

"Check this out," the man said. "Their teeth are like little triangles. That's real teeth—dentine and enamel. Little razors, two rows of them.

Paul leaned down with his hands on his knees. The man put his index finger against the aquarium glass and pointed, absurdly, at the moving fish. "Teeth," he said. "Vicious little suckers."

"How much are they?" Paul asked.

The man looked at him. He took off his glasses, then looked again. He kept blinking.

"You're interested," he said. "Well, let me tell you something. Piranhas are a *habit,* okay? You get dedicated or you flush them. There's no in between. You feed them meat they get expensive, you don't they get boring—just another fish. You understand what I'm saying?"

"I think I do," Paul answered.

"Good," said the man. "Fine."

They stood there for a moment looking in at the piranhas. "Well," said the man. "I'll leave you alone here so you can mull it over. You let me know what you decide."

"I'll take eight," Paul told him. "How much are they?"

"Eight?" said the man. "You'll need another tank for that, you know. Eight? That's a lot to start with."

"I like them," Paul said. "They're interesting."

KEN STOOD LOOKING into the new aquarium, situated next to the first one. "All right," he said, bending down to look more closely. "Just like the ones in the *movie*."

Paul sat down on the edge of his bed. The piranhas spoke for themselves.

"What do you feed them?" Ken said.

"Whatever," Paul said. "You know."

"Like what?"

"Like tuna fish, mainly. Other stuff."

"Insects?"

"No."

"Like what then?"

"Tadpoles," Paul said. "I got them at school. They're in that jar over there."

"Cool," Ken said. "I want to see."

"It's not that big a deal," Paul said.

Ken picked up the jar of tadpoles. "Can I dump some in?" he asked. "Please?"

"Go ahead," Paul answered.

They watched together while the piranhas ate. It was quite leisurely, finally. No mad frenzy. They maneuvered, the tadpoles wriggled to no avail. Calm feeding.

"See?" Paul said. "I think it's from living in the tank or something. They don't go crazy like in the movie."

"The movie was better," Ken agreed.

"I read about them in the encyclopedia," Paul said. "They live in this river somewhere. A cow comes in, they turn it into a skeleton. They swim around in big groups, hunting. They find another fish, they eat it. People, too, sometimes. Natives washing their clothes and stuff."

"No kidding?" Ken said. "For real?"

Paul didn't answer. He lay back on his bed.

"Hey," said Ken. "Why don't you feed them something big, maybe? Maybe they'll go crazy eating it."

"Like what?" Paul said.

"Like a goldfish or something. You know, a fish. Throw one in and see what happens."

"What for?" said Paul.

"You know," said Ken. "So they can *eat* it."

"I thought about that," Paul said.

THEY WERE EVIL, he saw at night, blind in their purpose, communally devoted to the shedding of blood. Watching them Paul understood the liberation that came with such a shared lust: the piranhas—it was their instinct—had stepped across an invisible boundary, relinquishing their identities in exchange for the assurances of cooperation with ten thousand others. He could not even feel, rightfully, that he owned them really; they defied proprietorship; their allegiance was to one another. They were a single organism, each a part of something larger than the self. And none was alone—they brought what made them whole with them into captivity, then clung to it in defiance of reality. As with the other fish, on nights before, he imagined them engaged in their former lives—undulating with thousands of other fish of like kind, the scent of meat propelling them all across the river currents, the warm, safe riot of the hunting attack, the rapture of blood. He dreamed that in some other life he had known this feeling, too: safe among masses of those like himself, engaged to the pit of his being in a world of purpose, passion, sustenance, action, and finding within its context that impossible thing, love, boundless acceptance, a rightful place in things.

One night, having watched them late, he went out onto the deck of the house. He wanted, if possible, to see the stars or moon—whatever was up there: anything. But instead his parents were in their hot tub kissing violently, and his father's hands were on his mother's breasts; they surged up out of the water together and his father's pale, starved rump emerged and his mother's brown heels were pinned against his father's hamstrings. He saw that theirs was an angry passion that would not be satisfied; that love was like everything else in their lives; he felt this, watching them—the violence of their dissatisfaction with everything.

His mother kissed his father's neck, his hairy shoulder, his earlobe, and then her cheek was against his and she was staring into Paul's eyes. "Get out of here," she snarled. "Honestly, Paul." Paul's father swiveled and stared at him, too. "Paul," he said. "Jesus Christ."

They fell apart into the water. His mother took a glass of wine from the edge of the tub. His father laughed into the darkness.

"What's so funny?" Paul said.

"How about giving us a little privacy?" said his mother.

"Sorry," Paul said. "It was an accident."

"Go to bed," said his father. "It's late, Paul. Okay?"

He laughed again. Paul's mother took another sip from her wine. She moved over onto his father's lap.

"Are you getting the message?" she said to Paul. "Leave already, okay?"

HE WENT IN and fed a blue gourami to the piranhas. They worked on it together, methodically. They nipped out a piece here, a piece there, tail and fins first, then along the flanks, finally at the back of the head. The gourami turned belly up before long. Later Paul fished out the skeleton.

He fed them the red-tailed shark the next night. It was no contest—they ate her with astonishing speed. The pair of severums went in together. The tiger barbs had to be tired out. The Dempsey fought, then died and was devoured. The elephant fish was the last to go. They accosted her from all sides; the blood was substantial. She floundered and the piranhas stripped flesh from her flanks until everything was gone but the bone.

Later the housecleaning woman, Molly, came into Paul's room and saw the empty tank with its hood left open, the water circulating through the filters, the pump humming along, the thermostat light glowing—but no fish, nothing, just water. She mentioned this curiosity to Paul's mother.

"They all died," Paul explained to her. "That's what."

"Well, did you take care of them?" said his mother. "Did you feed them?"

"I took care of them," Paul said. "Sure I fed them."

"Well, then what happened?"

"I don't know."

"Well, what did you do with them?"

"I flushed them down the toilet."

"Oh, God," said his mother. "Honestly."

HIS FATHER CAME into his room that night. He sat on Paul's desk and put his feet on Paul's chair. He looked at the fish tanks and sighed.

"I see you split up the piranhas," he said. "How come, Paul? What's the deal?"

"They'll get bigger," said Paul. "This gives them more room."

"Don't you think they're big enough already?" asked his father. "They're getting *huge*."

"No way," said Paul.

They were silent for a moment. The filter pumps hummed. The television was on upstairs.

"You have to get rid of these piranhas," said his father. "And I'm not asking you. I'm telling you."

"How come?" said Paul.

"Because they're *strange*," said his father. "That's why."

"What's strange about them?"

"They're just strange. They're strange, Paul, you can't have them in your room like this. They—"

"Come on," Paul said. "Please?"

His father shook his head. "You have to get rid of them," he said. "That's all there is to it."

"No way," Paul said. "Come on, Dad."

His father leaned around the doorjamb. "Kim!" he yelled. "Come down here!"

"Come on, Dad," Paul said one more time.

His mother came in. She looked at each of them, one at a time. "Now what?" she said. "What is it?"

"Confrontation," said his father. "You're better at it, Kim."

"He's twelve," said Paul's mother. "You can handle it."

"I'm keeping my piranhas," Paul said.

"No you're not," said his mother.

"Yes I am," said Paul. "They're not hurting anything."

"Listen," said his mother. "The piranhas are going. Is that understood? Just remember who paid for all those fish in the first place. I paid, I'm going to make the decisions."

"I wanted to use my Christmas money," Paul said. "All right, fine—I'll get rid of them. Then I'll buy some more with my *own* money."

"No you won't," said his mother. "This is it with the tropical fish, Paul. You'll have to find a more appropriate hobby."

She went over and pulled the plug on the electric pumps. The bubbles stopped running through the filters.

"Leave it unplugged," she said. "I'm serious."

"Maybe Paul can take them back to the pet store," said his father. "Wouldn't that be better?"

"Paul can resolve this however he sees fit," said his mother. "Just as long as he gets them out of here."

There was silence then. Paul curled up on his bed. He pulled the pillow over his head, tucked his knees against his chest and swore under his breath at both of them.

"Did you hear me, Paul?" said his mother.

"Get out of here," Paul yelled. "I mean it."

PAUL, IN THE morning, put the piranhas in the hot tub. They died immediately; he left them there.

He told Ken about it. They skipped school in memory of the dead fish. "My parents suck," Paul said.

"So do mine," answered Ken.

"I hate them," said Paul. "Big time."

"Same here," Ken said.

They walked across the golf course together. They cut across a sand trap to the ninth green. It had begun to rain; no one was golfing.

"I just want to *kill* them," Paul said.

"I want to kill mine, too."

"What's the best way?"

"Poison their food."

"Cut them up with an ax while they're asleep."

"Cut the brake line in the car."

"Shoot them in the back while they're taking a shower."

"We can trade," Ken said. "Like on television. You kill mine while I kill yours."

"I know," said Paul. "With a *chainsaw*."

They sat on a bench. It was raining harder now. Cars went by on the road. Paul imagined how it might be to kill his parents. The thought caused him only minor remorse, because he felt certain they deserved it, somehow.

"Let's head over to the arcade," Ken said. "Maybe someone else'll be there."

Paul got up and pulled the collar of his coat against his neck, but the rain was inside of it now.

"All right," he said. "Let's."

from *Krik? Krak!*

Born in 1969 in Haiti, Edwidge Danticat published her first writings in English at the age of fourteen, just two years after moving to the United States. She is the author of two works published by Vintage Contemporaries—the novel Breath, Eyes, Memory, *published in 1995, and her story collection* Krik! Krak!, *published in 1996, which was a finalist for the National Book Award. Edwidge Danticat's new novel,* The Farming of Bones, *is due from Soho Press in Fall 1998.*

■ BETWEEN THE POOL AND GARDENIAS

SHE WAS VERY pretty. Bright shiny hair and dark brown skin like mahogany cocoa. Her lips were wide and purple, like those African dolls you see in tourist store windows but could never afford to buy.

I thought she was a gift from Heaven when I saw her on the dusty curb, wrapped in a small pink blanket, a few inches away from a sewer as open as a hungry child's yawn. She was like Baby Moses in the Bible stories they read to us at the Baptist Literary Class. Or Baby Jesus, who was born in a barn and died on a cross, with nobody's lips to kiss before he went. She was just like that. Her still round face. Her eyes closed as though she was dreaming of a far other place.

Her hands were bony, and there were veins so close to the surface that it looked like you could rupture her skin if you touched her too hard. She probably belonged to someone, but the street had no one in it. There was no one there to claim her.

At first I was afraid to touch her. Lest I might disturb the early-morning sun rays streaming across her forehead. She might have been some kind of *wanga*, a charm sent to trap me. My enemies were many and crafty. The girls who slept with my husband while I was still grieving over my miscarriages. They might have sent that vision of loveliness to blind me so that I would never find my way back to the place that I yanked out my head when I got on that broken down minibus and left my village months ago.

The child was wearing an embroidered little blue dress with the letters *R-O-S-E* on a butterfly collar. She looked the way that I had imagined all my little girls would look. The ones my body could never hold. The ones that somehow got suffocated inside me and made my husband wonder if I was killing them on purpose.

I called out all the names I wanted to give them: Eveline, Josephine, Jacqueline, Hermine, Marie Magdalène, Célianne. I could give her all the clothes that I had sewn for them. All these little dresses that went unused.

At night, I could rock her alone in the hush of my room, rest her on my belly, and wish she were inside.

When I had just come to the city, I saw on Madame's television that a lot of poor city women throw out their babies because they can't afford to feed them. Back in Ville Rose you cannot even throw out the bloody clumps that shoot out of your body after your child is born. It is a crime, they say, and your whole family would consider you wicked if you did it. You have to save every piece of flesh and give it a name and bury it near the roots of a tree so that the world won't fall apart around you.

In the city, I hear they throw out whole entire children. They throw them out anywhere: on doorsteps, in garbage cans, at gas pumps, sidewalks. In the time that I had been in Port-au-Prince, I had never seen such a child until now.

But Rose. My, she was so clean and warm. Like a tiny angel, a little cherub, sleeping after the wind had blown a lullaby into her little ears.

I picked her up and pressed her cheek against mine.

I whispered to her, "Little Rose, my child," as though that name was a secret.

She was like the palatable little dolls we played with as children—mango seeds that we drew faces on and then called by our nicknames. We christened them with prayers and invited all our little boy and girl friends for colas and cassavas and—when we could get them—some nice butter cookies.

Rose didn't stir or cry. She was like something that was thrown aside after she became useless to someone cruel. When I pressed her face against my heart, she smelled like the scented powders in Madame's cabinet, the mixed scent of gardenias and fish that Madame always had on her when she stepped out of her pool.

I HAVE ALWAYS said my mother's prayers at dawn. I welcomed the years that were slowly bringing me closer to her. For no matter how much distance death tried to put between us, my mother would often come to visit me. Sometimes in the short sighs and whispers of somebody else's voice. Sometimes in somebody else's face. Other times in brief moments in my dreams.

There were many nights when I saw some old women leaning over my bed.

"That there is Marie," my mother would say. "She is now the last one of us left."

Mama had to introduce me to them, because they had all died before I was born. There was my great grandmother Eveline who was killed by Dominican soldiers at the Massacre River. My grandmother Défilé who died with a bald head in a prison, because God had given her wings. My godmother Lili who killed herself in old age because her husband had jumped out of a flying balloon and her grown son left her to go to Miami.

We all salute you Mary, Mother of God. Pray for us poor sin-ners, from now until the hour of our death. Amen.

I always knew they would come back and claim me to do some good for somebody. Maybe I was to do some good for this child.

I carried Rose with me to the outdoor market in Croix-Bossale. I swayed her in my arms like she was and had always been mine.

In the city, even people who come from your own village don't know you or care about you. They didn't notice that I had come the day before with no child. Suddenly, I had one, and nobody asked a thing.

IN THE MAID'S room, at the house in Pétion-Ville, I laid Rose on my mat and rushed to prepare lunch. Monsieur and Madame sat on their terrace and welcomed the coming afternoon by sipping the sweet out of my sour-sop juice.

They liked that I went all the way to the market every day before dawn to get them a taste of the outside country, away from their protected bourgeois life.

"She is probably one of those *manbos*," they say when my back is turned. "She's probably one of those stupid people who think that they have a spell to make themselves invisible and hurt other people. Why can't none of them get a spell to make themselves rich? It's that voodoo nonsense that's holding us Haitians back."

I lay Rose down on the kitchen table as I dried the dishes. I had a sudden desire to explain to her my life.

"You see, young one, I loved that man at one point. He was very nice to me. He made me feel proper. The next thing I know, it's ten years with him. I'm old like a piece of dirty paper people used to wipe their behinds, and he's got ten different babies with ten different women. I just had to run."

I pretended that it was all mine. The terrace with that sight of the private pool and the holiday ships cruising in the distance. The large television system and all those French love songs and *rara* records, with the talking drums and conch shell sounds in them. The bright paintings with white winged horses and snakes as long and wide as lakes. The pool that the sweaty Dominican man cleaned three times a week. I pretended that it belonged to us: him, Rose, and me.

The Dominican and I made love on the grass once, but he never spoke to me again. Rose listened with her eyes closed even though I was telling her things that were much too strong for a child's ears.

I wrapped her around me with my apron as I fried some plantains for the evening meal. It's so easy to love somebody, I tell you, when there's nothing else around.

Her head fell back like any other infant's. I held out my hand and let her three matted braids tickle the lifelines in my hand.

"I am glad you are not one of those babies that cry all day long," I told her. "All little children should be like you. I am glad that you don't cry and make a lot of noise. You're just a perfect child, aren't you?"

I put her back in my room when Monsieur and Madame came home for their supper. As soon as they went to sleep, I took her out by the pool so we could talk some more.

You don't just join a family not knowing what you're getting into. You have to know some of the history. You have to know that they pray to Erzulie, who loves men like men love her, because she's mulatto and some Haitian men seem to love her kind. You have to look into your looking glass on the day of the dead because you might see faces there that knew you even before you ever came into this world.

I fell asleep rocking her in a chair that wasn't mine. I knew she was real when I woke up the next day and she was still in my arms. She looked the same as she did when I found her. She continued to look like that for three days. After that, I had to bathe her constantly to keep down the smell.

I once had an uncle who bought pigs' intestines in Ville Rose to sell at the markets in the city. Rose began to smell like the intestines after they hadn't sold for a few days.

I bathed her more and more often, sometimes three or four times a day in the pool. I used some of Madame's perfume, but it was not helping. I wanted to take her back to the street where I had found her, but I'd already disturbed her rest and had taken on her soul as my own personal responsibility.

I left her in a shack behind the house, where the Dominican kept his tools. Three times a day, I visited her with my hand over my nose. I watched her skin grow moist, cracked, and sunken in some places, then ashy and dry in others. It seemed like she had aged in four days as many years as there were between me and my dead aunts and grandmothers.

I knew I had to act with her because she was attracting flies and I was keeping her spirit from moving on.

I gave her one last bath and slipped on a little yellow dress that I had sewn while praying that one of my little girls would come along further than three months.

I took Rose down to a spot in the sun behind the big house. I dug a hole in the garden among all the gardenias. I wrapped her in the little pink blanket that I had found her in, covering everything but her face. She smelled so bad that I couldn't even bring myself to kiss her without choking on my breath.

I felt a grip on my shoulder as I lowered her into the small hole in the ground. At first I thought it was Monsieur or Madame, and I was real afraid that Madame would be angry with me for having used a whole bottle of her perfume without asking.

Rose slipped and fell out of my hands as my body was forced to turn around.

"What are you doing?" the Dominican asked.

His face was a deep Indian brown but his hands were bleached and wrinkled from the chemicals in the pool. He looked down at the baby lying in the dust. She was already sprinkled with some of the soil that I had dug up.

"You see, I saw these faces standing over me in my dreams—"

I could have started my explanation in a million of ways.

"Where did you take this child from?" he asked me in his Spanish Creole.

He did not give me a chance to give an answer.

"I go already." I thought I heard a little *méringue* in the sway of his voice. "I call the gendarmes. They are coming. I smell that rotten flesh. I know you kill the child and keep it with you for evil."

"You acted too soon," I said.

"You kill the child and keep it in your room."

"You know me," I said. "We've been together."

"I don't know you from the fly on a pile of cow manure," he said. "You eat little children who haven't even had time to earn their souls."

He only kept his hands on me because he was afraid that I would run away and escape.

I looked down at Rose. In my mind I saw what I had seen for all my other girls. I imagined her teething, crawling, crying, fussing, and just misbehaving herself.

Over her little corpse, we stood, a country maid and a Spaniard grounds man. I should have asked his name before I offered him my body.

We made a pretty picture standing there. Rose, me, and him. Between the pool and the gardenias, waiting for the law.

|||| T O B I A S   W O L F F

from *The Night in Question*

Tobias Wolff's memoir of Vietnam, In Pharaoh's Army, *was a National Book Award finalist and won the prestigious Esquire/Volvo/Waterstone's Nonfiction Award. His childhood memoir, the bestselling* This Boy's Life, *won the* Los Angeles Times *Book Award. He is also the author of three story collections, including* The Night in Question, *and a short novel,* The Barracks Thief. *Tobias Wolff is at work on his first novel, forthcoming from Knopf.*

■ MORTALS

THE METRO EDITOR called my name across the newsroom and beckoned to me. When I got to his office he was behind the desk. A man and a woman were there with him, the man nervous on his feet, the woman in a chair, bony-faced and vigilant, holding the straps of her bag with both hands. Her suit was the same bluish gray as her hair. There was something soldierly about her. The man was short, doughy, rounded off. The burst vessels in his cheeks gave him a merry look until he smiled.

"I didn't want to make a scene," he said. "We just thought you should know." He looked at his wife.

"You bet I should know," the metro editor said. "This is Mr. Givens," he said to me, "Mr. Ronald Givens. Name ring a bell?"

"Vaguely."

"I'll give you a hint. He's not dead."

"Okay," I said. "I've got it."

"Another hint," the metro editor said. Then he read aloud, from that morning's paper, the obituary I had written announcing Mr. Givens's death. I'd written a whole slew of obits the day before, over twenty of them, and I didn't remember much of it,

but I did remember the part about him working for the IRS for
thirty years. I'd recently had problems with the IRS, so that stuck
in my mind.

As Givens listened to his obituary he looked from one to the
other of us. He wasn't as short as I'd first thought. It was an
impression he created by hunching his shoulders and thrusting
his neck forward like a turtle. His eyes were soft, restless. He
used them like a peasant, in swift measuring glances with his
face averted.

He laughed when the metro editor was through. "Well, it's
accurate," he said. "I'll give you that."

"Except for one thing." The woman was staring at me.

"I owe you an apology," I told Givens. "It looks like somebody
pulled the wool over my eyes."

"Apology accepted!" Givens said. He rubbed his hands
together as if we'd all just signed something. "You have to see the
humor, Dolly. What was it Mark Twain said? 'The reports of my
death—'"

"So what happened?" the metro editor said to me.

"I wish I knew."

"That's not good enough," the woman said.

"Dolly's pretty upset," Givens said.

"She has every right to be upset," the metro editor said. "Who
called in the notice?" he asked me.

"To tell the truth, I don't remember. I suppose it was somebody from the funeral home."

"You call them back?"

"I don't believe I did, no."

"Check with the family?"

"He most certainly did not," Mrs. Givens said.

"No," I said.

The metro editor said, "What do we do before we run an
obituary?"

"Check back with the funeral home and the family."

"But you didn't do that."

"No, sir. I guess I didn't."

"Why not?"

I made a helpless gesture with my hands and tried to appear properly stricken, but I had no answer. The truth was, I never followed those procedures. People were dying all the time. I hadn't seen the point in asking their families if they were really dead, or calling funeral parlors back to make sure the funeral parlors had just called me. All this procedural stuff was a waste of time, I'd decided; it didn't seem possible that anyone could amuse himself by concocting phony death notices and impersonating undertakers. Now I saw that this was foolish of me, and showed a radical failure of appreciation for the varieties of human pleasure.

But there was more to it than that. Since I was still on the bottom rung in metro, I wrote a lot of obituaries. Some days they gave me a choice between that and marriage bulletins, but most of the time obits were all I did, one after another, morning to night. After four months of this duty I was full of the consciousness of death. It soured me. It puffed me up with morbid snobbery, the feeling that I knew a secret nobody else had even begun to suspect. It made me wearily philosophical about the value of faith and passion and hard work, at a time when my life required all of these. It got me down.

I should have quit, but I didn't want to go back to the kind of jobs I'd had before a friend's father fixed me up with this one—waiting on tables, mostly, pulling night security in apartment buildings, anything that would leave my days free for writing. I'd lived like this for three years, and what did I have to show for it? A few stories in literary journals that nobody read, including me. I began to lose my nerve. I'd given up a lot for my writing, and it wasn't giving anything back—not respectability, nor money, nor love. So when this job came up I took it. I hated it and did it badly, but I meant to keep it. Someday I'd move over to the police beat. Things would get better.

I was hoping that the metro editor would take his pound of flesh and let me go, but he kept after me with questions, probably showing off for Givens and his wife, letting them see a real news-hound at work. In the end I was forced to admit that I hadn't called any other families or funeral homes that day, nor, in actual fact, for a good long time.

Now that he had his answer, the metro editor didn't seem to know what to do with it. It seemed to be more than he'd bargained for. At first he just sat there. Then he said, "Let me get this straight. Just how long has this paper been running unconfirmed obituaries?"

"About three months," I said. And as I made this admission I felt a smile on my lips, already there before I could fight it back or dissemble it. It was the rictus of panic, the same smile I'd given my mother when she told me my father had died. But of course the metro editor didn't know that.

He leaned forward in his chair and gave his head a little shake, the way a horse will, and said, "Clean out your desk." I don't think he'd meant to fire me; he looked surprised by his own words. But he didn't take them back.

Givens looked from one to the other of us. "Now hold on here," he said. "Let's not blow this all out of proportion. This is a live-and-learn situation. This isn't something a man should lose his job over."

"He wouldn't have," Mrs. Givens said, "if he'd done it right."

Which was a truth beyond argument.

I CLEANED OUT my desk. As I left the building I saw Givens by the newsstand, watching the door. I didn't see his wife. He walked up to me, raised his hands, and said, "What can I say? I'm at a loss for words."

"Don't worry about it," I told him.

"I sure as heck didn't mean to get you fired. It wasn't even my idea to come in, if you want to know the truth."

"Forget it. It was my own fault." I was carrying a box full of notepads and files, several books. It was heavy. I shifted it under my other arm.

"Look," Givens said, "how about I treat you to lunch. What do you say? It's the least I can do."

I looked up and down the street.

"Dolly's gone on home," he said. "How about it?"

I didn't especially want to eat lunch with Givens, but it seemed to mean a lot to him, and I didn't feel ready to go home yet. What would I do there? Sure, I said, lunch sounded fine. Givens asked me if I knew anyplace reasonable nearby. There was a Chinese joint a few doors down, but it was always full of reporters. I didn't want to watch them try to conjure up sympathy over my situation, which they'd laugh about anyway the minute I left, not that I blamed them. I suggested Tad's Steakhouse over by the cable car turnaround. You could get a six-ounce sirloin, salad, and baked potato for a buck twenty-nine. This was 1974.

"I'm not that short," Givens said. But he didn't argue, and that's where we went.

Givens picked at his food, then pushed the plate away and contemplated mine. When I asked if his steak was okay, he said he didn't have much appetite.

"So," I said, "who do you think called it in?"

His head was bent. He looked up at me from under his eyebrows. "Boy, you've got me there. It's a mystery."

"You must have some idea."

"Nope. Not a one."

"Think it could've been someone you worked with?"

"Nah." He shook a toothpick out of the dispenser. His hands were pale and sinewy.

"It had to be somebody who knows you. You have friends, right?"

"Sure."

"Maybe you had an argument, something like that. Somebody's mad at you."

He kept his mouth covered with one hand while he worked the toothpick with the other. "You think so? I had it figured for more of a joke."

"Well, it's a pretty serious joke, calling in a death notice on someone. Pretty threatening. I'd sure feel threatened, if it was me."

Givens inspected the toothpick, then dropped it in the ashtray. "I hadn't thought of it like that," he said. "Maybe you're right."

I could see he didn't believe it for a second—didn't understand what had happened. The words of death had been pronounced on him, and now his life would be lived in relation to those words, in failing opposition to them, until they overpowered him and became true. Someone had put a contract out on Givens, with words as the torpedoes. Or so it appeared to me.

"You're sure it isn't one of your friends," I said. "It could be a little thing. You played cards, landed some big ones, then folded early before he had a chance to recoup."

"I don't play cards," Givens said.

"How about your wife? Any problems in that department?"

"Nope."

"Everything smooth as silk, huh?"

He shrugged. "Same as ever."

"How come you call her Dolly? That wasn't the name in the obit."

"No reason. I've always called her that. Everybody does."

"I don't feature her as a Dolly," I said.

He didn't answer. He was watching me.

"Let's say Dolly gets mad at you, really mad . . . She wants to send you a message—something outside normal channels."

"Not a chance." Givens said this without bristling. He didn't try to convince me, so I figured he was probably right.

"You're survived by a daughter, right? What's her name again?"

"Tina," he said, with some tenderness.

"That's it, Tina. How are things with Tina?"

"We've had our problems. But I can guarantee you, it wasn't her."

"Well, hell's bells," I said. "Somebody did it."

I finished my steak, watching the show outside: winos, evangelists, outpatients, whores, fake hippies selling oregano to tourists in white shoes. Pure theater, even down to the smell of popcorn billowing out of Woolworth's. Richard Brautigan often came here. Tall and owlish, he stooped to his food and ate slowly, ruminating over every bite, his eyes on the street. Some funny things happened here, and some appalling things. Brautigan took it all in and never stopped eating.

I told Givens that we were sitting at the same table where Richard Brautigan sometimes sat.

"Sorry?"

"Richard Brautigan, the writer."

Givens shook his head.

I was ready to go home. "Okay," I said, "you tell me. Who wants you dead?"

"No one wants me dead."

"Somebody's imagining you dead. Thinking about it. The wish is father to the deed."

"Nobody wants me dead. Your problem is, you think everything has to mean something."

That was one of my problems, I couldn't deny it.

"Just out of curiosity," he said, "what did you think of it?"

"Think of what?"

"My obituary." He leaned forward and started fooling with the salt and pepper shakers, tapping them together and sliding them around like partners in a square dance. "I mean, did you get any feeling for who I was? The kind of person I am?"

I shook my head.

"Nothing stood out?"

I said no.

"I see. Maybe you wouldn't mind telling me, what exactly does it take for you to remember someone?"

"Look," I said, "you write obituaries all day, they sort of blur into each other."

"Yes, but you must remember some of them."

"Some of them—sure."

"Which ones?"

"Writers I like. Great baseball players. Movie stars I've been in love with."

"Celebrities, in other words."

"Some of them, yes. Not all."

"You can lead a good life without being a celebrity," he said. "People with big names aren't always big people."

"That's true," I said, "but it's sort of a little person's truth."

"Is that so? And what does that make you?"

I didn't answer.

"If the only thing that impresses you is having a big name, then you must be a regular midget. At least that's the way I see it." He gave me a hard look and gripped the salt and pepper shakers like a machine gunner about to let off a burst.

"That's not the only thing that impresses me."

"Oh yeah? What else, then?"

I let the question settle. "Moral distinction," I said.

He repeated the words. They sounded pompous.

"You know what I mean," I said.

"Correct me if I'm wrong," he said, "but I have a feeling that's not your department, moral distinction."

I didn't argue.

"And you're obviously not a celebrity."

"Obviously."

"So where does that leave you?" When I didn't answer, he said, "Think you'd remember your own obituary?"

"Probably not."

"No probably about it! You wouldn't even give it a second thought."

"Okay, definitely not."

"You wouldn't even give it a second thought. And you'd be wrong. Because you probably have other qualities that would stand out if you were looking closely. Good qualities. Everybody has something. What do you pride yourself on?"

"I'm a survivor," I said. But I didn't think that claim would carry much weight in an obituary.

Givens said, "With me it's loyalty. Loyalty is a very clear pattern in my life. You would've noticed that if you'd had your eyes open. When you read that a man has served his country in time of war, stayed married to the same woman forty-two years, worked at the same job, by God, that should tell you something. That should give you a certain picture."

He stopped to nod at his own words. "And it hasn't always been easy," he said.

I had to laugh, mostly at myself for being such a dim bulb. "It was you," I said. "You did it."

"Did what?"

"Called in the obit."

"Why would I do that?"

"You tell me."

"That would be saying I did it." Givens couldn't help smiling, proud of what a slyboots he was.

I said, "You're out of your ever-loving mind," but I didn't mean it. There was nothing in what Givens had done that I couldn't make sense of or even, in spite of myself, admire. He had dreamed up a way of going to his own funeral. He'd tried on his last suit, so to speak, seen himself rouged up and laid out, and listened to his own eulogy. And the best part was, he resurrected afterward. That was the real point, even if he thought he was doing it to throw a scare into Dolly or put his virtues on display. Resurrection was what it was all about, and this tax collector had gotten himself a taste of it. It was biblical.

"You're a caution, Mr. Givens. You're a definite caution."

"I didn't come here to be insulted."

"Relax," I told him. "I'm not mad."

He scraped his chair back and stood up. "I've got better things to do than sit here and listen to accusations."

I followed him outside. I wasn't ready to let him go. He had to give me something first. "Admit you did it," I said.

He turned away and started up Powell.

"Just admit it," I said. "I won't hold it against you."

He kept walking, head stuck forward in that turtlish way, navigating the crowd. He was slippery and fast. Finally I took his arm and pulled him into a doorway. His muscles bunched under my fingers. He almost jerked free, but I tightened my grip and we stood there frozen in contention.

"Admit it."

He shook his head.

"I'll break your neck if I have to," I told him.

"Let go," he said.

"If something happened to you right now, your obituary would be solid news. Then I could get my job back."

He tried to pull away again but I held him there.

"It'd make a hell of a story," I said.

I felt his arm go slack. Then he said, almost inaudibly, "Yes." Just that one word.

This was the best I was going to get out of him. It had to be enough. When I let go of his arm he turned and ducked his head and took his place in the stream of people walking past. I started back to Tad's for my box. Just ahead of me a mime was following a young swell in a three-piece suit, catching to the life his leading-man's assurance, the supercilious tilt of his chin. A girl laughed raucously. The swell looked back and the mime froze. He was still holding his pose as I came by. I slipped him a quarter, hoping he'd let me pass.

from *Selected Stories*

Cynthia Ozick has praised Alice Munro as "our Chekhov," and she is revered by her devoted read-
ers and critics alike as the most original writer of short stories working today. Munro is the author
of eight collections of stories and one novel, among them The Beggar Maid, Friend of My Youth,
The Moons of Jupiter, Open Secrets, *and* Selected Stories.

■ WILD SWANS

FLO SAID TO watch for White Slavers. She said this was how they operated: an old woman, a motherly or grandmotherly sort, made friends while riding beside you on a bus or train. She offered you candy, which was drugged. Pretty soon you began to droop and mumble, were in no condition to speak for yourself. Oh, help, the woman said, my daughter (granddaughter) is sick, please some-body help me get her off so that she can recover in the fresh air. Up stepped a polite gentleman, pretending to be a stranger, offer-ing assistance. Together, at the next stop, they hustled you off the train or bus, and that was the last the ordinary world ever saw of you. They kept you a prisoner in the White Slave place (to which you had been transported drugged and bound so you wouldn't even know where you were), until such time as you were thor-oughly degraded and in despair, your insides torn up by drunken men and invested with vile disease, your mind destroyed by drugs, your hair and teeth fallen out. It took about three years for you to get to this state. You wouldn't want to go home then; maybe couldn't remember home, or find your way if you did. So they let you out on the streets.

Flo took ten dollars and put it in a little cloth bag, which she sewed to the strap of Rose's slip. Another thing likely to happen was that Rose would get her purse stolen.

Watch out, Flo said as well, for people dressed up as ministers. They were the worst. That disguise was commonly adopted by White Slavers, as well as those after your money.

Rose said she didn't see how she could tell which ones were disguised.

Flo had worked in Toronto once. She had worked as a waitress in a coffee shop in Union Station. That was how she knew all she knew. She never saw sunlight, in those days, except on her days off. But she saw plenty else. She saw a man cut another man's stomach with a knife, just pull out his shirt and do a tidy cut, as if it was a watermelon not a stomach. The stomach's owner just sat looking down surprised, with no time to protest. Flo implied that that was nothing, in Toronto. She saw two bad women (that was what Flo called whores, running the two words together, like badminton) get into a fight, and a man laughed at them, other men stopped and laughed and egged them on, and they had their fists full of each other's hair. At last the police came and took them away, still howling and yelping.

She saw a child die of a fit too. Its face was black as ink.

"Well, I'm not scared," said Rose provokingly. "There's the police, anyway."

"Oh, them! They'd be the first ones to diddle you!"

She did not believe anything Flo said on the subject of sex. Consider the undertaker.

A little bald man, very neatly dressed, would come into the store sometimes and speak to Flo with a placating expression.

"I only wanted a bag of candy. And maybe a few packages of gum. And one or two chocolate bars. Could you go to the trouble of wrapping them?"

Flo in her mock-deferential tones would assure him that she

could. She wrapped them in heavy-duty white paper, so they were something like presents. He took his time with the selection, humming and chatting, then dawdled for a while. He might ask how Flo was feeling. And how Rose was, if she was there.

"You look pale. Young girls need fresh air." To Flo he would say, "You work too hard. You've worked hard all your life."

"No rest for the wicked," Flo would say agreeably.

When he went out she hurried to the window. There it was—the old black hearse with its purple curtains.

"He'll be after them today!" Flo would say as the hearse rolled away at a gentle pace, almost a funeral pace. The little man had been an undertaker, but he was retired now. The hearse was retired too. His sons had taken over the undertaking and bought a new one. He drove the old hearse all over the country, looking for women. So Flo said. Rose could not believe it. Flo said he gave them the gum and the candy. Rose said he probably ate them himself. Flo said he had been seen, he had been heard. In mild weather he drove with the windows down, singing, to himself or to somebody out of sight in the back.

> *"Her brow is like the snowdrift*
> *Her throat is like the swan . . ."*

Flo imitated him singing. Gently overtaking some woman walking on a back road, or resting at a country crossroads. All compliments and courtesy and chocolate bars, offering a ride. Of course every woman who reported being asked said she had turned him down. He never pestered anybody, drove politely on. He called in at houses, and if the husband was home he seemed to like just as well as anything to sit and chat. Wives said that was all he ever did anyway but Flo did not believe it.

"Some women are taken in," she said. "A number." She liked to speculate on what the hearse was like inside. Plush. Plush on the walls and the roof and the floor. Soft purple, the color of the curtains, the color of dark lilacs.

All nonsense, Rose thought. Who could believe it, of a man that age?

ROSE WAS GOING to Toronto on the train for the first time by herself. She had been once before, but that was with Flo, long before her father died. They took along their own sandwiches and bought milk from the vendor on the train. It was sour. Sour chocolate milk. Rose kept taking tiny sips, unwilling to admit that something so much desired could fail her. Flo sniffed it, then hunted up and down the train until she found the old man in his red jacket, with no teeth and the tray hanging around his neck. She invited him to sample the chocolate milk. She invited people nearby to smell it. He let her have some ginger ale for nothing. It was slightly warm.

"I let him know," Flo said, looking around after he had left. "You have to let them know."

A woman agreed with her but most people looked out the window. Rose drank the warm ginger ale. Either that, or the scene with the vendor, or the conversation Flo and the agreeing woman now got into about where they came from, why they were going to Toronto, and Rose's morning constipation which was why she was lacking color, or the small amount of chocolate milk she had got inside her, caused her to throw up in the train toilet. All day long she was afraid people in Toronto could smell vomit on her coat.

This time Flo started the trip off by saying, "Keep an eye on her, she's never been away from home before!" to the conductor, then looking around and laughing, to show that was jokingly meant. Then she had to get off. It seemed the conductor had no more need for jokes than Rose had, and no intention of keeping an eye on anybody. He never spoke to Rose except to ask for her ticket. She had a window seat, and was soon extraordinarily happy. She felt Flo receding, West Hanratty flying away from her, her own wearying self discarded as easily as everything else. She loved the towns less and less known. A woman was standing at her back door in her nightgown, not caring if everybody on the train saw her. They were travelling south, out of the snowbelt, into an earlier spring, a tenderer sort of landscape. People could grow peach trees in their back yards.

Rose collected in her mind the things she had to look for in Toronto. First, things for Flo. Special stockings for her varicose veins. A special kind of cement for sticking handles on pots. And a full set of dominoes.

For herself Rose wanted to buy hair-remover to put on her arms and legs, and if possible an arrangement of inflatable cushions, supposed to reduce your hips and thighs. She thought they probably had hair-remover in the drugstore in Hanratty, but the woman in there was a friend of Flo's and told everything. She told Flo who bought hair dye and slimming medicine and French safes. As for the cushion business, you could send away for it but there was sure to be a comment at the Post Office, and Flo knew people there as well. She also planned to buy some bangles, and an angora sweater. She had great hopes of silver bangles and powder-blue angora. She thought they could transform her, make her calm and slender and take the frizz out of her hair, dry her underarms and turn her complexion to pearl.

The money for these things, as well as the money for the trip, came from a prize Rose had won, for writing an essay called "Art and Science in the World of Tomorrow." To her surprise, Flo asked if she could read it, and while she was reading it, she remarked that they must have thought they had to give Rose the prize for swallowing the dictionary. Then she said shyly, "It's very interesting."

She would have to spend the night at Cela McKinney's. Cela

McKinney was her father's cousin. She had married a hotel manager and thought she had gone up in the world. But the hotel manager came home one day and sat down on the dining-room floor between two chairs and said, "I am never going to leave this house again." Nothing unusual had happened, he had just decided not to go out of the house again, and he didn't, until he died. That had made Cela McKinney odd and nervous. She locked her doors at eight o'clock. She was also very stingy. Supper was usually oatmeal porridge, with raisins. Her house was dark and narrow and smelled like a bank.

The train was filling up. At Brantford a man asked if she would mind if he sat down beside her.

"It's cooler out than you'd think," he said. He offered her part of his newspaper. She said no thanks.

Then, lest he think her rude, she said it really was cooler. She went on looking out the window at the spring morning. There was no snow left, down here. The trees and bushes seemed to have a paler bark than they did at home. Even the sunlight looked different. It was as different from home, here, as the coast of the Mediterranean would be, or the valleys of California.

"Filthy windows, you'd think they'd take more care," the man said. "Do you travel much by train?"

She said no.

Water was lying in the fields. He nodded at it and said there was a lot this year.

"Heavy snows."

She noticed his saying "snows," a poetic-sounding word. Anyone at home would have said "snow."

"I had an unusual experience the other day. I was driving out in the country. In fact, I was on my way to see one of my parishioners, a lady with a heart condition—"

She looked quickly at his collar. He was wearing an ordinary shirt and tie and a dark-blue suit.

"Oh, yes," he said. "I'm a United Church minister. But I don't always wear my uniform. I wear it for preaching in. I'm off duty today.

"Well, as I said, I was driving through the country and I saw some Canada geese down on a pond, and I took another look, and there were some swans down with them. A whole great flock of swans. What a lovely sight they were. They would be on their spring migration, I expect, heading up North. What a spectacle. I never saw anything like it."

Rose was unable to think appreciatively of the wild swans because she was afraid he was going to lead the conversation from them to Nature in general and then to God, the way a minister would feel obliged to do. But he did not, he stopped with the swans.

"A very fine sight. You would have enjoyed them."

He was between fifty and sixty years old, Rose thought. He was short, and energetic-looking, with a square ruddy face and bright waves of gray hair combed straight up from his forehead. When she realized he was not going to mention God she felt she ought to show her gratitude.

She said they must have been lovely.

"It wasn't even a regular pond, it was only some water lying in a field. It was just luck the water was lying there and they came down and I came driving by at the right time. Just luck. They come in at the east end of Lake Erie, I think. But I never was lucky enough to see them before."

She turned by degrees to the window, and he returned to his paper. She remained slightly smiling, so as not to seem rude, not to seem to be rejecting conversation altogether. The morning really was cool, and she had taken down her coat off the hook where she put it when she first got on the train; she had spread it over herself, like a lap robe. She had set her purse on the floor when the minister sat down, to give him room. He took the sections of the paper apart, shaking and rustling them in a leisurely, rather showy way. He seemed to her the sort of person who does everything in a showy way. A ministerial way. He brushed aside the sections he didn't want at the moment. A corner of newspaper touched her leg, just at the edge of her coat.

She thought for some time that it was the paper. Then she said to herself, What if it is a hand? That was the kind of thing she could imagine. She would sometimes look at men's hands, at the fuzz on their forearms, their concentrating profiles. She would think about everything they could do. Even the stupid ones. For instance, the driver-salesman who brought the bread to Flo's store. The ripeness and confidence of manner, the settled mixture of ease and alertness with which he handled the bread truck. A fold of mature belly over the belt did not displease her. Another time she had her eye on the French teacher at school. Not a Frenchman at all, really, his name was McLaren, but Rose thought teaching French had rubbed off on him, made him look like one. Quick and sallow; sharp shoulders; hooked nose and sad eyes. She saw him lapping and coiling his way through slow pleasures, a perfect autocrat of indulgences. She had a considerable longing to be somebody's object. Pounded, pleasured, reduced, exhausted.

But what if it was a hand? What if it really was a hand? She shifted slightly, moved as much as she could toward the window. Her imagination seemed to have created this reality, a reality she was not prepared for at all. She found it alarming. She was concentrating on that leg, that bit of skin with the stocking over it. She could not bring herself to look. Was there a pressure, or was there not? She shifted again. Her legs had been, and remained, tightly closed. It was. It was a hand. It was a hand's pressure.

Please don't. That was what she tried to say. She shaped the words in her mind, tried them out, then couldn't get them past her lips. Why was that? The embarrassment, was it, the fear that people might hear? People were all around them, the seats were full.

It was not only that.

She did manage to look at him, not raising her head but turning it cautiously. He had tilted his seat back and closed his eyes. There was his dark-blue suit sleeve, disappearing under the newspaper. He had arranged the paper so that it overlapped Rose's coat. His hand was underneath, simply resting, as if flung out in sleep.

Now, Rose could have shifted the newspaper and removed her coat. If he was not asleep, he would have been obliged to draw back his hand. If he was asleep, if he did not draw it back, she could have whispered *Excuse me* and set his hand firmly on his own knee. This solution, so obvious and foolproof, did not occur to her. And she would have to wonder, Why not? The minister's hand was not, or not yet, at all welcome to her. It made her feel uncomfortable, resentful, slightly disgusted, trapped, and wary. But she could not take charge of it, to reject it. She could not insist that it was there, when he seemed to be insisting that it was not. How could she declare him responsible, when he lay there so harmless and trusting, resting himself before his busy day, with such a pleased and healthy face? A man older than her father would be, if he were living, a man used to deference, an appreciator of Nature, delighter in wild swans. If she did say *Please don't* she was sure he would ignore her, as if overlooking some silliness or impoliteness on her part. She knew that as soon as she said it she would hope he had not heard.

But there was more to it than that. Curiosity. More constant, more imperious, than any lust. A lust in itself, that will make you draw back and wait, wait too long, risk almost anything, just to see what will happen. *To see what will happen.*

The hand began, over the next several miles, the most delicate, the most timid, pressures and investigations. Not asleep. Or if he was, his hand wasn't. She did feel disgust. She felt a faint, wandering nausea. She thought of flesh: lumps of flesh, pink snouts, fat tongues, blunt fingers, all on their way trotting and creeping and lolling and rubbing, looking for their comfort. She thought of cats in heat rubbing themselves along the top of board fences, yowling with their miserable complaint. It was pitiful, infantile, this itching and shoving and squeezing. Spongy tissues, inflamed membranes, tormented nerve-ends, shameful smells; humiliation.

All that was starting. His hand, that she wouldn't ever have wanted to hold, that she wouldn't have squeezed back, his stubborn patient hand was able, after all, to get the ferns to rustle and the streams to flow, to waken a sly luxuriance.

Nevertheless, she would rather not. She would still rather not. Please remove this, she said out the window. Stop it, please, she said to the stumps and barns. The hand moved up her leg past the top of her stocking to her bare skin, had moved higher, under her suspender, reached her underpants and the lower part of her belly. Her legs were still crossed, pinched together. While her legs stayed crossed she could lay claim to innocence, she had not admitted anything. She could still believe that she would stop this in a minute. Nothing was going to happen, nothing more. Her legs were never going to open.

But they were. They were. As the train crossed the Niagara Escarpment above Dundas, as they looked down at the preglacial valley, the silver-wooded rubble of little hills, as they came sliding down to the shores of Lake Ontario, she would make this slow, and silent, and definite declaration, perhaps disappointing as much as satisfying the hand's owner. He would not lift his eyelids, his face would not alter, his fingers would not hesitate, but would go powerfully and discreetly to work. Invasion, and welcome, and sunlight flashing far and wide on the lake water; miles of bare orchards stirring round Burlington.

This was disgrace, this was beggary. But what harm in that, we say to ourselves at such moments, what harm in anything, the worse the better, as we ride the cold wave of greed, of greedy assent. A stranger's hand, or root vegetables or humble kitchen tools that people tell jokes about; the world is tumbling with innocent-seeming objects ready to declare themselves, slippery and obliging. She was careful of her breathing. She could not believe this. Victim and accomplice she was borne past Glassco's Jams and Marmalades, past the big pulsating pipes of oil refineries. They glided into suburbs where bedsheets, and towels used to wipe up intimate stains, flapped leeringly on the clotheslines, where even the children seemed to be frolicking lewdly in the schoolyards, and the very truck drivers stopped at the railway crossings must be thrusting their thumbs gleefully into curled hands. Such cunning antics now, such popular visions. The gates and towers of the Exhibition Grounds came into view, the painted domes and pillars floated marvellously against her eyelids' rosy sky. Then flew apart in celebration. You could have had such a flock of birds, wild swans, even, wakened under one big dome together, exploding from it, taking to the sky.

She bit the edge of her tongue. Very soon the conductor passed through the train, to stir the travellers, warm them back to life.

In the darkness under the station the United Church minister, refreshed, opened his eyes and got his paper folded together, then asked if she would like some help with her coat. His gallantry was self-satisfied, dismissive. No, said Rose, with a sore tongue. He hurried out of the train ahead of her. She did not see him in the station. She never saw him again in her life. But he remained on call, so to speak, for years and years, ready to slip into place at a critical moment, without even any regard, later on, for husband or lovers. What recommended him? She could never understand it. His simplicity, his arrogance, his perversely appealing lack of handsomeness, even of ordinary grown-up masculinity? When he stood up she saw that he was shorter even than she had thought, that his face was pink and shiny, that there was something crude and pushy and childish about him.

Was he a minister, really, or was that only what he said? Flo had mentioned people who were not ministers, dressed up as if they were. Not real ministers dressed as if they were not. Or, stranger still, men who were not real ministers pretending to be real but dressed as if they were not. But that she had come as close as she had, to what could happen, was an unwelcome thing. Rose walked through Union Station feeling the little bag with the ten dollars rubbing at her, knew she would feel it all day long, rubbing its reminder against her skin.

She couldn't stop getting Flo's messages, even with that. She remembered, because she was in Union Station, that there was a girl named Mavis working here, in the gift shop, when Flo was working in the coffee shop. Mavis had warts on her eyelids that looked like they were going to turn into sties but they didn't, they went away. Maybe she had them removed, Flo didn't ask. She was very good-looking, without them. There was a movie star in those days she looked a lot like. The movie star's name was Frances Farmer.

Frances Farmer. Rose had never heard of her.

That was the name. And Mavis went and bought herself a big hat that dipped over one eye and a dress entirely made of lace. She went off for the weekend to Georgian Bay, to a resort up there. She booked herself in under the name of Florence Farmer. To give everybody the idea she was really the other one, Frances Farmer, but calling herself Florence because she was on holiday and didn't want to be recognized. She had a little cigarette holder that was black and mother-of-pearl. She could have been arrested, Flo said. For the *nerve*.

Rose almost went over to the gift shop to see if Mavis was still there and if she could recognize her. She thought it would be an especially fine thing to manage a transformation like that. To dare it; to get away with it, to enter on preposterous adventures in your own, but newly named, skin.

|||| E R N E S T   J .   G A I N E S

from *Bloodline*

Ernest J. Gaines is the author of the novels A Lesson Before Dying, *winner of the 1993 National Book Critics Circle Award;* A Gathering of Old Men; In My Father's House; Of Love and Dust; *and* Catherine Carmier, *and the 1968 story collection* Bloodline.

■ THREE MEN

TWO OF THEM was sitting in the office when I came in there. One was sitting in a chair behind the desk, the other one was sitting on the end of the desk. They looked at me, but when they saw I was just a nigger they went back to talking like I wasn't even there. They talked like that two or three more minutes before the one behind the desk looked at me again. That was T. J. I didn't know who the other one was.

"Yeah, what you want?" T. J. said.

They sat inside a little railed-in office. I went closer to the gate. It was one of them little gates that swung in and out.

"I come to turn myself in," I said.

"Turn yourself in for what?"

"I had a fight with somebody. I think I hurt him."

T. J. and the other policeman looked at me like I was crazy. I guess they had never heard of a nigger doing that before.

"You Proctor Lewis?" T. J. said.

"Yes, sir."

"Come in here."

I pushed the little gate open and went in. I made sure it didn't swing back too hard and make noise. I stopped a little way from the desk. T. J. and the other policeman was watching me all the time.

"Give me some papers," T. J. said. He was looking up at me like he was still trying to figure out if I was crazy. If I wasn't crazy, then I was a smart aleck.

I got my wallet out my pocket. I could feel T. J. and the other policeman looking at me all the time. I wasn't supposed to get any papers out, myself, I was supposed to give him the wallet and let him take what he wanted. I held the wallet out to him and he jerked it out of my hand. Then he started going through everything I had in there, the money and all. After he looked at everything, he handed them to the other policeman. The other one looked at them, too; then he laid them on the desk. T. J. picked up the phone and started talking to somebody. All the time he was talking to the other person, he was looking up at me. He had a hard time making the other person believe I had turned myself in. When he hung up the phone, he told the policeman on the desk to get my records. He called the other policeman "Paul." Paul slid away from the desk and went to the file cabinet against the wall. T. J. still looked at me. His eyes was the color of ashes. I looked down at the floor, but I could still feel him looking at me. Paul came back with the records and handed them to him. I looked up again and saw them looking over the records together. Paul was standing behind T. J., looking over his shoulder.

"So you think you hurt him, huh?" T. J. asked, looking up at me again.

I didn't say anything to him. He was a mean, evil sonofabitch. He was big and red and he didn't waste time kicking your ass if you gived him the wrong answers. You had to weigh every word he said to you. Sometimes you answered, other times you kept your mouth shut. This time I passed my tongue over my lips and kept quiet.

It was about four o'clock in the morning, but it must've been seventy-five in there. T. J. and the other policeman had on short-sleeve khaki shirts. I had on a white shirt, but it was all dirty and torn. My sleeves was rolled up to the elbows, and both of my elbows was skinned and bruised.

"Didn't I bring you in here one time, myself?" Paul said.

"Yes, sir, once, I think," I said. I had been there two or three times, but I wasn't go'n say it if he didn't. I had been in couple other jails two or three times, too, but I wasn't go'n say anything about them either. If they hadn't put it on my record that was they hard luck.

"A fist fight," Paul said. "Pretty good with your fists, ain't you?"

"I protect myself," I said.

It was quiet in there for a second or two. I knowed why; I hadn't answered the right way.

"You protect yourself, what?" T. J. said.

"I protect myself, *sir*," I said.

They still looked at me. But I could tell Paul wasn't anything like T. J. He wasn't mean at all, he just had to play mean because T. J. was there. Couple Sundays ago I had played baseball with a boy who looked just like Paul. But he had brown eyes; Paul had blue eyes.

"You'll be sorry you didn't use your fists this time," T. J. said. "Take everything out your pockets."

I did what he said.

"Where's your knife?" he asked.

"I never car' a knife," I said.

"You never car' a knife, what, boy?" T. J. said.

"I never car' a knife, *sir*," I said.

He looked at me hard again. He didn't think I was crazy for turning myself in, he thought I was a smart aleck. I could tell from his big, fat, red face he wanted to hit me with his fist.

He nodded to Paul and Paul came toward me. I moved back some.

"I'm not going to hurt you," Paul said.

I stopped, but I could still feel myself shaking. Paul started patting me down. He found a pack of cigarettes in my shirt pocket. I could see in his face he didn't want take them out, but he took them out, anyhow.

"Thought I told you empty your pockets?" T. J. said.

"I didn't know—"

"Paul, if you can't make that boy shut up, I can," T. J. said.

"He'll be quiet," Paul said, looking at me. He was telling me with his eyes to be quiet or I was go'n get myself in a lot of trouble.

"You got one more time to butt in," T. J. said. "One more time now."

I was getting a swimming in the head, and I looked down at the floor. I hoped they would hurry up and lock me up so I could have a little peace.

"Why'd you turn yourself in?" T. J. asked.

I kept my head down. I didn't answer him.

"Paul, can't you make that boy talk?" T. J. said. "Or do I have to get up and do it?"

"He'll talk," Paul said.

"I figured y'all was go'n catch me sooner or later—sir."

"That's not the reason you turned yourself in," T. J. said.

I kept my head down.

"Look up when I talk to you," T. J. said.

I raised my head. I felt weak and shaky. My clothes was wet and sticking to my body, but my mouth felt dry as dust. My eyes wanted to look down again, but I forced myself to look at T. J.'s big red face.

"You figured if you turned yourself in, Roger Medlow was go'n get you out, now, didn't you?"

I didn't say anything—but that's exactly what I was figuring on.

"Sure," he said. He looked at me a long time. He knowed how I was feeling; he knowed I was weak and almost ready to fall. That's why he was making me stand there like that. "What you think we ought to do with niggers like you?" he said. "Come on now—what you think we ought to do with you?"

I didn't answer him.

"Well?" he said.

"I don't know," I said. "Sir."

"I'll tell you," he said. "See, if I was gov'nor, I'd run every damned one of you off in that river out there. Man, woman and child. You know that?"

I was quiet, looking at him. But I made sure I didn't show in my face what I was thinking. I could've been killed for what I was thinking then.

"Well, what you think of that?" he said.

"That's up to the gov'nor, sir," I said.

"Yeah," he said. "That's right. That's right. I think I'll write him a little telegram and tell him 'bout my idea. Can save this state a hell of a lot trouble."

Now he just sat there looking at me again. He wanted to hit me in the mouth with his fist. Not just hit me, he wanted to beat me. But he had to have a good excuse. And what excuse could he have when I had already turned myself in.

"Put him in there with Munford," he said to Paul.

We went out. We had to walk down a hall to the cell block. The niggers' cell block was on the second floor. We had to go up some concrete steps to get there. Paul turned on the lights and a woman hollered at him to turn them off. "What's this supposed to be—Christmas?" she said. "A person can't sleep in this joint." The women was locked up on one end of the block and the men was at the other end. If you had a mirror or a piece of shiny tin, you could stick it out the cell and fix it so you could see the other end of the block.

The guard opened the cell door and let me in, then he locked it back. I looked at him through the bars.

"When will y'all ever learn?" he said, shaking his head.

He said it like he meant it, like he was sorry for me. He kept reminding me of that boy I had played baseball with. They called that other boy Lloyd, and he used to show up just about every Sunday to play baseball with us. He used to play the outfield so he could do a lot of running. He used to buy Cokes for everybody after the game. He was the only white boy out there.

"Here's a pack of cigarettes and some matches," Paul said. "Might not be your brand, but I doubt if you'll mind it too much in there."

I took the cigarettes from him.

"You can say 'Thanks,'" he said.

"Thanks," I said.

"And you can say 'sir' sometimes," he said.

"Sir," I said.

He looked at me like he felt sorry for me, like he felt sorry for everybody. He didn't look like a policeman at all.

"Let me give you a word of warning," he said. "Don't push T. J. Don't push him, now."

"I won't."

"It doesn't take much to get him started—don't push him."

I nodded.

"Y'all g'n turn out them goddamn lights?" the woman hollered from the other end of the block.

"Take it easy," Paul said to me and left.

After the lights went out, I stood at the cell door till my eyes got used to the dark. Then I climbed up on my bunk. Two other people was in the cell. Somebody on the bunk under mine, somebody on the lower bunk 'cross from me. The upper bunk 'cross from me was empty.

"Cigarette?" the person below me said.

He said it very low, but I could tell he was talking to me

and not to the man 'cross from us. I shook a cigarette out the pack and dropped it on the bunk. I could hear the man scratching the match to light the cigarette. He cupped his hands close to his face, because I didn't see too much light. I could tell from the way he let that smoke out he had wanted a cigarette very bad.

"What you in for?" he said, real quiet.

"A fight," I said.

"First time?"

"No, I been in before."

He didn't say any more and I didn't, either. I didn't feel like talking, anyhow. I looked up at the window on my left, and I could see a few stars. I felt lonely and I felt like crying. But I couldn't cry. Once you started that in here you was done for. Everybody and his brother would run over you.

The man on the other bunk got up to take a leak. The toilet was up by the head of my bunk. After the man had zipped up his pants, he just stood there looking at me. I tightened my fist to swing at him if he tried any funny stuff.

"Well, hello there," he said.

"Get your ass back over there, Hattie," the man below me said. He spoke in that quiet voice again. "Hattie is a woman," he said to me. "Don't see how come they didn't put him with the rest of them whores."

"Don't let it worry your mind," Hattie said.

"Caught him playing with this man dick," the man below me said. "At this old flea-bitten show back of town there. Up front— front row—there he is playing with this man dick. Bitch."

"Is that any worse than choking somebody half to death?" Hattie said.

The man below me was quiet. Hattie went back to his bunk.

"Oh, these old crampy, stuffy, old ill-smelling beds," he said, slapping the mattress level with the palm of his hand. "How do they expect you to sleep." He laid down. "What are you in for, honey?" he asked me. "You look awful young."

"Fighting," I said.

"You poor, poor thing," Hattie said. "If I can help you in any way, don't hesitate to ask."

"Shit," the man below me said. I heard him turning over so he could go to sleep.

"The world has given up on the likes of you," Hattie said. "You jungle beast."

"Bitch, why don't you just shut up," the man said.

"Why don't both of y'all shut up," somebody said from another cell.

It was quiet after that.

I looked up at the window and I could see the stars going out in the sky. My eyes felt tired and my head started spinning, and I wasn't here any more, I was at the Seven Spots. And she was there in red, and she had two big dimples in her jaws. Then she got up and danced with him, and every time she turned my way she looked over his shoulder at me and smiled. And when she turned her back to me, she rolled her big ass real slow and easy—just for me, just for me. Grinning Boy was sitting at the table with me, saying: "Poison, poison—nothing but poison. Look at that; just look at that." I was looking, but I wasn't thinking about what he was saying. When she went back to that table to sit down, I went there and asked her to dance. That nigger sitting there just looked at me, rolling his big white eyes like I was supposed to break out of the joint. I didn't pay him no mind, I was looking at that woman. And I was looking down at them two big pretty brown things poking that dress way out. They looked so soft and warm and waiting, I wanted to touch them right there in front of that ugly nigger. She shook her head, because he was sitting there, but little bit later when she went back in the kitchen, I went back there, too. Grinning Boy tried to stop me, saying, "Poison, poison, poison," but I didn't pay him no mind. When I came back in the kitchen, she was standing at the counter ordering a chicken sandwich. The lady back of the counter had to fry the chicken, so she had to wait a while. When she saw me, she started smiling. Them two big dimples came in her jaws. I smiled back at her.

"She go'n take a while," I said. "Let's step out in the cool till she get done."

She looked over her shoulder and didn't see the nigger peeping, and we went outside. There was people talking out there, but I didn't care, I had to touch her.

"What's your name?" I said.

"Clara."

"Let's go somewhere, Clara."

"I can't. I'm with somebody," she said.

"That nigger?" I said. "You call him somebody?"

She just looked at me with that little smile on her face—them two big dimples in her jaws. I looked little farther down, and I could see how them two warm, brown things was waiting for somebody to tear that dress open so they could get free.

"You must be the prettiest woman in the world," I said.

"You like me?"

"Lord, yes."

"I want you to like me," she said.

"Then what's keeping us from going?" I said. "Hell away with that nigger."

"My name is Clara Johnson," she said. "It's in the book. Call me tomorrow after four."

She turned to go back inside, but just then that big sweaty nigger bust out the door. He passed by her like she wasn't even there.

"No, Bayou," she said. "No."

But he wasn't listening to a thing. Before I knowed it, he had cracked me on the chin and I was down on my back. He raised his foot to kick me in the stomach, and I rolled and rolled till I was out of the way. Then I jumped back up.

"I don't want fight you, Bayou," I said. "I don't want fight you, now."

"You fight or you fly, nigger," somebody else said. "If you run, we go'n catch you."

Bayou didn't say nothing. He just came in swinging. I backed away from him.

"I wasn't doing nothing but talking to her," I said.

He rushed in and knocked me on a bunch of people. They picked me clear off the ground and throwed me back on him. He hit me again, this time a glancing blow on the shoulder. I moved back from him, holding the shoulder with the other hand.

"I don't want fight you," I told him. "I was just talking to her."

But trying to talk to Bayou was like trying to talk to a mule. He came in swinging wild and high, and I went under his arm and rammed my fist in his stomach. But it felt like ramming your fist into a hundred-pound sack of flour. He stopped about a half a second, then he was right back on me again. I hit him in the face this time, and I saw the blood splash out of his mouth. I was still backing away from him, hoping he would quit, but the nigger kept coming on me. He had to, because all his friends and that woman was there. But he didn't know how to fight, and every time he moved in I hit him in the face. Then I saw him going for his knife.

"Watch it, now, Bayou," I said. "I don't have a knife. Let's keep this fair."

But he didn't hear a thing I was saying; he was listening to the others who was sicking him on. He kept moving in on me. He had both of his arms 'way out—that blade in his right hand. From the way he was holding it, he didn't have nothing but killing on his mind.

I kept moving back, moving back. Then my foot touched a bottle and I stooped down and picked it up. I broke it against the corner of the building, but I never took my eyes off Bayou. He started circling me with the knife, and I moved round him with the bottle. He made a slash at me, and I jumped back. He was all opened and I could've gotten him then, but I was still hoping for him to change his mind.

"Let's stop it, Bayou," I kept saying to him. "Let's stop it, now."

But he kept on circling me with the knife, and I kept on going round him with the bottle. I didn't look at his face any more, I kept my eyes on that knife. It was a Texas jack with a pearl handle, and that blade must've been five inches long.

"Stop it, Bayou," I said. "Stop it, stop it."

He slashed at me, and I jumped back. He slashed at me again, and I jumped back again. Then he acted like a fool and ran on me, and all I did was stick the bottle out. I felt it go in his clothes and in his stomach and I felt the hot, sticky blood on my hand and I saw his face all twisted and sweaty. I felt his hands brush against mine when he throwed both of his hands up to his stomach. I started running. I was running toward the car, and Grinning Boy was running there, too. He got there before me and jumped in on the driving side, but I pushed him out the way and got under that ste'r'n' wheel. I could hear that gang coming after me, and I shot that Ford out of there a hundred miles an hour. Some of them ran up the road to cut me off, but when they saw I wasn't stopping they jumped out of the way. Now, it was nobody but me, that Ford and that gravel road. Grinning Boy was sitting over there crying, but I wasn't paying him no mind. I wanted to get much road between me and Seven Spots as I could.

After I had gone a good piece, I slammed on the brakes and told Grinning Boy to get out. He wouldn't get out. I opened the door and pushed on him, but he held the ste'r'n' wheel. He was crying and holding the wheel with both hands. I hit him and pushed on him and hit him and pushed on him, but he wouldn't turn it loose. If they was go'n kill me, I didn't want them to kill him, too, but he couldn't see that. I shot away from there with the door still opened, and after we had gone a little piece, Grinning Boy reached out and got it and slammed it again.

I came out on the pave road and drove three or four miles 'long the river. Then I turned down a dirt road and parked the car under a big pecan tree. It was one of these old plantation quarter and the place was quiet as a graveyard. It was pretty bright, though, because the moon and the stars was out. The dust in that long, old road was white as snow. I lit a cigarette and tried to think. Grinning Boy was sitting over there crying. He was crying real quiet with his head hanging down on his chest. Every now and then I could hear him sniffing.

"I'm turning myself in," I said.

I had been thinking and thinking and I couldn't think of nothing else to do. I knowed Bayou was dead or hurt pretty bad, and I knowed either that gang or the law was go'n get me, anyhow. I backed the car out on the pave road and drove to Bayonne. I told Grinning Boy to let my uncle know I was in trouble. My uncle would go to Roger Medlow—and I was hoping Roger Medlow would get me off like he had done once before. He owned the plantation where I lived.

"HEY," SOMEBODY WAS calling and shaking me. "Hey, there, now; wake up."

I opened my eyes and looked at this old man standing by the head of my bunk. I'm sure if I had woke up anywhere else and found him that close to me I would've jumped back screaming. He must've been sixty; he had reddish-brown eyes, and a stubby gray beard. 'Cross his right jaw, from his cheekbone to his mouth, was a big shiny scar where somebody had gotten him with a razor. He was wearing a derby hat, and he had it cocked a little to the back of his head.

"They coming," he said.

"Who?"

"Breakfast."

"I'm not hungry."

"You better eat. Never can tell when you go'n eat again in this joint."

His breath didn't smell too good either, and he was standing so close to me, I could smell his breath every time he breathed in and out. I figured he was the one they called Munford. Just before they brought me down here last night, I heard T. J. tell Paul to put me in there with Munford. Since he had called the other one Hattie, I figured he was Munford.

"Been having yourself a nice little nightmare," he said. "Twisting and turning there like you wanted to fall off. You can have this bunk of mine tonight if you want."

I looked at the freak laying on the other bunk. He looked back at me with a sad little smile on his face.

"I'll stay here," I said.

The freak stopped smiling, but he still looked sad—like a sad woman. He knowed why I didn't want get down there. I didn't want no part of him.

Out on the cell block, the nigger trustee was singing. He went from one cell to the other one singing, "Come and get it, it's hot. What a lovely, lovely day, isn't it? Yes, indeed," he answered himself. "Yes, indeed . . . Come and get it, my children, come and get it. Unc' Toby won't feel right if y'all don't eat his lovely food."

He stopped before the cell with his little shiny pushcart. A white guard was with him. The guard opened the cell door and Unc' Toby gave each one of us a cup of coffee and two baloney sandwiches. Then the guard shut the cell again and him and Unc' Toby went on up the block. Unc' Toby was singing again.

"Toby used to have a little stand," Munford said to me. "He

think he still got it. He kinda loose up here," he said, tapping his head with the hand that held the sandwiches.

"They ought to send him to Jackson if he's crazy."

"They like keeping him here," Munford said. "Part of the scheme of things."

"You want this?" I asked.

"No, eat it," he said.

I got back on my bunk. I ate one of the sandwiches and drank some of the coffee. The coffee was nothing but brown water. It didn't have any kind of taste—not even bitter taste. I drank about half and poured the rest in the toilet.

The freak, Hattie, sat on his bunk, nibbling at his food. He wrapped one slice of bread round the slice of baloney and ate that, then he did the same thing with the other sandwich. The two extra slices of bread, he dipped down in his coffee and ate it like that. All the time he was eating, he was looking at me like a sad woman looks at you.

Munford stood between the two rows of bunks, eating and drinking his coffee. He pressed both of the sandwiches together and ate them like they was just one. Nobody said anything all the time we was eating. Even when I poured out the coffee, nobody said anything. The freak just looked at me like a sad woman. But Munford didn't look at me at all—he was looking up at the window all the time. When he got through eating, he wiped his mouth and throwed his cup on his bunk.

"Another one of them smokes," he said to me.

The way he said it, it sounded like he would've took it if I didn't give it to him. I got out the pack of cigarettes and gived him one. He lit it and took a big draw. I was laying back against the wall, looking up at the window; but I could tell that Munford was looking at me.

"Killed somebody, huh?" Munford said, in his quiet, calm voice.

"I cut him pretty bad," I said, still looking up at the window.

"He's dead," Munford said.

I wouldn't take my eyes off the window. My throat got tight, and my heart started beating so loud, I'm sure both Munford and that freak could hear it.

"That's bad," Munford said.

"And so young," Hattie said. I didn't have to look at the freak to know he was crying. "And so much of his life still before him—my Lord."

"You got people?" Munford asked.

"Uncle," I said.

"You notified him?"

"I think he knows."

"You got a lawyer?"

"No."

"No money?"

"No."

"That's bad," he said.

"Maybe his uncle can do something," Hattie said. "Poor thing." Then I heard him blowing his nose.

I looked at the bars in the window. I wanted them to leave me alone so I could think.

"So young, too," Hattie said. "My Lord, my Lord."

"Oh shut up," Munford said. "I don't know why they didn't lock you up with the rest of them whores."

"Is it too much to have some feeling of sympathy?" Hattie said, and blew his nose again.

"Morris David is a good lawyer," Munford said. "Get him if you can. Best for colored round here."

I nodded, but I didn't look at Munford. I felt bad and I wanted them to leave me alone.

"Was he a local boy?" Munford asked.

"I don't know," I said.

"Where was it?"

I didn't answer him.

"Best to talk 'bout it," Munford said. "Keeping it in just make it worse."

"Seven Spots," I said.

"That's a rough joint," Munford said.

"They're all rough joints," Hattie said. "That's all you have— rough joints. No decent places for someone like him."

"Who's your uncle?" Munford asked.

"Martin Baptiste. Medlow plantation."

"Martin Baptiste?" Munford said.

I could tell from the way he said it, he knowed my uncle. I looked at him now. He was looking back at me with his left eye half shut. I could tell from his face he didn't like my uncle.

"You same as out already," he said.

He didn't like my uncle at all, and now he was studying me to see how much I was like him.

"Medlow can get you out of here just by snapping his fingers," he said. "Big men like that run little towns like these."

"I killed somebody," I said.

"You killed another old nigger," Munford said. "A nigger ain't nobody."

He drawed on the cigarette, and I looked at the big scar on the side of his face. He took the cigarette from his mouth and patted the scar with the tip of one of his fingers.

"Bunch of them jumped on me one night," he said. "One caught me with a straight razor. Had the flesh hanging so much, I coulda ripped it off with my hands if I wanted to. Ah, but before I went down you shoulda seen what I did the bunch of 'em." He stopped and thought a while. He even laughed a little to himself. "I been in this joint so much, everybody from the judge on down know me. 'How's it going, Munford?' 'Well, you back with us again, huh, Munt?' 'Look, y'all, old Munt's back with us again, just like he said he'd be.' They all know me. All know me. I'll get out little later on. What time is it getting to be—'leven? I'll give 'em till twelve and tell 'em I want get out. They'll let me out. Got in Saturday night. They always keep me from Saturday till Monday. If it rain, they keep me till Tuesday—don't want me get out and catch cold, you know. Next Saturday, I'm right back. Can't stay out of here to save my soul."

"Places like these are built for people like you," Hattie said. "Not for decent people."

"Been going in and out of these jails here, I don't know how long," Munford said. "Forty, fifty years. Started out just like you—kilt a boy just like you did last night. Kilt him and got off— got off scot-free. My pappy worked for a white man who got me off. At first I didn't know why he had done it—I didn't think; all I knowed was I was free, and free is how I wanted to be. Then I got in trouble again, and again they got me off. I kept on getting in trouble, and they kept on getting me off. Didn't wake up till I got to be nearly old as I'm is now. Then I realized they kept getting me off because they needed a Munford Bazille. They need me to prove they human—just like they need that thing over there. They need us. Because without us, they don't know what they is—they don't know what they is out there. With us around, they can see us and they know what they ain't. They ain't us. Do you see? Do you see how they think?"

I didn't know what he was talking about. It was hot in the cell and he had started sweating. His face was wet, except for that big scar. It was just laying there smooth and shiny.

"But I got news for them. They us. I never tell them that, but inside I know it. They us, just like we is ourselves. Cut any of them open and you see if you don't find Munford Bazille or Hattie Brown there. You know what I mean?"

"I guess so."

"No, you don't know what I mean," he said. "What I mean is

not one of them out there is a man. Not one. They think they men. They think they men 'cause they got me and him in here who ain't men. But I got news for them—cut them open; go 'head and cut one open—you see if you don't find Munford Bazille or Hattie Brown. Not a man one of them. 'Cause face don't make a man—black or white. Face don't make him and fucking don't make him and fighting don't make him—neither killing. None of this prove you a man. 'Cause animals can fuck, can kill, can fight—you know that?"

I looked at him, but I didn't answer him. I didn't feel like answering.

"Well?" he said.

"Yeah."

"Then answer me when I ask you a question. I don't like talking to myself."

He stopped and looked at me a while.

"You know what I'm getting at?"

"No," I said.

"To hell if you don't," he said. "Don't let Medlow get you out of here so you can kill again."

"You got out," I said.

"Yeah," he said, "and I'm still coming back here and I'm still getting out. Next Saturday I'm go'n hit another nigger in the head, and Saturday night they go'n bring me here, and Monday they go'n let me out again. And Saturday after that I'm go'n hit me another nigger in the head—'cause I'll hit a nigger in the head quick as I'll look at one."

"You're just an animal out the black jungle," Hattie said. "Because you have to hit somebody in the head every Saturday night don't mean he has to do the same."

"He'll do it," Munford said, looking at me, not at Hattie. "He'll do it 'cause he know Medlow'll get him out. Won't you?"

I didn't answer him. Munford nodded his head.

"Yeah, he'll do it. They'll see to that."

He looked at me like he was mad at me, then he looked up at the bars in the window. He frowned and rubbed his hand over his chin, and I could hear the gritty sound his beard made. He studied the bars a long time, like he was thinking about something 'way off; then I saw how his face changed: his eyes twinkled and he grinned to himself. He turned to look at Hattie laying on the bunk.

"Look here," he said. "I got a few coppers and a few minutes—what you say me and you giving it a little whirl?"

"My God, man," Hattie said. He said it the way a young girl would've said it if you had asked her to pull down her drawers. He even opened his eyes wide the same way a young girl would've done it. "Do you think I could possibly ever sink so low?" he said.

"Well, that's what you do on the outside," Munford said.

"What I do on the outside is absolutely no concern of yours, let me assure you," the freak said. "And furthermore, I have friends that I associate with."

"And them 'sociating friends you got there—what they got Munford don't have?" Munford said.

"For one thing, manners," Hattie said. "Of all the nerve."

Munford grinned at him and looked at me.

"You know what make 'em like that?" he asked.

"No."

He nodded his head. "Then I'll tell you. It start in the cradle when they send that preacher there to christen you. At the same time he's doing that mumbo-jumbo stuff, he's low'ing his mouth to your little nipper to suck out your manhood. I know, he tried it on me. Here, I'm laying in his arms in my little white blanket and he suppose to be christening me. My mammy there, my pappy there; uncle, aunt, grandmammy, grandpappy; my nan-nane, my pa-ran—all of them standing there with they head bowed.

This preacher going, 'Mumbo-jumbo, mumbo-jumbo,' but all the time he's low'ing his mouth toward my little private. Nobody else don't see him, but I catch him, and I haul 'way back and hit him right smack in the eye. I ain't no more than three months old but I give him a good one. 'Get your goddamn mouth away from my little pecker, you no-teef, rotten, egg-sucking sonofabitch. Get away from here, you sister-jumper, God-calling, pulpit-spitting, mother-huncher. Get away from here, you chicken-eating, catfish-eating, gin-drinking sonofabitch. Get away, goddamn it, get away . . .'"

I thought Munford was just being funny, but he was serious as he could ever get. He had worked himself up so much, he had to stop and catch his breath.

"That's what I told him," he said. "That's what I told him. . . . But they don't stop there, they stay after you. If they miss you in the cradle, they catch you some other time. And when they catch you, they draw it out of you or they make you a beast—make you use it in a brutish way. You use it on a woman without caring for her, you use it on children, you use it on other men, you use it on yourself. Then when you get so disgusted with everything round you, you kill. And if your back is strong, like your back is strong, they get you out so you can kill again." He stopped and looked at me and nodded his head. "Yeah, that's what they do with you— exactly. . . . But not everybody end up like that. Some of them make it. Not many—but some of them do make it."

"Going to the pen?" I said.

"Yeah—the pen is one way," he said. "But you don't go to the pen for the nigger you killed. Not for him—he ain't worth it. They told you that from the cradle—a nigger ain't worth a good gray mule. Don't mention a white mule: fifty niggers ain't worth a good white mule. So you don't go to the pen for killing the nigger, you go for yourself. You go to sweat out all the crud you got in your system. You go, saying, 'Go fuck yourself, Roger Medlow, I want to be a man, and by God I will be a man. For once in my life I will be a man.'"

"And a month after you been in the pen, Medlow tell them to kill you for being a smart aleck. How much of a man you is then?"

"At least you been a man a month—where if you let him get you out you won't be a man a second. He won't 'low it."

"I'll take that chance," I said.

He looked at me a long time now. His reddish-brown eyes was sad and mean. He felt sorry for me, and at the same time he wanted to hit me with his fist.

"You don't look like that whitemouth uncle of yours," he said. "And you look much brighter than I did at your age. But I guess every man must live his own life. I just wish I had mine to live all over again."

He looked up at the window like he had given up on me. After a while, he looked back at Hattie on the bunk.

"You not thinking 'bout what I asked you?" he said.

Hattie looked up at him just like a woman looks at a man she can't stand.

"Munford, if you dropped dead this second, I doubt if I would shed a tear."

"Put all that together, I take it you mean no," Munford said.

Hattie rolled his eyes at Munford the way a woman rolls her eyes at a man she can't stand.

"Well, I better get out of here," Munford said. He passed his hand over his chin. It sounded like passing your hand over sandpaper. "Go home and take me a shave and might go out and do little fishing," he said. "Too hot to pick cotton."

He looked at me again.

"I guess I'll be back next week or the week after—but I suppose you'll be gone to Medlow by then."

"If he come for me—yes."

"He'll come for you," Munford said. "How old you is—twenty?"

"Nineteen."

"Yeah, he'll come and take you back. And next year you'll kill another old nigger. 'Cause they grow niggers just to be killed, and they grow people like you to kill 'em. That's all part of the—the culture. And every man got to play his part in the culture, or the culture don't go on. But I'll tell you this; if you was kin to anybody else except that Martin Baptiste, I'd stay in here long enough to make you go to Angola. 'Cause I'd break your back 'fore I let you walk out of this cell with Medlow. But with Martin Baptiste blood in you, you'll never be worth a goddamn no matter what I did. With that, I bid you adieu."

He tipped his derby to me, then he went to the door and called for the guard. The guard came and let him out. The people on the block told him good-bye and said they would see him when they got out. Munford waved at them and followed the guard toward the door.

"That Munford," Hattie said. "Thank God we're not all like that." He looked up at me. "I hope you didn't listen to half of that nonsense."

I didn't answer the freak—I didn't want have nothing to do with him. I looked up at the window. The sky was darkish blue and I could tell it was hot out there. I had always hated the hot sun, but I wished I was out there now. I wouldn't even mind picking cotton, much as I hated picking cotton.

I got out my other sandwich: nothing but two slices of light bread and a thin slice of baloney sausage. If I wasn't hungry, I wouldn't 'a' ate it at all. I tried to think about what everybody was doing at home. But hard as I tried, all I could think about was here. Maybe it was best if I didn't think about outside. That could run you crazy. I had heard about people going crazy in jail. I tried to remember how it was when I was in jail before. It wasn't like this if I could remember. Before, it was just a brawl—a fight. I had never stayed in more than a couple weeks. I had been in about a half dozen times, but never more than a week or two. This time it was different, though. Munford said Roger Medlow was go'n get me out, but suppose Munford was wrong. Suppose I had to go up? Suppose I had to go to the pen?

Hattie started singing. He was singing a spiritual and he was singing it in a high-pitched voice like a woman. I wanted to tell him to shut up, but I didn't want have nothing to do with that freak. I could feel him looking at me; a second later he had quit singing.

"That Munford," he said. "I hope you didn't believe everything he said about me."

I was quiet. I didn't want to talk to Hattie. He saw it and kept his mouth shut.

If Medlow was go'n get me out of here; why hadn't he done so? If all he had to do was snap his fingers, what was keeping him from snapping them? Maybe he wasn't go'n do anything for me. I wasn't one of them Uncle Tom-ing niggers like my uncle, and maybe he was go'n let me go up this time.

I couldn't make it in the pen. Locked up—caged. Walking round all day with shackles on my legs. No woman, no pussy—I'd die in there. I'd die in a year. Not five years—one year. If Roger Medlow came, I was leaving. That's how old people is: they always want you to do something they never did when they was young. If he had his life to live all over—how come he didn't do it then? Don't tell me do it when he didn't do it. If that's part of the culture, then I'm part of the culture, because I sure ain't for the pen.

That black sonofabitch—that coward. I hope he didn't have religion. I hope his ass burn in hell till eternity.

Look how life can change on you—just look. Yesterday this time I was poon-tanging like a dog. Today—that black sonofabitch—behind these bars maybe for the rest of my life. And look at me, look at me. Strong. A man. A damn good man. A hard dick—a pile of muscles. But look at me—locked in here like a caged animal.

Maybe that's what Munford was talking about. You spend much time in here like he done spent, you can't be nothing but a' animal.

I wish somebody could do something for me. I can make a phone call, can't I? But call who? That ass-hole uncle of mine? I'm sure Grinning Boy already told him where I'm at. I wonder if Grinning Boy got in touch with Marie. I suppose this finish it. Hell, why should she stick her neck out for me. I was treating her like a dog, anyhow. I'm sorry, baby; I'm sorry. No, I'm not sorry; I'd do the same thing tomorrow if I was out of here. Maybe I'm a' animal already. I don't care who she is, I'd do it with her and don't give a damn. Hell, let me stop whining; I ain't no goddamn animal. I'm a man, and I got to act and think like a man.

I got to think, I got to think. My daddy is somewhere up North—but where? I got more people scattered around, but no use going to them. I'm the black sheep of this family—and they don't care if I live or die. They'd be glad if I died so they'd be rid of me for good.

That black sonofabitch—I swear to God. Big as he was, he had to go for a knife. I hope he rot in hell. I hope he burn—goddamn it—till eternity come and go.

Let me see, let me see, who can I call? I don't know a soul with a dime. Them white people out there got it, but what do they care 'bout me, a nigger. Now, if I was a' Uncle Tom-ing nigger—oh, yes, they'd come then. They'd come running. But like I'm is, I'm fucked. Done for.

Five years, five years—that's what they give you. Five years for killing a nigger like that. Five years out of my life. Five years for a rotten, no good sonofabitch who didn't have no business being born in the first place. Five years . . .

Maybe I ought to call Medlow myself. . . . But suppose he come, then what? Me and Medlow never got along. I couldn't never bow and say, "Yes sir," and scratch my head. But I'd have to do it now. He'd have me by the nuts and he'd know it; and I'd have to kiss his ass if he told me to.

Oh Lord, have mercy. . . . They get you, don't they. They let you run and run, then they get you. They stick a no-good, trashy nigger up there, and they get you. And they twist your nuts and twist them till you don't care no more.

I got to stop this, I got to stop it. My head'll go to hurting after while and I won't be able to think anything out.

"Oh, you're so beautiful when you're meditating," Hattie said. "And what were you meditating about?"

I didn't answer him—I didn't want have nothing to do with that freak.

"How long you're going to be in here, is that it?" he said. "Sometimes they let you sit for days and days. In your case they might let you sit here a week before they say anything to you. What do they care—they're inhuman."

I got a cigarette out of the pack and lit it.

"I smoke, too," Hattie said.

I didn't answer that freak. He came over and got the pack out of my shirt pocket. His fingers went down in my pocket just like a woman's fingers go in your pocket.

"May I?" he said.

I didn't say nothing to him. He lit his cigarette and laid the pack on my chest just like a woman'd do it.

"Really, I'm not all that awful," he said. "Munford has poisoned your mind with all sorts of notions. Let go—relax. You need friends at a time like this."

I stuffed the pack of cigarettes in my pocket and looked up at the window.

"These are very good," the freak said. "Very, very good. Well, maybe you'll feel like talking a little later on. It's always good to let go. I'm understanding; I'll be here."

He went back to his bunk and laid down.

Toward three o'clock, they let the women out of the cells to walk around. Some of the women came down the block and talked to the men through the bars. Some of them even laughed and joked. Three-thirty, the guard locked them up and let the men out. From the way the guard looked at me, I knowed I wasn't going anywhere. I didn't want to go anywhere, either, because I didn't want people asking me a pile of questions. Hattie went out to stretch, but few minutes later he came and laid back down. He was grumbling about some man on the block trying to get fresh with him.

"Some of them think you'll stoop to anything," he said.

I looked out of the window at the sky. I couldn't see too much, but I liked what I could see. I liked the sun, too. I hadn't ever liked the sun before, but I liked it now. I felt my throat getting tight, and I turned my head.

Toward four o'clock, Unc' Toby came on the block with dinner. For dinner, we had stew, mashed potatoes, lettuce and tomatoes. The stew was too soupy; the mashed potatoes was too soupy; the lettuce and tomatoes was too soggy. Dessert was three or four dried-up prunes with black water poured over them. After Unc' Toby served us, the guard locked up the cell. By the time we finished eating, they was back there again to pick up the trays.

I laid on my bunk, looking up at the window. How long I had been there? No more than about twelve hours. Twelve hours— but it felt like three days, already.

They knowed how to get a man down. Because they had me now. No matter which way I went—plantation or pen—they had me. That's why Medlow wasn't in any hurry to get me out. You don't have to be in any hurry when you already know you gotta man by the nuts.

Look at the way they did Jack. Jack was a man, a good man. Look what they did him. Let a fifteen-cents Cajun bond him out of jail—a no-teeth, dirty, overall-wearing Cajun get him out. Then they broke him. Broke him down to nothing—to a grinning, bowing fool. . . . We loved Jack. Jack could do anything. Work, play ball, run women—anything. They knowed we loved him, that's why they did him that. Broke him—broke him the way you break a wild horse. . . . Now everybody laughs at him. Gamble with him and cheat him. He know you cheating him, but he don't care—just don't care any more . . .

Where is my father? Why my mama had to die? Why they brought me here and left me to struggle like this? I used to love my mama so much. Her skin was light brown; her hair was silky. I used to watch her powdering her face in the glass. I used to always cry when she went out—and be glad when she came back because she always brought me candy. But you gone for good now, Mama; and I got nothing in this world but me.

A man in the other cell started singing. I listened to him and looked up at the window. The sky had changed some more. It was lighter blue now—gray-blue almost.

The sun went down, a star came out. For a while it was the only star; then some more came to join it. I watched all of them. Then I watched just a few, then just one. I shut my eyes and opened them and tried to find the star again. I couldn't find it. I wasn't too sure which one it was. I could've pretended and choosed either one, but I didn't want lie to myself. I don't believe in lying to myself. I don't believe in lying to nobody else, either. I believe in being straight with a man. And I want a man to be straight with me. I wouldn't 'a' picked up that bottle for nothing if that nigger hadn't pulled his knife. Not for nothing. Because I don't believe in that kind of stuff. I believe in straight stuff. But a man got to protect himself . . . But with stars I wasn't go'n cheat. If I didn't know where the one was I was looking at at first, I wasn't go'n say I did. I picked out another one, one that wasn't too much in a cluster. I measured it off from the bars in the window, then I shut my eyes. When I opened them, I found the star right away. And I didn't have to cheat, either.

The lights went out on the block. I got up and took a leak and got back on my bunk. I got in the same place I was before and looked for the star. I found it right away. It was easier to find now because the lights was out. I got tired looking at it after a while and looked at another one. The other one was much more smaller and much more in a cluster. But I got tired of it after a while, too.

I thought about Munford. He said if they didn't get you in the cradle, they got you later. If they didn't suck all the manhood out of you in the cradle, they made you use it on people you didn't love. I never messed with a woman I didn't love. I always loved all these women I ever messed with. . . . No, I didn't love them. Because I didn't love her last night—I just wanted to fuck her. And I don't think I ever loved Marie, either. Marie just had the best pussy in the world. She had the best—still got the best. And that's why I went to her, the only reason I went. Because God knows she don't have any kind a face to make you come at her . . .

Maybe I ain't never loved nobody. Maybe I ain't never loved nobody since my mama died. Because I loved her, I know I loved her. But the rest—no, I never loved the rest. They don't let you love them. Some kind of way they keep you from loving them . . .

I have to stop thinking. That's how you go crazy—thinking. But what else can you do in a place like this—what? I wish I knowed somebody. I wish I knowed a good person. I would be good if I knowed a good person. I swear to God I would be good.

All of a sudden the lights came on, and I heard them bringing in somebody who was crying. They was coming toward the cell where I was; the person was crying all the way. Then the cell door opened and they throwed him in there and they locked the door again. I didn't look up—I wouldn't raise my head for nothing. I could tell nobody else was looking up, either. Then the footsteps faded away and the lights went out again.

I raised my head and looked at the person they had throwed in there. He was nothing but a little boy—fourteen or fifteen. He had on a white shirt and a pair of dark pants. Hattie helped him up off the floor and laid him on the bunk under me. Then he sat on the bunk 'side the boy. The boy was still crying.

"Shhh now, shhh now," Hattie was saying. It was just like a woman saying it. It made me sick a' the stomach. "Shhh now, shhh now," he kept on saying.

I swung to the floor and looked at the boy. Hattie was sitting on the bunk, passing his hand over the boy's face.

"What happened?" I asked him.

He was crying too much to answer me.

"They beat you?" I asked him.

He couldn't answer.

"A cigarette?" I said.

"No—no—sir," he said.

I lit one, anyhow, and stuck it in his mouth. He tried to smoke it and started coughing. I took it out.

"Shhh now," Hattie said, patting his face. "Just look at his clothes. The bunch of animals. Not one of them is a man. A bunch of pigs—dogs—philistines."

"You hurt?" I asked the boy.

"Sure, he's hurt," Hattie said. "Just look at his clothes, how they beat him. The bunch of dogs."

I went to the door to call the guard. But I stopped; I told myself to keep out of this. He ain't the first one they ever beat and he won't be the last one, and getting in it will just bring you a dose of the same medicine. I turned around and looked at the boy. Hattie was holding the boy in his arms and whispering to him. I hated what Hattie was doing much as I hated what the law had done.

"Leave him alone," I said to Hattie.

"The child needs somebody," he said. "You're going to look after him?"

"What happened?" I asked the boy.

"They beat me," he said.

"They didn't beat you for nothing, boy."

He was quiet now. Hattie was patting the side of his face and his hair.

"What they beat you for?" I asked him.

"I took something."

"What you took?"

"I took some cakes. I was hungry."

"You got no business stealing," I said.

"Some people got no business killing, but it don't keep them from killing," Hattie said.

He started rocking the boy in his arms the way a woman rocks a child.

"Why don't you leave him alone?" I said.

He wouldn't answer me. He kept on.

"You hear me, whore?"

"I might be a whore, but I'm not a merciless killer," he said.

I started to crack him side the head, but I changed my mind. I had already raised my fist to hit him, but I changed my mind. I started walking. I was smoking the cigarette and walking. I walked, I walked, I walked. Then I stood at the head of the bunk and look up at the window at the stars. Where was the one I was looking at a while back? I smoked on the cigarette and looked for it—but where was it? I threw the cigarette in the toilet and lit another one. I smoked and walked some more. The rest of the place was quiet. Nobody had said a word since the guards throwed that little boy in the cell. Like a bunch of roaches, like a bunch of mices, they had crawled in they holes and pulled the cover over they head.

All of a sudden I wanted to scream. I wanted to scream to the top of my voice. I wanted to get them bars in my hands and I wanted to shake, I wanted to shake that door down. I wanted to let all these people out. But would they follow me—would they? Y'all go'n follow me? I screamed inside. Y'all go'n follow me?

I ran to my bunk and bit down in the cover. I bit harder, harder, harder. I could taste the dry sweat, the dry piss, the dry vomit. I bit harder, harder, harder . . .

I got on the bunk. I looked out at the stars. A million little white, cool stars was out there. I felt my throat hurting. I felt the water running down my face. But I gripped my mouth tight so I wouldn't make a sound. I didn't make a sound, but I cried. I cried and cried and cried.

I KNOWED I was going to the pen now. I knowed I was going, I knowed I was going. Even if Medlow came to get me, I wasn't leaving with him. I was go'n do like Munford said. I was going there and I was go'n sweat it and I was go'n take it. I didn't want have to pull cover over my head every time a white man did something to a black boy—I wanted to stand. Because they never let you stand if they got you out. They didn't let Jack stand—and I had never heard of them letting anybody else stand, either.

I felt good. I laid there feeling good. I felt so good I wanted to sing. I sat up on the bunk and lit a cigarette. I had never smoked a cigarette like I smoked that one. I drawed deep, deep, till my chest got big. It felt good. It felt good deep down in me. I jumped to the floor feeling good.

"You want a cigarette?" I asked the boy.

I spoke to him like I had been talking to him just a few minutes ago, but it was over an hour. He was laying in Hattie's arms quiet like he was half asleep.

"No, sir," he said.

I had already shook the cigarette out of the pack.

"Here," I said.

"No, sir," he said.

"Get up from there and go to your own bunk," I said to Hattie.

"And who do you think you are to be giving orders?"

I grabbed two handsful of his shirt and jerked him up and slammed him 'cross the cell. He hit against that bunk and started crying—just laying there, holding his side and crying like a woman. After a while he picked himself up and got on that bunk.

"Philistine," he said. "Dog—brute."

When I saw he wasn't go'n act a fool and try to hit me, I turned my back on him.

"Here," I said to the boy.

"I don't smoke—please, sir."

"You big enough to steal?" I said. "You'll smoke it or you'll eat it." I lit it and pushed it in his mouth. "Smoke it."

He smoked and puffed it out. I sat down on the bunk 'side him. The freak was sitting on the bunk 'cross from us, holding his side and crying.

"Hold that smoke in," I said to the boy.

He held it in and started coughing. When he stopped coughing I told him to draw again. He drawed and held it, then he let it out. I knowed he wasn't doing it right, but this was his first time, and I let him slide.

"If Medlow come to get me, I'm not going," I said to the boy. "That means T. J. and his boys coming, too. They go'n beat me up because they think I'm a smart aleck trying to show them up. Now you listen to me, and listen good. Every time they come for me I want you to start praying. I want you to pray till they bring me back in this cell. And I don't want you praying like a woman, I want you to pray like a man. You don't even have to get on your knees; you can lay on your bunk and pray. Pray quiet and to yourself. You hear me?"

He didn't know what I was talking about, but he said, "Yes, sir," anyhow.

"I don't believe in God," I said. "But I want you to believe. I want you to believe He can hear you. That's the only way I'll be able to take those beatings—with you praying. You understand what I'm saying?"

"Yes, sir."

"You sure, now?"

"Yes, sir."

I drawed on the cigarette and looked at him. Deep in me I felt some kind of love for this little boy.

"You got a daddy?" I asked him.

"Yes, sir."

"A mama?"

"Yes, sir."

"Then how come you stealing?"

"'Cause I was hungry."

"Don't they look after you?"

"No, sir."

"You been in here before?"

"Yes, sir."

"You like it in here?"

"No, sir. I was hungry."

"Let's wash your back," I said.

We got up and went to the facebowl. I helped him off with his shirt. His back was cut from where they had beat him.

"You know Munford Bazille?" I asked him.

"Yes, sir. He don't live too far from us. He kin to you?"

"No, he's not kin to me. You like him?"

"No, sir, I don't like him. He stay in fights all the time, and they always got him in jail."

"That's how you go'n end up."

"No, sir, not me. 'Cause I ain't coming back here no more."

"I better not ever catch you in here again," I said. "Hold onto that bunk—this might hurt."

"What you go'n do?"

"Wash them bruises."

"Don't mash too hard."

"Shut up," I told him, "and hold on."

I wet my handkerchief and dabbed at the bruises. Every time I touched his back, he flinched. But I didn't let that stop me. I washed his back good and clean. When I got through, I told him to go back to his bunk and lay down. Then I rinched out his shirt and spread it out on the foot of my bunk. I took off my own shirt and rinched it out because it was filthy.

I lit a cigarette and looked up at the window. I had talked big, but what was I going to do when Medlow came? Was I going to change my mind and go with him? And if I didn't go with Medlow, I surely had to go with T. J. and his boys. Was I going to be able to take the beatings night after night? I had seen what T. J. could do to your back. I had seen it on this kid and I had seen it on other people. Was I going to be able to take it?

I don't know, I thought to myself. I'll just have to wait and see.

from *Dancing After Hours*

The author of ten books of fiction and a collection of essays, Andre Dubus "restores the faith in the survival of the short story" (Los Angeles Times). Vintage Contemporaries has published his Selected Stories *and the collection* Dancing After Hours, *which won the Rea Award for the Short Story, was a finalist for the National Book Critics Circle, and was one of the* New York Times Book Review's Notable Books of 1996.

■ ALL THE TIME IN THE WORLD

IN COLLEGE, LUANN was mirthful and romantic, an attractive girl with black hair and dark skin and eyes. She majored in American Studies, and her discipline kept her on the dean's list. Her last name was Arceneaux; her mother's maiden name was Voorhies, and both families had come to Maine from Canada. Her parents and sister and brother and LuAnn often gestured with their hands as they talked. Old relatives in Canada spoke French.

LuAnn's college years seemed a fulfillment of her adolescence; she lived with impunity in a dormitory in Boston, with both girls and boys, with drinking and marijuana and cocaine; at the same time, she remained under the aegis of her parents. They were in a small town three hours north by bus; she went there on a few weekends, and during school vacations, and in summer. She was the middle child, between a married sister and a brother in high school. Her parents were proud of her work, they enjoyed her company, and they knew or pretended they knew as little about her life with friends as they had when she lived at home and walked a mile to school. In summer during college she was a lifeguard at a lake with a public beach. She saved some money and her parents paid her tuition and gave her a small allowance when she lived in the dormitory. They were neither strict nor lenient; they trusted her and, at home, she was like a young woman of their own generation: she drank and smoked with them, and on Sundays went to Mass with them and her brother. She went to Sunday Mass in Boston, too, and sometimes at noon on weekdays in the university chapel, and sitting in the pew she felt she was at home: that there, among strangers, she was all of herself, and only herself, forgiven and loved.

This was a time in America when courting had given way to passion, and passion burned without vision; this led to much postcoital intimacy, people revealing themselves to each other after they were lovers, and often they were frightened or appalled by what they heard as they were lying naked on a bed. Passion became smoke and left burned grass and earth on the sheets. The couple put on their clothes, fought for a few months, or tried with sincere and confessional negotiation to bring back love's blinding heat, then parted from each other and waited for someone else. While LuAnn was in college, she did not understand all of this, though she was beginning to, and she did not expect her parents to understand any of it. She secretly took birth control pills and, when she was at home, returned from dates early enough to keep at bay her parents' fears. At Mass she received Communion, her conscience set free by the mores of her contemporaries and the efficacy of the pill. When her parents spoke of drugs and promiscuity among young people, she turned to them an innocent face. This period of enjoying adult pleasures and at times suffering their results, while still living with her parents as a grown child, would end with the commencement she yearned for, strove for, and dreaded.

When it came, she found an apartment in Boston and a job

with an insurance company. She worked in public relations. June that year was lovely, and some days she took a sandwich and cookies and fruit to work, and ate lunch at the Public Garden so she could sit in the sun among trees and grass. For the first time in her life she wore a dress or skirt and blouse five days a week, and this alone made her feel that she had indeed graduated to adult life. So did the work: she was assistant to a woman in her forties, and she liked the woman and learned quickly. She liked having an office and a desk with a telephone and typewriter on it. She was proud of her use of the telephone. Until now a telephone had been something she held while talking with friends and lovers and her family. At work she called people she did not know and spoke clearly in a low voice.

The office was large, with many women and men at desks, and she learned their names, and presented to them an amiability she assumed upon entering the building. Often she felt that her smiles, and her feigned interest in people's anecdotes about commuting and complaints about colds, were an implicit and draining part of her job. A decade later she would know that spending time with people and being unable either to speak from her heart or to listen with it was an imperceptible bleeding of her spirit.

Always in the office she felt that she was two people at once. She believed that the one who performed at the desk and chatted with other workers was the woman she would become as she matured, and the one she concealed was a girl destined to atrophy, and become a memory. The woman LuAnn worked for was an intense, voluble blonde who colored her hair and was cynical, humorous, and twice-divorced. When she spoke of money, it was with love, even passion; LuAnn saw money as currency to buy things with and pay bills, not an acquisition to accumulate and compound, and she felt like a lamb among wolves. The woman had a lover, and seemed happy.

LuAnn appreciated the practical function of insurance and

bought a small policy on her own life, naming her parents as ben-
eficiaries; she considered it a partial payment of her first child's
tuition. But after nearly a year with the insurance company, on a
Saturday afternoon while she was walking in Boston, wearing
jeans and boots and a sweatshirt and feeling the sun on her face
and hair, she admitted to herself that insurance bored her. Soon
she was working for a small publisher. She earned less money but
felt she was closer to the light she had sometimes lived in during
college, had received from teachers and books and other students
and often her own work. Now she was trying to sell literature,
the human attempt to make truth palpable and delightful. There
was, of course, always talk of money; but here, where only seven
people worked and book sales were at best modest, money's end
was much like its end in her own life: to keep things going. She
was the publicity director and had neither assistants nor a secretary. She worked with energy and was not bored; still, there were
times each day when she watched herself, and listened to herself,
and the LuAnn Arceneaux she had known all her life wanted to
say aloud: *Fuck* this; and to laugh.

   She had lovers, one at a time; this had been happening since
she was seventeen. After each one, when her sorrow passed and
she was again resilient, she hoped for the next love; and her
unspoken hope, even to herself, was that her next love would be
her true and final one. She needed a name for what she was doing
with this succession of men, and what she was doing was not
clear. They were not affairs. An affair had a concrete parameter:
the absence of all but physical love; or one of the lovers was married; or both of them were; or people from different continents
met on a plane flying to a city they would never visit again; something hot and sudden like that. What LuAnn was doing was more
complicated, and sometimes she called it naked dating: you went
out to dinner, bared your soul and body, and in the morning went
home to shower and dress for work. But she needed a word whose

connotation was serious and deep, so she used the word everyone else used, and called it a relationship. It was not an engagement, or marriage; it was entered without vows or promises, but existed from one day to the next. Some people who were veterans of many relationships stopped using the word, and said things like: *I'm seeing Harry,* and *Bill and I are fucking.*

The men saw marriage as something that might happen, but not till they were well into their thirties. One, a tall, blond, curly-haired administrator at the insurance company, spoke of money; he believed a man should not marry until paying bills was no longer a struggle, until he was investing money that would grow and grow, and LuAnn saw money growing like trees, tulips, wild grass and vines. When she loved this man, she deceived herself and believed him. When she no longer loved him, she knew he was lying to her and to himself as well. Money had become a lie to justify his compromise of the tenderness and joy in his soul; these came forth when he was with her. At work he was ambitious and cold, spoke of precedent and the bottom line, and sometimes in the office she had to see him naked in her mind in order to see him at all.

One man she briefly loved, a sound engineer who wrote poems, regarded children as spiteful ingrates, fatherhood as bad for blood pressure, and monogamy as absurd. The other men she loved talked about marriage as a young and untried soldier might talk of war: sometimes they believed they could do it, and survive as well; sometimes they were afraid they could not; but it remained an abstraction that would only become concrete with the call to arms, the sound of drums and horns and marching feet. She knew with each man that the drumroll of pregnancy would terrify him; that even the gentlest—the vegetarian math teacher who would not kill the mice that shared his apartment—would gratefully drive her to an abortion clinic and tenderly hold her hand while she opened her legs. She knew this so deeply in her heart that it was hidden from her; it lay in the dark, along with her knowledge that she would die.

But her flesh knew the truth, and told her that time and love were in her body, not in a man's brain. In her body a man ejaculated, and the plastic in her uterus allowed him to see time as a line rising into his future, a line his lovemaking would not bend toward the curve of her body, the circle of love and time that was her womb and heart. So she loved from one day to the next, blinded herself to the years ahead, until hope was tired legs climbing a steep hill, until hope could no longer move upward or even stand aching in one flat and solid place. Then words came to her, and she said them to men, with derision, with anger, and with pain so deep that soon she could not say them at all, but only weep and, through the blur of tears, look at her lover's angry and chastened eyes. The last of her lovers before she met her final one was a carpenter with Greek blood, with dark skin she loved to see and touch; one night while they ate dinner in his kitchen, he called commitment "the *c* word." LuAnn was twenty-eight then. She rose from her chair, set down her glass of wine, and contained a scream while she pointed at him and said in a low voice: "You're not a man. You're a boy. You all are. You're all getting milk through the fence. You're a thief. But you don't have balls enough to take the cow."

This was in late winter, and she entered a period of abstinence, which meant that she stopped dating. When men asked her out, she said she needed to be alone for a while, that she was not ready for a relationship. It was not the truth. She wanted love, but she did not want her search for it to begin in someone's bed. She had been reared by both parents to know that concupiscence was at the center of male attention; she learned it soon enough anyway in the arms of frenzied boys. In high school she also learned that her passion was not engendered by a boy, but was part of her, as her blood and spirit were, and then she knew the words and actions she used to keep boys out of her body were also containing her own fire, so it would not spread through her flesh until its time. Knowing its time was not simple, and that is why she stopped dating after leaving the carpenter sitting at his table, glaring at her, his breath fast, his chest puffed with words that did not come soon enough for LuAnn to hear. She walked home on lighted sidewalks with gray snow banked on their curbs, and she did not cry. For months she went to movies and restaurants with women. On several weekends she drove to her parents' house, where going to sleep in her room and waking in it made her see clearly the years she had lived in Boston; made her feel that, since her graduation from college, only time and the age of her body had advanced, while she had stood on one plane, repeating the words and actions she regarded as her life.

On a Sunday morning in summer, she put on a pink dress and white high-heeled shoes and, carrying a purse, walked in warm sunlight to the ten o'clock Mass. The church was large and crowded. She did not know this yet, but she would in her thirties: the hot purity of her passion kept her in the Church. When she loved, she loved with her flesh, and to her it was fitting and right, and did not need absolving by a priest. So she had never abandoned the Eucharist; without it, she felt the Mass, and all of the Church, would be only ideas she could get at home from books; and because of it, she overlooked what was bureaucratic or picayune about the Church. Abortion was none of these; it was in the air like war. She hoped never to conceive a child she did not want, and she could not imagine giving death to a life in her womb. At the time for Communion she stepped into the line of people going to receive the mystery she had loved since childhood. A woman with gray hair was giving the Hosts; she took a white disk from the chalice, held it before her face, and said: "The Body of Christ." LuAnn said: "Amen," and the woman placed it in her palms and LuAnn put it in her mouth and for perhaps six minutes then, walking back to her pew and kneeling, she felt in harmony with the entire and timeless universe. This came to her every Sunday, and never at work; sometimes she could achieve it if she drove out of the city on a sunlit day and walked alone on a trail in woods, or on the shore of a lake.

After Mass she lingered on the church steps till she was alone. Few cars passed, and scattered people walked or jogged on the sidewalk, and a boy on a skateboard clattered by. She descended, sliding her hand down the smooth stone wall. A few paces from the steps, she turned her face up to the sun; then the heel of her left shoe snapped, and her ankle and knee gave way: she gained her balance and raised her foot and removed the broken shoe, then the other one. Her purse in one hand and her shoes in the other, she went to the steps and sat and looked at the heel hanging at an angle from one tiny nail whose mates were bent, silver in the sunlight. A shadow moved over her feet and up her legs and she looked at polished brown loafers and a wooden cane with a shining brass tip, and a man's legs in jeans, then up at his face: he had a trimmed brown beard and blue eyes and was smiling; his hair was brown and touched the collar of his navy blue shirt. His chest was broad, his waist was thick and bulged over his belt, and his bare arms were large; he said: "I could try to fix it."

"With what?"

He blushed, and said: "It was just a way of talking to you."

"I know."

"Would you like brunch?"

"Will they let me in barefoot?"

"When they see the shoe."

He held out his hand, and she took it and stood; her brow was the height of his chin. They told each other their names; he was

Ted Briggs. They walked, and the concrete was warm under her bare feet. She told him he had a pretty cane, and asked him why.

"Artillery, in the war. A place called Khe Sanh."

"I know about Khe Sanh."

He looked at her.

"You do?"

"Yes."

"Good," he said.

"Why?"

"You were very young then."

"So were you."

"Nineteen."

"I was twelve."

"So how do you know about Khe Sanh?"

"I took a couple of courses. It's the best way to go to war."

He smiled, and said: "I believe it."

At a shaded corner they stopped to cross the street and he held her elbow as she stepped down from the curb. She knew he was doing this because of the filth and broken glass, and that he wanted to touch her, and she liked the feel of his hand. She liked the gentle depth of his voice, and his walk; his right knee appeared inflexible, but he walked smoothly. It was his eyes she loved; she could see sorrow in them, something old he had lived with, and something vibrant and solid, too. She felt motion in him, and she wanted to touch it. He was a lawyer; he liked to read and he liked movies and deep-sea fishing. On their left, cars stopped for a red light; he glanced at her, caught her gazing at his profile, and she said: "It was bad, wasn't it?"

He stopped and looked down at her.

"Yes. I was a corpsman. You know, the nurse, the EMT—" She nodded. "With the Marines. I got hurt in my twelfth month. Ten years later I started dealing with the eleven and a half months before that."

"How's it going?"

"Better. My knee won't bend, but my head is clear in the morning."

They walked; his hand with the cane was close to her left arm, and she could feel the air between their hands and wrists and forearms and biceps, a space with friction in it, and she veered slightly closer so their skin nearly touched. They reached the street where she lived and turned onto it, facing the sun, and she did not tell him this was her street. On the first block was the restaurant; she had walked or driven past it but had not been inside. He held the door for her and she went into the dark cool air and softened lights, the smells of bacon and liquor. She was on a carpet now, and she could see the shapes of people at tables, and hear low voices; then he moved to her right side, lightly placed his hand on her forearm, and guided her to a booth. They ordered: a Bloody Mary for her and orange juice for him, and cantaloupes and omelettes and Canadian bacon with English muffins. When the drinks came, she lit a cigarette and said: "I drink. I smoke. I eat everything."

"I go to meetings. I'm in my sixth year without a drink. My second without smoking." His hand came midway across the table. "But I'd love a hit off yours."

She gave him the cigarette, her fingers sliding under his. She left her hand there, waited for his fingers again, and got them, his knuckles beneath hers, and she paused for a moment before squeezing the cigarette and withdrawing her hand. She said: "Doesn't cheating make you miss it more?"

"Oh, I'm always missing something."

"Drinking?"

"Only being able to. Or thinking I was."

"Nothing horrible has ever happened to me."

"I hope nothing does."

"I suppose if I live long enough something will."

"If you don't live long enough, *that* would be horrible. Are you seeing anyone?"

"No. Are you?"

"No. I'm waiting. I limp. I get frightened suddenly, when there's no reason to be. I get sad too, when nothing has happened. I know its name now, and—"

"What is its name?"

"It. It's just it, and I go about my day or even my week sometimes, then it's gone. The way a fever is there, and then it isn't. I want a home with love in it, with a woman and children."

"My God," she said, and smiled, nearly laughing, her hands moving up from the table. "I don't think I've *ever* heard those words from the mouth of a man."

"I love the way you talk with your hands."

They stayed in the booth until midafternoon; he invited her to a movie that night; they stepped out of the restaurant into the bright heat, and he walked with her to the door of her apartment building, and stood holding her hand. She raised her bare heels and kissed his cheek, the hair of his beard soft on her chin, then went inside. She showered for a long time and washed her hair and, sitting at her mirror, blew it dry. She put on a robe and slept for an hour and woke happily. She ate a sandwich and soup, and dressed and put on makeup. He lived near the church, and he walked to her building and they walked to the movie; the sun was very low, and the air was cooling. After the movie he took her hand and held it for the four blocks to her apartment, where, standing on the sidewalk, he put his arms around her, the cane touching her right calf, and they kissed. She heard passing cars, and people talking as they walked by; then for a long time she heard only their lips and tongues, their breath, their moving arms and hands. Then she stepped away and said: "Not yet."

"That's good."

"You keep saying that."

"I keep meaning it."

He waited until she was inside both doors, and she turned and waved and he held up his hand till she was on the elevator, and she waved again as the door closed. In her apartment she went to her closet and picked up the white shoe with the broken heel. She did not believe in fate, but she believed in gifts that came; they moved with angels and spirits in the air, were perhaps delivered by them. Her red fingernails were lovely on the white leather; her hands warmed the heel.

In the morning she woke before the clock radio started, and made the bed; tonight she would see him. In her joy was fear, too, but it was a good fear of the change coming into her life. It had already come, she knew that; but she would yield slowly to it. She felt her months alone leaving her; she was shedding a condition; it was becoming her past. Outside in the sun, walking to work, she felt she could see the souls of people in their eyes. The office was bright; she could feel air touching her skin, and the warmth of electric lights. With everyone she felt tender and humorous and patient, and happily mad. She worked hard, with good concentration, and felt this, too, molting: this trying to plunder from an empty cave a treasure for her soul. She went to lunch with two women, and ordered a steak and a beer. Her friends were amused; she said she was very hungry, and kept her silence.

What she had now was too precious and flammable to share with anyone. She knew that some night with Ted it would burst and blaze, and it would rise in her again and again, would course in her blood, burn in her face, shine in her eyes. And this time love was taking her into pain, yes, quarrels and loneliness and boiling rage; but this time there was no time, and love was taking her as far as she would go, as long as she would live, taking her strongly and bravely with this Ted Briggs, holding his pretty cane; this man who was frightened by what had happened to him, but not by the madness she knew he was feeling now. She was hungry, and she talked with her friends and waited for her steak, and for all that was coming to her: from her body, from the earth, from radiant angels poised in the air she breathed.

from *Push*

Performance poet Sapphire introduced readers to sixteen-year-old Precious Jones—one of the most devastating and inspirational heroines in contemporary American fiction—in her first novel, Push, published by Vintage Contemporaries in 1997. Winner of the American Library Association's Black Caucus Award, the novel was praised for its raw candor and its deeply affecting portrait of a brave young woman striving to beat the odds and overcome her illiteracy. In addition, Sapphire is the author of the gritty, artful collection of poetry and prose American Dreams, also available from Vintage.

I WAS LEFT back when I was twelve because I had a baby for my fahver. That was in 1983. I was out of school for a year. This gonna be my second baby. My daughter got Down Sinder. She's retarded. I had got left back in the second grade too, when I was seven, 'cause I couldn't read (and I still peed on myself). I should be in the eleventh grade, getting ready to go into the twelf' grade so I can gone 'n graduate. But I'm not. I'm in the ninfe grade.

I got suspended from school 'cause I'm pregnant which I don't think is fair. I ain' did nothin'!

My name is Claireece Precious Jones. I don't know why I'm telling you that. Guess 'cause I don't know how far I'm gonna go with this story, or whether it's even a story or why I'm talkin'; whether I'm gonna start from the beginning or right from here or two weeks from now. Two weeks from now? Sure you can do anything when you talking or writing, it's not like living when you can only do what you doing. Some people tell a story 'n it don't make no sense or be true. But I'm gonna try to make sense and tell the truth, else what's the fucking use? Ain' enough lies and shit out there already?

So, OK, it's Thursday, September twenty-four 1987 and I'm walking down the hall. I look good, smell good—fresh, clean. It's hot but I do not take off my leather jacket even though it's hot, it might get stolen or lost. Indian summer, Mr Wicher say. I don't know why he call it that. What he mean is, it's *hot*, 90 degrees, like summer days. And there is no, none, I mean *none*, air conditioning in this mutherfucking building. The building I'm talking about is, of course, I.S. 146 on 134th Street between Lenox Avenue and Adam Clayton Powell Jr Blvd. I am walking down the hall from homeroom to first period maff. Why they put some shit like maff first period I do not know. Maybe to gone 'n git it over with. I actually don't mind maff as much as I had thought I would. I jus' fall in Mr Wicher's class sit down. We don't have assigned seats in Mr Wicher's class, we can sit anywhere we want. I sit in the same seat everyday, in the back, last row, next to the door. Even though I know that back door be locked. I don't say nuffin' to him. He don't say nuffin' to me, *now*. First day he say, "Class turn the book pages to page 122 please." I don't move. He say, "Miss Jones, I *said* turn the book pages to page 122." I say, "Mutherfucker I ain't deaf!" The whole class laugh. He turn red. He slam his han' down on the book and say, "Try to have some discipline." He a skinny little white man about five feets four inches. A peckerwood as my mother would say. I look at him 'n say, "I can slam too. You wanna slam?" 'N I pick up my book 'n slam it down on the desk hard. The class laugh some more. He say, "Miss Jones I would appreciate it if you would leave the room right NOW." I say, "I ain' going nowhere mutherfucker till the bell ring. I came here to learn maff and you gon' teach me." He look like a bitch just got a train pult on her. He don't know what to do. He try to recoup, be cool, say, "Well, if you want to learn, calm down—" "I'm calm,"

I tell him. He say, "If you want to learn, shut up and open your book." His face is red, he is shaking. I back off. I have won. I guess.

I didn't want to hurt him or embarrass him like that you know. But I couldn't let him, anybody, know, page 122 look like page 152, 22, 3, 6, 5—all the pages look alike to me. 'N I really do want to learn. Everyday I tell myself something gonna happen, some shit like on TV. I'm gonna break through or somebody gonna break through to me—I'm gonna learn, catch up, be normal, change my seat to the front of the class. But again, it has not been that day.

But thas the first day I'm telling you about. Today is not the first day and like I said I was on my way to maff class when Mrs Lichenstein snatch me out the hall to her office. I'm really mad 'cause actually I like maff even though I don't do nuffin', don't open my book even. I jus' sit there for fifty minutes. I don't cause trouble. In fac' some of the other natives get restless I break on 'em. I say, "Shut up mutherfuckers I'm tryin' to learn something." First they laugh like trying to pull me into fuckin' with Mr Wicher and disrupting the class. Then I get up 'n say, "Shut up mutherfuckers I'm tryin' to learn something." The coons clowning look confuse, Mr Wicher look confuse. But I'm big, five feet nine-ten, I weigh over two hundred pounds. Kids is scared of me. "Coon fool," I tell one kid done jumped up. "Sit down, stop ackin' silly." Mr Wicher look at me confuse but grateful. I'm like the polices for Mr Wicher. I keep law and order. I like him, I pretend he is my husband and we live together in Weschesser, wherever that is.

I can see by his eyes Mr Wicher like me too. I wish I could tell him about all the pages being the same but I can't. I'm getting pretty good grades. I usually do. I just wanna gone get the fuck out of I.S. 146 and go to high school and get my diploma.

Anyway I'm in Mrs Lichenstein's office. She's looking at me,

I'm looking at her. I don't say nuffin'. Finally she say, "So Claireece, I see we're expecting a little visitor." But it's not like a question, she's telling me. I still don't say nuffin'. She staring at me, from behind her big wooden desk, she got her white bitch hands folded together on top her desk.

"Claireece."

Everybody call me Precious. I got three names—Claireece Precious Jones. Only mutherfuckers I hate call me Claireece.

"How old are you Claireece?"

White cunt box got my file on her desk. I see it. I ain't that late to lunch. Bitch know how old I am.

"Sixteen is ah rather ahh"—she clear her throat—"*old* to still be in junior high school."

I still don't say nuffin'. She know so much let her ass do the talking.

"Come now, you are pregnant, aren't you Claireece?"

She asking now, a few seconds ago the hoe just *knew* what I was.

"Claireece?"

She tryin' to talk all gentle now and shit.

"Claireece, I'm talking to you."

I still don't say nuffin'. This hoe is keeping me from maff class. I like maff class. Mr Wicher like me in there, need me to keep those rowdy niggers in line. He nice, wear a dope suit *every* day. He do not come to school looking like some of these other nasty ass teachers.

"I don't want to miss no more of maff class," I tell stupid ass Mrs Lichenstein.

She look at me like I said I wanna suck a dog's dick or some shit. What's with this cunt bucket? (That's what my muver call women she don't like, cunt buckets. I kinda get it and I kinda don't get it, but I like the way it sounds so I say it too.)

I get up to go, Mrs Lichenstein ax me to please sit down, she not through with me yet. But I'm through with her, thas what she don't get.

"This is your *second* baby?" she says. I wonder what else it say in that file with my name on it. I hate her.

"I think we should have a parent-teacher conference Clair-eece—me, you, and your mom."

"For what?" I say. "I ain' done nuffin'. I doose my work. I ain' in no trouble. My grades is good."

Mrs Lichenstein look at me like I got three arms or a bad odor out my pussy or something.

What my muver gon' do I want to say. What is she gonna do? But I don't say that. I jus' say, "My muver is busy."

"Well maybe I could arrange to come to your house—" The look on my face musta hit her, which is what I was gonna do if she said one more word. Come to my house! Nosy ass white bitch! I don't think so! We don't be coming to your house in Weschesser or wherever the fuck you freaks live. Well I be damned, I done heard everything, white bitch wanna visit.

"Well then Claireece, I'm afraid I'm going to have to suspend you—"

"For what!"

"You're pregnant and—"

"You can't suspend me for being pregnant, I got rights!"

"Your attitude Claireece is one of total uncooperation—"

I reached over the desk. I was gonna yank her fat ass out that chair. She fell backwards trying to get away from me 'n started screaming, "SECURITY SECURITY!"

I was out the door and on the street and I could still hear her stupid ass screaming, "SECURITY SECURITY!"

"PRECIOUS!" THAT'S MY mother calling me.

I don't say nothin'. She been staring at my stomach. I know

what's coming. I keep washing dishes. We had fried chicken, mashed potatoes, gravy, green beans, and Wonder bread for dinner. I don't know how many months pregnant I am. I don't wanna stand here 'n hear Mama call me slut. Holler 'n shout on me all day like she did the last time. Slut! Nasty ass tramp! What you been doin'! Who! Who! WHOoooo like owl in Walt Disney movie I seen one time. Whooo! Ya wanna know who—

"Claireece Precious Jones I'm talkin' to you!"

I still don't answer her. I was standing at this sink the last time I was pregnant when them pains hit, *wump!* Ahh wump! I never felt no shit like that before. Sweat was breaking out on my forehead, pain like fire was eating me up. I jus' standing there 'n pain hit me, then pain go sit down, then pain git up 'n hit me harder! 'N she standing there *screaming* at me, "Slut! Goddam slut! You fuckin' cow! I don't believe this, right under my nose. You been high tailing it round here." Pain hit me again, then *she* hit me. I'm on the floor groaning, "Mommy please, Mommy please, please Mommy! Mommy! Mommy! MOMMY!" Then she KICK me side of my face! "Whore! Whore!" she screamin'. Then Miz West live down the hall pounding on the door, hollering "Mary! Mary! What you doin'! You gonna kill that chile! She need help not no beating, is you crazy!"

Mama say, "She shoulda tole me she was pregnant!"

"Jezus Mary, you didn't know. *I* knew, the whole building knew. Are you crazy—"

"Don't tell me nothin' about my own chile—"

"Nine-one-one! Nine-one-one! Nine-one-one!" Miz West screaming' now. She call Mama a fool.

Pain walking on me now. Jus' stomping on me. I can't see hear, I jus' screaming', "Mommy! Mommy!"

Some mens, these ambulance mens, I don't see 'em or hear 'em come in. But I look up from the pain and he dere. This Spanish guy in EMS uniform. He push me back on a cushion. I'm like in a ball from the pain. He say, "RELAX!" The pain stabbing me wif a knife and this spic talking 'bout relax.

He touch my forehead put his other hand on the side of my belly. "What's your name?" he say. "Huh?" I say. "Your name?" "Precious," I say. He say, "Precious, it's almost here. I want you to push, you hear me momi, when that shit hit you again, go with it and push, Preshecita. *Push.*"

And I did.

from *Little Kingdoms*

Steven Millhauser won the 1996 Pulitzer Prize for Martin Dressler: The Tale of an American Dreamer. A finalist for the National Book Award, the recipient of a Lannan Award, and honored by the American Academy of Arts and Letters, Millhauser is the author of several books, including Edwin Mullhouse *and* Little Kingdoms, *both available from Vintage Contemporaries. His other books include* The Barnum Museum, From the Realm of Morpheus, The Penny Arcade, Portrait of a Romantic, *and, most recently,* The Knife Thrower and Other Stories.

■ FROM THE LITTLE KINGDOM OF J. FRANKLIN PAYNE

ONE WARM BLUE night toward the middle of July, in the year 1920, John Franklin Payne, a newspaper cartoonist by trade, looked up from his desk in the third-floor study of his home in Mount Hebron, New York, and saw with surprise that it was three o'clock in the morning. The world was absolutely still. Through the windows the sky was a deep, glowing blue, as if there must be a bright moon somewhere, and Franklin felt a sudden desire to burst through the window into the blue night sky. The desire startled him, for he liked to work alone in his tower study late into the night. The study was warm, uncomfortably warm; despite the new screen in the lower half of the center window, the small room held the heat of the roof.

In the hot stillness Franklin took off his vest and looked again at the glass-cased clock on top of his high-backed desk. The glass door with the brass handle, the lacy clock-hands, the exposed cogwheels, the big metal key lying under the swinging pendulum, all this seemed strange and unseen before, though the clock had stood on the mantelpiece of his parents' home in Ohio since his earliest childhood; and the familiar, strange clock, the glowing sky, the mysterious hour, all seemed connected with something inside him that was about to burst. As he stared at the pendulum he began to notice that the stillness of the hour was really a secret riot of sound: the dark tick of the clock, like drops of water dripping from an eave, the shrill of crickets beyond the screen, and under it all, clearer and clearer, the gentle rasp of his wife's breathing as it came through the open window of the second-floor bedroom. He had told Cora he would be done in an hour or so, but the six-panel strip had proved unexpectedly stubborn. And then he had laid aside his drawing board, that smooth-worn dark board with a faint shine that reminded him of the shine of a well-handled pipe, and with a sense of excitement he had brought out the packet of carefully trimmed rice paper, set up his other board with its glass window, pulled over his jar of Venus pencils and a fresh bottle of black drawing ink, and set to work on his secret, exhilarating project.

What to do? If he went down to his bedroom next to Cora's on the second floor, and fell asleep instantly, he would get only two and a half hours of sleep before the rattle of milk bottles in the wire box on the front porch announced his five-thirty rising. But Franklin was too excited to sleep. He was excited by the glowing blue sky, by the clamorous silence, by his lamplit tower room high above the rest of the house, by the sense that he was creating a world far more enchanting than the world of his comic strips, which had already brought him a certain notoriety. He was bursting with energy. He thought how nice it would be to creep downstairs and slip into bed with Cora—but she would be angry if he woke her. For though Cora was given to passionate whims of her own, she did not like to be surprised. Franklin remembered that a colleague was coming up for a visit on Saturday, and he had a sudden misgiving about Max: suppose Cora—but there was no use worrying about it now. He decided to work straight through the night. Immediately he decided not to. His eyes ached, his temples throbbed, his hand had become slightly unsteady—the last drawing had almost been spoiled.

Franklin numbered the piece of rice paper carefully in the lower right-hand corner and added it to the pile of thirty-two new drawings, each of which had been traced over the preceding drawing and exactly resembled it except for a small departure. Each of the separate drawings still had to be gone over in ink and then mounted on a piece of cardboard in order to be examined in his viewing machine. He now had 1,826 India-ink drawings, which had taken him almost three months to complete. At sixteen frames per second he would need nearly 4,000 drawings for a four-minute animated cartoon.

Franklin pushed back his chair carefully, for Cora complained that she could hear his chair scrape even though her room was not directly below the tower study, and walked over to the center window. He had inserted the adjustable screen only three weeks ago, after a hard-shelled insect had come in at night through the raised sash and struck his drawing hand like a piece of flying tin. Down below, the shadow of the house fell halfway across the sloping lawn. He saw plainly the elongated tower with the pointed roof, from which he was looking down into the yard, and for a moment he had the odd sensation that he was down there, strewn across the lawn—at any moment his shadow-form would emerge from the shadow-tower and pass into the brightness of the moon. Under one of the high old maples a child's table, set with cups and saucers and teapot, lay half in light and half in shade: one chair, pulled back slightly, glowed almost white, while the other chair lay in black shadow. The brilliant spout of the teapot looked like the raised trunk of an elephant. He would have to remind Stella to bring in her toys before dark—or maybe the dolls had come out to have a tea party under the summer moon.

In his childhood home in Plains Farms, Ohio, he had heard things come alive at night: dolls woke from their daylight spell, teapots poured tea, dishes came down from their cupboards and walked about the house, clowns in jigsaw puzzles rose up and danced, the little boy in the wallpaper caught a fish with his yellow fishing pole. Franklin had lain very still, listening to the secret life in the house, and twenty years later he had put it all in a Sunday color strip—but in the last panel the boy had wakened from his dream. And one summer night in Ohio, Franklin himself had sat up in bed and pushed aside the curtain and the stiff, heavy shade to stare at the brilliant backyard. He had longed to pass through the window into the dark enchantment of the summer night; and in the morning when he opened his eyes he found he had fallen asleep with his head against the window frame. Franklin was restless. The tower study was unbearably hot. All at once he had a marvelous idea.

With a thrust of his palms he pushed up the half-open lower sash. The adjustable screen, framed in maple, fit snugly against the vertical parting-strips that ran the length of the window frame and separated the upper and lower sashes. He released the stiff spring, carefully removed the screen, and placed it on the floor against the side of his desk. Then with dream-ease he stepped out into the blue summer night.

A narrow roofslope lay directly beneath the window. On his knees, backward, Franklin made his way to the edge. There, as if he knew what he was doing, he slid over the roof edge and swung down; for a moment he hung wildly before dropping to the wide and nearly flat roof of the front porch.

He was standing beside the tall window of his own bedroom, directly beneath his tower study. The shade was pulled down all the way, as if he were inside, fast asleep. And for a moment he imagined himself lying fast asleep in his bed, dreaming this other Franklin, who had stepped out of a tower into the sky. Franklin strode past the window, noticing himself passing jauntily in the dark pane of the upper sash—and how easy it was to walk this way, along the shingles of a roof, with one's hands in one's pockets at the magic hour of three in the morning; he felt like kicking up his heels. But he slowed as he drew near Cora's window.

Through the adjustable screen he saw Cora lying on her back with her unbound hair strewn over the pillow. He could make out the proud line of her forehead and thought he could see, escaping from her thick pale tumble of hair, the bottom of an ear. Franklin felt a little sharp burst of longing, and with a feeling of dream-freedom he released the steel spring that held the screen tight against the window frame. At that moment Cora turned slightly in her sleep, half opened an eye, and seemed to look at him.

"I'm only a dream," Franklin whispered, and held his breath. The eye closed. Franklin adjusted the screen and tiptoed away along the porch roof.

The roof turned with the wraparound porch, and as he stepped around the corner Franklin walked into the brightness of the moon. The moon startled him: it was much larger than it ought to be. It seemed to be growing bigger and bigger—at any moment it would engulf him and he would dissolve in an exhilaration of whiteness. In an old strip he had shown the moon setting on top of a saloon on Vine Street, rolling drunkenly across rooftops, toppling into the Ohio River with a splash. Franklin continued around the corner and came to a moon-flooded window. In the room his three-year-old daughter lay sleeping on her back. One leg rested on top of the covers and one arm was flung back on the pillow and bent over her head, as if she had fallen asleep suddenly in the midst of an ecstatic dance.

Franklin eased out the screen and climbed inside. At the bed he pulled the sheet and bedspread over Stella's legs, removed a lump that turned out to be a white one-eyed bear, and lay down beside Stella with his hands clasped behind his head. "It's a wonderful night," he said. "I think the moon's going to land on the roof in a few minutes. We can climb up on it and have moon pie. Won't that be fun?" Stella stirred in her sleep and slowly rolled against him. "Shhh, now," Franklin said. "Just another dream." He kissed her forehead and sat up. Creatures with moon-glittering eyes looked at him from shelves and chairs, watched him as they leaned against each other's shoulders. "I'm surprised at you," Franklin said. "This is no time for loafing." He rose from the bed and began gathering up the dolls and animals, which he placed on the floor in two lines facing Stella's bed. In the center of the front row sat a Raggedy Ann doll, a kangaroo, a ballerina in silver slippers, and a donkey with one ear. "Night," Franklin said to no one in particular, then climbed out the window onto the porch roof. The moon had returned to its proper size. Franklin bent into the room and replaced the screen.

He continued to the end of the porch roof, where he came to a projecting bay formed by an empty guest room. Above the bay rose a third-floor gable. The roofline was above his reach, but a brilliant white downspout, gleaming as if the paint were still wet, climbed a corner of the bay. Franklin placed one toe on the louver of a shutter and one toe on a brace of the rainspout, grasped the roof edge, and pulled himself up onto a steep slope.

Slowly, bent over to his fingertips, he made his moonlit way along the peaks and valleys of his jumbled roof, passing through gable-shadows and bursts of brightness. He felt as if he had come down from the moon, an enchanted visitor, to walk on the bumpy top of a town. Once he slipped on a strip of flashing, once he sat straddling a crest of roof, and once he passed a tall, thin chimney that widened at the top and made him think of a pedestal with a missing bust. In a burst of high spirits he imagined chimney statues: a bust of Homer with his bald head gleaming under the moon, a Civil War general with raised sword on a rearing horse, a white marble Venus stepping out of her bath. He had become quite used to his up-and-down journey under the spell of the moon when he found himself in a sudden valley beside a polygonal tower.

Dreamily he made his way down to the skirt of roof beneath the open window and entered his warm study.

Nothing had changed. The mahogany desk-chair with its padded leather seat was turned slightly from the desk, the pendulum swung slowly above the key in the glass-cased clock, a collection of cedarwood penholders standing in a square jar looked like a handful of pick-up-sticks about to fall. On the faded wallpaper with its pattern of repeated haystacks, the little reapers lay asleep with their hats over their eyes. Franklin laid his last drawing on top of the glass rectangle in the sloping animation board. He turned on the light bulb beneath the glass, placed a blank piece of rice paper over the drawing, and lined up the two pieces of glowing paper by matching the crossmarks in the four corners. He tried to recall his mood of moonlit exhilaration, but it all seemed to have happened long ago. Choosing a blunt-tipped Venus pencil from his pencil jar, Franklin began to trace the background for drawing number 1,827 as the first little ache of tiredness rippled along his temples and began to beat softly with the beat of his blood.

|||| MICHELLE HUNEVEN

from *Round Rock*

A restaurant critic for the Los Angeles Times, *Michelle Huneven dazzled readers and critics alike with her wise, generous, and captivating portrait of a group of recovering alcoholics who are as appealing as they are deeply troubled, in this, her first novel. Vintage Contemporaries will publish* Round Rock *in September 1998.*

LEWIS FLETCHER WAS waiting to be discharged from the Ventura County Social Model Detoxification Facility. Nobody could explain this name to him. "Social" as opposed to what? Asocial? Antisocial? *Un*social? Yesterday, they—or at least this guy Bobby—told him he'd be able to walk right out come nine o'clock this morning. Walk right out to freedom. Sky. Sidewalk underfoot. Well-aimed sun. Coffee shops. Then, Bobby said, some stuff about him came in over the computer, and now it was known he'd had too many alcohol-related offenses to be released on his own recognizance.

Lewis had trouble accepting this development. Six years had passed since he'd had that drunk-and-disorderly, which wasn't at all what it sounded like, and three years since the DUI, or almost three, and that was a fluke too. The day he got the DUI, he'd been at the beach with friends and hadn't had a thing to drink until a minute before they left. They'd been rolling up blankets, gathering trash, when a girl handed him a screwdriver. He drank it down like orange juice, only she must have put a lot of vodka in it that he didn't taste, because when he was tested, he had a really high blood-alcohol count. Point two.

The drunk-and-disorderly was even more ridiculous. He and

one of his mother's boyfriends had been drinking a little beer and got into an argument in the driveway. They were yelling away, with Lewis's mother coming out every few minutes to beg them to stop. He didn't have any idea what was so important that they had to stand there and yell for the whole neighborhood to hear, but he did recall that there was some pleasure in it, a big, freeing fuck-everybody feeling, and neither one of them was willing to give it up. His mom called the cops, and they took both of them to the station. They were joking around in the patrol car on the way down, and probably wouldn't even have been booked if Elkhart—that was the boyfriend's stupid name—hadn't called the cops a couple of pindicks to their faces.

Of all the times Lewis had really tied one on, been truly angry at someone or on the verge of doing something profoundly disorderly, it was absurd that these two incidents were the ones that came over the computer to complicate his discharge from detox. Bobby said he had a few choices: his wife or a relative could come and sign him out, or he had to check himself into some kind of treatment program for alcoholism.

Lewis didn't have a wife, so he called his mother, who lived sixty miles away, in Sunland. She was on her way to work, she told him, and couldn't come. She couldn't come after work, either, or tomorrow, which was Saturday. She couldn't come get him at all, in fact. "This time, you have to count on somebody else, because I'm letting you down and making a point of it," she said. "This is a big step for me and I want you to respect it." Okay then, Lewis said, goodbye, and stood there trying to think why she was so mad at him. He had this guilty, sick-at-heart feeling and kept going through his memories until he found one that matched. Sure enough, he remembered the hundred dollars he borrowed from her three months ago for what was supposed to be three days. Funny thing was, he'd had the money the whole time.

He could've paid her back. He never got around to finding an envelope, addressing it, buying a stamp.

He sat back down on the plaid couch in the waiting room swamped with shame that he was such a constant disappointment to his mother. Instead of a son, she had a black hole for an offspring, and in their every encounter, he saw, he had never failed to cause her anguish.

Bobby came over and said if Lewis didn't have any other relatives, or if he didn't have a hospital program or halfway house in mind, he could always take a bed upstairs for a month. Lewis had no relatives and didn't know of any programs, but he would kill himself before spending a whole month in detox. Still, to get Bobby off his back, he agreed to go upstairs and have a look.

The detox center, along with other county agencies, was housed in an old junior high school. As he pulled himself upstairs, Lewis saw initials cut into the wooden banister. Some were enclosed in lopsided hearts. Lewis wondered if anybody who ever went together in junior high school actually got married and stayed married all their lives. He thought about a girl he went steady with in junior high, a black girl named June with a French last name he couldn't recall. She was very dark, though her hair was naturally straight. She was the first black girl he'd ever kissed. That he had a black girlfriend was a big deal to everybody. White girls had black boyfriends, but not the other way around. This girl had fine, sharp teeth and liked to bite down on his tongue and lips. A few times, she drew blood. At first, he was surprised and excited by her biting, but soon his mouth was so sore that he lost any desire to kiss her. They broke up, and although they went on to the same high school together, they eventually stopped acknowledging each other. Within two years, they were strangers again. Lewis had run into an old friend who went to their tenth reunion and reported that June what's-her-name, the biter, had won the award for having the most children: six.

In the first old classroom at the top of the stairs, Lewis found half a dozen beds, each with a dresser/nightstand unit in an area made separate, if not exactly private, by chin-high white Formica partitions. The room looked like a secretary pool, only with beds instead of desks. Three guys had gathered in the first tiny bedroom space, two Latinos and a little guy who was white except for arms and shoulders covered with green tattoos. Lewis recognized them from the AA meeting last night. They took this AA stuff seriously and needed to, because to hear them tell it, their lives were all messed up with crack cocaine, heroin, prison, insane women, you name it.

The next classroom didn't have any partitions, just five beds in a row, like an old-fashioned hospital ward. None of these beds was taken. Every surface in the room itself, including the bottom half of the windows, had been painted the same dull pale green. Hand-lettered cardboard plaques were stuck on the walls, each with a saying: EASY DOES IT. LET GO, LET GOD. ONE DAY AT A TIME.

Lewis lay down on one of the beds and lit a cigarette. Somebody had written JESUS CARES on the pillow in blue ballpoint pen. He tried to make this meaningful, something that someone had written just for him to find—a divine message, humbly drawn— but he didn't have the energy for such creative thinking. He didn't believe in Jesus, except as a man and maybe a spiritual genius, a Buddha for literal white people. Once he had a dream about Jesus and Jesus was nicer than anybody Lewis had ever met, and his hair was long and glossy like in ads for cheap shampoo. Jesus also had long fingernails, fetishistically long. Frankly, even though he seemed so nice, Jesus had creeped Lewis out.

Lewis smoked his cigarette and listened to his heart thump. He could see the shadow of a tree through the painted glass. Traffic surged outside. The central furnace rumbled. There was a sweet chemical scent of floor wax he recalled from every school he'd known.

No matter how hard he tried, Lewis couldn't remember how he ended up here, in Ventura County Social Model Detox. Bobby told him that a woman in Oxnard named Clarice Martin had called an ambulance because he was having convulsions in her front yard. "Flopping like a fish in her dichondra," Bobby put it. Lewis had never heard of Clarice Martin and didn't have any idea how he got to Oxnard.

The last thing he did remember was being in Westwood at a small party in married-student housing. He didn't recall whose party it was or what he was doing there, but he was in a knotty-pine kitchen talking to a short, plump girl. Her face was rapt and bright with hope and coming at him like a bucket of fresh milk.

To hold her at bay, Lewis ranted about Rilke, erected a wall of words. Or no, come to think of it, maybe he was lecturing on Goethe. Of course it was Goethe, whom he'd never read. The only thing he knew about Goethe was from an old Time/Life book that said he was the most intelligent man who had ever lived. Someone had estimated Goethe's IQ and it was higher than everybody else's, even Einstein's. Higher by some thirty-odd points than Lewis's, at any rate. Not that anybody was really sure. Goethe, after all, had never taken an IQ test. His IQ and the IQs of other long-dead geniuses had been based on their capacity for abstraction. Goethe's abstractions were the most abstract of all, which is why Lewis had avoided reading him: why read someone just to make yourself feel stupid?

If he'd been boring Miss Bright-Eyed Milkmaid, she didn't show it. She touched his arm. Her face spewed light. Her eyes urged him on. Had he pounced? He had a vague sense of pulling her to him, scrubbing his beard against her incandescent cheeks, stuffing his tongue into her tiny mouth. Yet he couldn't say for sure if he was remembering this or just imagining it.

He finished his cigarette, then stood up so fast his eyesight exploded into sparks of wormy light. He put one hand on the bedstead and waited for the air to clear.

Back downstairs, Lewis shook his head at Bobby. "Can't do it," he said. He resumed his seat on the ugly plaid couch. He kept thinking there were bugs on him, that a line of ants was crawling up his neck and into his hair, but he couldn't catch one. After a while, Bobby came over and said that there was a man who might take Lewis in his halfway house. He was lucky, Bobby said, because normally there was a waiting list for this drunk farm, as he called it, but he'd just found out there were a couple of empty beds. How did that sound to Lewis—a month in the country on a sliding scale?

ABOUT THE TIME Lewis was staggering down the old schoolhouse stairs, Red Ray was trying to coax Frank Jamieson into the cab of his '46 Ford pickup. Frank was more interested in the sky, which was full of fast-moving horsetail clouds. Frank, it occurred to Red, was looking more and more like Walt Whitman every day: surging gray beard, disheveled, hoary, vaguely vagrant. Unlike Whitman, Frank always had a cigarette in his mouth. Also, Frank never spoke; he hadn't said a word to anybody in eleven and a half years.

"C'mon, you old sacka corn." Red had his arm around Frank's shoulders and was attempting to steer him over to the truck's open door. "Upsa-daisy, into the cab."

Frank was too big to move when he didn't feel like it. Even though Red probably matched him pound for pound—they both weighed in at over 230—Frank had a lower center of gravity and a way of turning his weight into concrete.

"Come *on,* Franky," said Red.

Frank raised his right hand, index finger extended, and touched the unlit tip of his cigarette.

"I'll light the damn thing," Red said, "if you get in the truck."

He next tried sitting in the truck as an example to Frank. Closing the driver's-side door, Red grasped the steering wheel resolutely. "Bus is leaving," he called, turning the key and gunning the engine. He was parked behind the Blue House, the old Victorian mansion that served as Round Rock's dormitory. Behind the mansion were orange groves, Washington navels. Plump, ripe, the oranges spun amid dark leaves like spheres of light.

Red lit a Pall Mall for himself, then extended the lighter toward Frank. Frank pointed to the tip of his cigarette.

My mouth tastes like an electrical short, Libby wrote. *My eyeballs are dry. My nose is packed with crystallized scabs which bleed when picked. I am not fishing—the first Sunday I've missed in a year.*

I'm depressed, thanks, I think, to the cocaine. I've forgotten why I live here in this valley-so-low. I can't find a decent job. Or a decent man. And my closest friend . . . How does Billie do it?

When Libby returned the following week, the lake was socked in with fog. The air was cool, even cold, but the weatherman said to expect temperatures in the high eighties by noon. She set up two poles, wrote in her journal, and caught one fish, which somehow slipped off her stringer. She dozed in the warming air, a slow bake.

Someone called her name and Lewis pulled out of the fog like creation itself. Her first reaction was, How dare he? Her second, pleased surprise. Or maybe the two thoughts were simultaneous: How dare he cause her pleased surprise?

"This is the second week I've come looking for you." Lewis squatted by her chair. He threw back his head and gulped air. "This *is* a cool thing too. I normally hate man-made lakes, but there is something to be said for large bodies of water. You're right—it *is* like going to church, only better." He touched the cane pole. "And murdering fish is the sacrament. Hey, want to go to Miserable Yolanda's for breakfast?"

"Can you go there?" she said.

"Why not?"

"Isn't it a bar?"

"What, you think I'm going to drink?"

"No, no . . ." she stammered stupidly. Alcoholism etiquette, she sensed, was a minefield for the uninitiated.

He punched her arm lightly. "I'll be safe with you. You won't let me partake, even if I want to, right?"

His dark eyes danced with what? Derision?

"Sorry," she said to him. "It's none of my business."

"Don't worry about it."

When they got to town, he was too hot and wanted to change out of his sweater. "It'll just take a sec," he said. "You want to see my room?"

She wasn't crazy about ducking into the Mills with a man in clear sight of Victor Ibañez's window, yet she'd always wondered about the fine white clapboard building with wide porches under tall, graceful deodar pines.

The lobby, though dingy, was clean, with scarred, stunted cacti in pots, an atmospheric plein-air painting of red rocks and cypress trees, and rugs so worn that their patterns were mere tracery. Lewis's room, at the top of creaky wooden stairs, was tinier, if possible, than her trailer's spare bedroom. He barely had space for a bed and a bureau. Thumbtacked to the wall was a T-shirt silkscreened with a caricature of Wallace Stevens. A post-card of a blue jar was tacked upside-down above the T-shirt's neck. "It's a joke," Lewis said. "Wallace Stevens wrote a famous poem about a blue jar."

The only poem of Stevens's that Libby had read, which a pianist friend had recommended, was about somebody at the clavier. The vocabulary had cowed her, and she lacked the train-ing, or possibly the patience, to decode the work. Lewis shuffled a stack of library books, suddenly determined to read this blue-jar poem to her.

Libby sat down on the bed since there was no place else to sit, unless she wanted to roost on a big clump of laundry in the room's only chair. Through a small window, she looked out on the bone-white limbs of a eucalyptus tree. Lewis began to read. She didn't understand this poem, either. Lewis's room smelled of old var-nish and dust. The tap in the bathroom sink dripped. Her hands were chapped and speckled with fish blood. Her hair snarled from wind. The room was hot. Lewis was reading another poem now, with more dizzying words. "The Idea of Order at Key West." At least she didn't have to think of anything to say. Then, he put the book down on the foot of the bed—she assumed he was going to rummage in the laundry chair for a shirt—but without a word, he placed his hands on her shoulders and then slid them down her arms. He came in close; it was a stare-down, an ophthalmic assault. Her mind sped. He couldn't kiss her when she was all fishy like this, and bundled up in shirts. But he did. He was relentless, even, nudging her down on the bed, kissing her neck and jaw, licking his way back to her lips. In no time he was undressing her, a series of insistent tugs. She didn't mind. In fact she liked this focused, no-nonsense approach. This was what she thought would happen, although maybe not so quickly, and she couldn't have predicted that he would have such authority. She was naked and he was still in that old wool sweater and jeans. He looked her straight in the eye. Scary, but fun. Really fun.

Sprawled across the bed, he pushed his pants down, rolled away from her to put on a condom, and re-establishing eye con-tact, promptly guided himself inside her. His eyes flickered. It was a little much, a little intense, so she looked over his shoulder to where a wall met the ceiling. Jean buttons snagged on her thigh. The musty sweater was itchy, abrasive, like his beard. She didn't even like beards, thought them slovenly. The whole grungy room was slovenly. She came fast and hard. Like I'm the man, she thought. Premature. He paused until she looked him square in the face. He smiled and, without pulling out of her or looking away, took off his sweater and T-shirt. His chest was hairless, the ribs pronounced. His olive skin was granular, like muscled sand.

"Do you want to talk about this?" he asked, still inside her.

"Not now!"

"We're doin' it," he said. "Shouldn't we talk about it?"

"God, Lewis." She bundled his butt in her hands and, to shut him up, pushed him into her.

"No?" Laughing a little. More in control than she ever dreamed he'd be. "You sure you don't want to talk about this?"

She couldn't talk if she wanted to, and he knew this. That was the point.

Afterward, they lay there like gasping fish. He held her forearm, squeezed it occasionally, kissed her ear. He got up first, and brought her back a mug of lukewarm tap water. They shared a cigarette. When she returned from the bathroom, his pants were on. "Breakfast," he said.

At Happy Yolanda's, they found Billie and the Bills sitting with Red Ray. Little Bill and Red jumped up to drag over another table. "We've been fishing," Lewis said. "It's so cool. Libby goes every Sunday."

Libby blushed and sat up straight. Did she smell like sex? The back of her hair was a bird's nest. Billie winked at her at least seven hundred times. Lewis and Red Ray talked about the softball game later that day. She drifted, chewing *machaca* and eggs, sipping burnt, weak coffee. Lewis grasped her hand under the table and placed it on his erection. She inhaled coffee, coughing until Red handed her a glass of water.

She and Lewis walked outside with everyone else. She hung

back, thinking he might want to say something to her. But suddenly he was half a block away—"Bye! So long! Thanks for the fishing!"—and she was still standing next to Billie outside of Happy Yolanda's.

"You're hooked," Billie said.

"I'm not hooked."

"You're hooked, all right. Your eyes have turned to goo."

from *Model Behavior*

From Jay McInerney's novel and story collection, Model Behavior, forthcoming from Knopf in October 1998, here is "How It Ended."

■ HOW IT ENDED

I LIKE TO ASK married couples how they met. It's always interesting to hear how two lives became intertwined, how of the nearly infinite number of possible conjunctions this or that one came into being, to hear the first chapter of a story in progress. As a matrimonial lawyer I deal extensively in endings, so it's a relief, a sort of holiday, to visit the realm of beginnings. And I ask because I've always enjoyed telling my own story—our story, I should say—which I'd always felt was unique.

My name is Donald Prout, rhymes with trout. My wife, Cameron, and I were on vacation in the Virgin Islands when we met Jack and Jean Van Heusen. At our tiny, expensive resort we would see them in the dining room and on the beach. Etiquette dictated respect for privacy, but there was a quiet, countervailing camaraderie born of the feeling that one's fellow guests shared a level of good taste and financial standing. And the Van Heusens stood out as the only other young couple.

I'd just won a difficult case, sticking it to a rich husband and coming out with a nice settlement despite considerable evidence that my client had been cheating on him with everything in pants for years. Of course I sympathized with the guy, but he had his own counsel, had many inherited millions left over, and it's my job, after all, to give whoever hires me the best counsel possible. Now I was taking what I thought of as, for lack of a better cliché, a well-earned rest. I'd never done much resting, going straight from Amherst—where I'd worked part time for my tuition—to Columbia Law to a big midtown firm, where I'd knocked myself out as an associate for six years.

It's a sad fact that the ability to savor long hours of leisure is a gift some of us have lost, or else never acquired. The first morning, within an hour of waking in paradise, I was restless, watching stalk-eyed land crabs skitter sideways across the sand, unwilling or unable to concentrate on the Updike I'd started on the plane. Lying on the beach in front of our cabana, I noticed the attractive young couple emerging from the water, splashing each other. She was a tall and elegant brunette. Sandy-haired and lanky, he looked like a boy who'd taken a semester off from prep school to go sailing. Over the next few days I couldn't help noticing them. They were very affectionate, which seemed to indicate a relatively new marriage (both wore wedding bands). And they had an aura of entitlement, of being very much at home and at ease on this very pricey patch of white sand, so I assumed they came from money. Also they seemed gloriously indifferent, unlike those couples who, after a few days of sun and sand in the company of the beloved, invite their neighbors for a daiquiri on the balcony to grope for mutual acquaintances and interests— anything to be spared the frightening monotony of each other.

In fact, I was feeling a little dissatisfied after several days, my wife and I having, more rapidly than I would have thought, exhausted our meager store of observations about the monotonously glorious weather and the subjects which we imagined we never had enough time to discuss at home, what with business and the social schedule. And after a relatively satisfying first night, our love-making was not as inspired as I had hoped it was going to be. I wanted to leave all the bullshit at home, rejuvenate our marriage and our sex life, tell Cameron my fantasies, pathetically simple and requitable as they were. Yet I found myself unable to broach this topic, stuck as I was in a four-year rut of communicating less and less directly, reluctant for some reason to execute the romantic flourishes—candlelight and flower petals in the bath water and such—she considered so inspiring. And seeing her in her two-piece, I honestly felt that Cameron needed to do a bit of toning and cut back on the sweets.

But the example of the Van Heusens was invigorating. After all, I reasoned, we were also an attractive young couple—an extra pound or two notwithstanding. I thought more highly of us for our ostensible resemblance to them, and when I overheard him tell an old gent that he'd recently passed the bar, I felt a rush of kinship and self-esteem, since I'd recently made partner at one of the most distinguished firms in New York.

On the evening of our fifth day we struck up a conversation at the poolside bar. I heard them speculating about a yacht out in the bay and told them who it belonged to, having been told myself when I'd seen it in Tortolla a few days earlier. I half-expected him to recognize the name, to claim friendship with the owners, but he only said, "Oh, really? Nice boat."

The sun was melting into the ocean, dyeing the water red and pink and gold. We all sat, hushed, watching the spectacle. I reluctantly broke the silence to remind the waiter that I had specified a piña colada on the rocks, not frozen, my teeth being sensitive to crushed ice. Within minutes the sun had slipped out of sight, sending up a last flare, and then we began to chat. Eventually they told us they lived in one of those eminently respectable communities on the North Shore of Boston.

They asked if we had kids and we said no, not yet. When I said, "You?" Jean blushed and referred the question to her husband.

After a silent exchange he turned to us and said, "Jeannie's pregnant."

"We haven't really told anyone yet," she added.

Cameron beamed at Jean and smiled encouragingly in my direction. We had been discussing this very topic lately. She was ready; I didn't feel quite so certain myself. Still, I think we both were pleased to be the recipients of this confidence, even though it was a function of our very lack of real intimacy, and of the place and time, for we learned, somewhat sadly, that this was their last night.

When I mentioned my profession, Jack solicited my advice; he would start applying to firms when they returned home. I was curious, of course, how he had come to the law so relatively late—he had just referred in passing to his recent thirtieth birthday celebration—and what he'd done with his twenties, but thought it would be indiscreet to ask.

We ordered a second round of drinks and talked until it was fully dark. "Why don't you join us for dinner," he said, as we all stood on the veranda, hesitant about going our separate ways. And so we did. I was grateful for the company, and Cameron seemed to be enlivened by the break in routine. I found Jean increasingly attractive—confident and funny—while her husband was wry and self-deprecating in a manner which suited a young man who was probably a little too rich and happy for anyone else's good. He seemed to be keeping his lights on dim.

As the dinner plates were cleared away, I said, "So tell me, how did you two meet?"

Cameron laughed at the introduction of my favorite parlor game. Jack and Jean exchanged a long look, seeming to consult about whether to reveal their great secret. He laughed through his nose and then she began to laugh; within moments they were both in a state of high hilarity. To be sure, we'd had several drinks and two bottles of wine with dinner and, excepting Jean, none of us was legally sober. Cameron in particular seemed to me to be getting a little sloppy, particularly in contrast to the abstinent Jean; when she reached again for the wine bottle, I tried to catch her eye but she was bestowing her bright, blurred attention on our companions. "How we met," Jack said to his wife. "God. You want to tackle this one?"

She shook her head. "I think you'd better."

"Cigar?" he asked, producing two metal tubes from his pocket. Though I've resisted the cigar fetish indulged in by so many of my colleagues, I occasionally smoke one with a client or an associate and I took one now. He handed me a cutter and lit us up, then leaned back and stroked his sandy bangs away from his eyes and released a spume of smoke.

"Maybe it's not such an unusual story," he proposed.

Jean laughed skeptically.

"You sure you don't mind, honey?" he asked.

She considered, shrugged her shoulders, then shook her head. "It's up to you."

"Well, I think this story begins when I got thrown out of Bowdoin," he said. "Not to put too fine a point on it, I was dealing pot. Well, pot and a little coke, actually." He stopped to check our reaction.

I, for one, tried to keep an open, inviting demeanor, eager for him to continue. I wouldn't say I was shocked, though I was certainly surprised.

"I got caught." He smiled. "By agreeing to pack up my old kit bag and go away forever I escaped prosecution. My parents were none too pleased about the whole thing, but unfortunately for them, virtually that week I'd come into a little bit of Gramps' filthy lucre and there wasn't much they could do about it. I was tired of school anyway. It's funny, I enjoyed it when I finally went back a few years ago to get my B.A. and then law school, but at the time it was wasted on me. Or I was wasted on it. Wasted in general. I'd wake up in the morning and fire up the old bong and then huff up a few lines to get through geology seminar."

He inhaled on his stogie, shaking his head ruefully at the memory of his youthful excess. He didn't seem particularly ashamed as much as bemused, as if he were describing the behavior of an incorrigible cousin.

"Well, I went sailing for about a year—spent some time in these waters, actually, some of the best sailing waters in the world—and then drifted back to Boston. I'd run through most of my capital but I didn't feel ready to hit the books again and somehow I just kind of naturally got back in touch with my suppliers from Bowdoin days. I still had a boat, a little thirty-six-footer. And I got back in the trade. It was different then— this was ten years ago, before the Colombians really moved in. Everything was more relaxed. We were gentleman outlaws, adrenaline junkies, sail bums, freaks with an entrepreneurial streak."

He frowned slightly, as if hearing the faint note of self-justification, of self-delusion, of sheer datedness. I'd largely avoided the drug culture of the seventies, but even I could remember when drugs were viewed as the sacraments of a vague liberation theology or, later, as a slightly risky form of recreation. But in this era the romance of drug dealing was a hard sell, and Jack seemed to realize it.

"Well, that's how we saw it then," he amended. "Let's just say that we were less ruthless and less financially motivated than the people who eventually took over the business."

Wanting to discourage his sudden attack of scruples, I waved to the waiter for another bottle of wine.

"Make sure it's not too chilled," Cameron shouted at the retreating waiter. "My husband has very sensitive teeth." I suppose she thought this was quite funny.

"Anyway, I did quite well," Jack continued. "Initially I was very hands on, rendezvousing with mother ships out in the water beyond Nantucket, hauling small loads in a hollow keel. Eventually my partner and I moved up the food chain. We were making money so fast we had a hard time thinking of ways to launder it. I mean, you can't just keep hiding it under your mattress. First we were buying cars and boats in cash and then we bought a bar in Cambridge to run some of the profits through. We were actually paying taxes on drug money just so we could show some legitimate income. We always used to say we'd get out before it got too crazy, once we'd really put aside a big stash, but there was so much more cash to be made and craziness is like anything else, you get into it one step at a time and no single step really feels like it's taking you over the cliff. Until you go right over the edge and then it's too late. You're smoking reefer in high school and then doing lines and all of a sudden you're buying AK-47s and bringing hundred-kilo loads into Boston Harbor."

I wasn't about to point out that some of us never even thought of dealing drugs, let alone buying firearms. I refilled his wine glass, nicely concealing my skepticism, secretly pleased to hear this golden boy revealing his baser metal. But I have to say I was intrigued.

"This goes on for two, three years. I wish I could say it wasn't fun, but it was. The danger, the secrecy, the money. . . ." He pulled on his cigar and looked out over the water. "So anyway, we set up one of our biggest deals ever, and our buyer's been turned. Facing fifteen-to-life on his own so he delivers us up on a platter. A *very* exciting moment. We're in a warehouse in Back Bay and suddenly twenty narcs are pointing thirty-eights at us."

"And one of them was Jean," Cameron proposed.

I shot her a look but she was gazing expectantly at her counterpart.

"For the sake of our new friends here," Jean said, "I wish I had been." She looked at her husband and touched his wrist and at that moment I found her extraordinarily desirable. "I think you're boring these nice people."

"Not at all," I protested, directing my reassurance at the story-teller's wife. I was genuinely sorry for her sake that she was party to this sordid tale. She turned and smiled at me, as I'd hoped she would, and for a moment I forgot about the story altogether as I conjured up a sudden vision: slipping from the cabana for a walk later that night, unable to sleep . . . and encountering her out at the edge of the beach, talking, both claiming insomnia, then confessing that we'd been thinking of each other, a long kiss and a slow recline to the soft sand. . . .

"You must think—" She smiled helplessly. "Well, I don't know what you must think. Jack's never really told anyone about all of this before. You're probably shocked."

"Please, go on," said Cameron. "We're dying to hear the rest. Aren't we, Don?"

I nodded, a little annoyed at this aggressive use of the marital pronoun. Her voice seemed loud and grating and the gaudy print blouse I've always hated seemed all the more garish beside Jeannie's elegant but sexy navy halter.

"Long story short," said Jack, "I hire Carson Baxter to defend me. And piece by piece he gets virtually every shred of evidence thrown out. Makes it disappear right before the jury's eyes. Then he sneers at the rest. I mean, the man's the greatest performer I've ever seen—"

"He's brilliant," I murmured. Baxter was one of the finest defense attorneys in the country. Although I didn't always share his political views, I admired his adherence to his principles and his legal scholarship. Actually, he was kind of a hero to me. I don't know why, but I was surprised to hear his name in this context.

"So I walked," Jack concluded.

316 | JAY McINERNEY

"You were acquitted?" I asked.

"Absolutely." He puffed contentedly on his cigar. "Of course, you'd think that would be the end of the story and the end of my illicit but highly profitable career. Alas, unfortunately not. Naturally, I told myself and everyone else I was going straight. But after six months the memory of prison and the bust had faded and a golden opportunity practically fell into my lap, a chance for one last big score. The retirement run. The one you should never make. Always a mistake, these farewell gigs." He laughed.

"That waiter's asleep on his feet," Jean said. "Like the waiter in that Hemingway story. He's silently jinxing you, Jack Van Heusen, with a special voodoo curse for long-winded white boys, because he wants to reset the table and go back to the cute little turquoise-and-pink staff quarters and make love to his wife, the chubby laundress who is waiting for him all naked on her fresh white linen."

"I wonder how the waiter and the laundress met," Jack said cheerfully, standing up and stretching. "That's probably the best story."

My beloved wife said, "Probably they met after Don yelled at her about a stain on his linen shirt and the waiter comforted her."

Jack looked at his watch. "Good God, ten-thirty already, way past official Virgin Islands bedtime."

"But you can't go to bed yet," Cameron said. "You haven't even met your wife."

"Oh, right. So anyway, a while later I met Jean and we fell in love and got married and lived happily ever after."

"No fair," Cameron shrieked.

"I'd be curious to hear your observations about Baxter," I said quietly.

"The hell with Baxter," Cameron said. When she was drinking, her voice took on a more pronounced nasal quality as it rose in volume. "I want to hear the love story."

"Let's at least take a walk on the beach," Jean suggested, standing up.

So we rolled out to the sand and dawdled along the water's edge as Jack resumed the tale.

"Well, my partner and I went down to the Keys and picked up a boat, a Hatteras Sixty-two with a false bottom. Had a kid in the Coast Guard on our payroll and another in Customs and they were going to talk us through the coastal net on our return. For show we load up the boat with a lot of big-game fishing gear, these huge Nakamichi rods and reels. And we stow the real payload—the automatic weapons with night scopes and the cash. The guns were part of the deal, thirty of them, enough for a small army. The Colombians were always looking for armament and we picked these up cheap from an Israeli who had to leave Miami real quick. It was a night like this, a warm winter starry Caribbean night, when the rudder broke about a hundred miles off Cuba. We started to drift and by morning we got reeled in by a Cuban naval vessel. Well, you can imagine how they reacted when they found the guns and the cash. I mean, think about it, an American boat loaded with guns and cash and high-grade electronics. We tried to explain that we were just drug dealers, but they weren't buying it."

We had come to the edge of the beach; farther on, a rocky ledge rose up from the gently lapping water of the cove. Jack knelt down and scooped up a handful of fine silvery sand. Cameron sat down beside him. I remained standing, looking up at the powdery spray of stars above us, feeling in my intoxicated state that I was exercising some important measure of autonomy by refusing to sit just because Jack was sitting. By this time I simply did not approve of Jack Van Heusen nor of the fact that this self-confessed drug runner was about to enter the practice of law. And I suppose I didn't sanction his happiness, either—with his obvious wealth—whether inherited or illicit—and his beautiful and charming wife.

"That was the worst time of my life," he said softly, the jauntiness receding. Jean, who had been standing beside him, knelt down and put a hand on his shoulder. Suddenly he smiled and patted her arm. "But hey—at least I learned Spanish, right?"

Cameron chuckled appreciatively.

"After six months in a Cuban prison, my partner, the captain and I were sentenced to death as American spies. They'd kept us apart the whole time, hoping to break us. And they would've, except that we couldn't tell them what they wanted to hear because we were just a couple of dumb drug runners and not CIA."

I sat down on the sand, finally, drawing my knees up against my chest, watching Jean's sympathetic face as if her husband's tawdry ordeal, reflected there, would become more compelling. I couldn't feel very sorry for him—he'd gotten himself into this mess. But I could see she knew at least some of the ghastly details that he was eliding for us, and that it pained her. And for that, I felt sorry for her.

"Anyway, we were treated better than most of the Cuban dissidents because they always had to consider the possibility of using us for barter or propaganda. A few weeks before we're supposed to be shot, I manage to get a message to Baxter, who flies down to Havana and uses his leftist cred to get an audience with fucking Fidel. This is when it's illegal to even *go* to Cuba. And Baxter has his files with him, and—here's the beauty part—he uses the same evidence he discredited in Boston to convince Castro and his defense ministry that we're honest to God drug dealers as opposed to dirty Yankee spies. And they release us into Baxter's custody. But when we fly back to Miami"—he paused, looked around at his audience—"the feds are waiting for us on the tarmac. A welcoming committee of G-men standing there sweating in their cheap suits. They arrest all four of us for violating the embargo by coming from Cuba. Of course, the Feds know the real story—they've been monitoring this for the better part of a year. Out of the fucking fritada pan—"

"The *sarten*, actually," Jean corrected impishly.

"Yeah, yeah." He stuck his tongue out at her, then resumed. "I thought I was going to lose it right there on the runway. After almost seven months in a cell without a window, thinking I was free and then—"

"God," Cameron blurted, "you must have been—"

"I was. So now the FBI contacts Havana to ask for the evidence which led to our acquittal as spies so that they can use it to bust us for a smuggling rap."

I heard the sounds of a thousand insects and the lapping of water as he paused and smiled.

"And the Cubans say, basically—fuck you, Yankee pigs. And we all walk. And Lord, it was sweet."

To my amazement, Cameron began to applaud. She was, I now realized, thoroughly drunk.

"We still haven't heard about Jean," I noted. As if I suspected, and was about to prove, your honor, that in point of fact they had never actually met at all.

Jean shared with her husband a conspiratorial smile that deflated me. Turning to me, she said, "My name is Jean Baxter Van Heusen."

I'm not a complete idiot. "Carson Baxter's daughter," I said and she nodded.

Cameron broke out laughing. "That's just great, I love it."

"How did your father feel about it?" I said, sensing a weak point.

Jean's smile disappeared. She picked up a handful of sand and let it slip through her fingers. "Not too good. Apparently, it's one thing to defend a drug dealer, prove his innocence and take his money. But it's quite another thing when he falls in love with your precious daughter."

"Jeannie used to come to my trial to watch her father perform. And that, to answer your question, finally, is how we met. In court. Exchanging steamy looks, then steamy notes, across a stuffy courtroom." Pulling her close against his shoulder he added, "God, you looked good."

"Right," she said. "Anything without a Y chromosome would've looked good to you after three months in custody."

"After I was acquitted we started seeing each other secretly. Carson didn't know when he flew to Cuba. He didn't have a clue until we walked out of the courthouse in Miami and Jean threw her arms around me. And except for a few scream-and-threat fests, he hasn't really spoken to us since that day." He paused. "He did send me a bill, though."

"The really funny thing," Jean said, "is that Jack was so impressed with my dad that he decided to go to law school."

Cameron laughed again. At least one of us found this funny. My response took me a long time to sort out. As a student of the law you learn to separate emotion from facts, but in this case I suffered a purely emotional reaction I cannot justify in rational terms. Unfairly, perhaps, I felt disillusioned with the great Carson Baxter. And I felt personally diminished, robbed of the pride I'd felt in discussing my noble profession with an acolyte only a few hours before, and cheated out of the righteous condescension I had felt only minutes before.

"What a great story," Cameron said.

"So what about you guys," said Jean, sitting on the moonlit sand with her arm around her husband. "What's your wildly romantic story? Tell us about how you two met."

Cameron turned to me eagerly, smiling with anticipation. "Tell them, Don."

I stared out into the bay at a light on the yacht we'd all admired earlier and I thought about the boy who'd been polishing brass on deck when we walked up the dock on Tortolla, a shirtless teenager with limp white hair hanging on his coppery shoulders, bobbing his head and humming, looking forward, I imagined, to a night on the town.

I turned back to my wife, grinning beside me in the cold sand. "You tell them," I said.

Meet new people.... *Enjoy* stimulating conversation.... *Discover* wonderful new books....

Join A READING GROUP

From informal get-togethers with friends to groups at bookstores and libraries to chat rooms on the Internet, people everywhere are talking about books. And Vintage Books is <u>the</u> source to turn to when you're looking for the broadest and finest selection of books to read and free guides to enhance group discussion.

Choose a Pulitzer Prize winner or a national bestseller, a woman's memoir or a courtroom drama, a mystery or a historical novel—from classic to contemporary, Vintage Books offers beautifully designed paperback editions of the highest quality.

Use the most informative and provocative reading group guides available—free from Vintage Books—to keep your discussions lively and informed. Each guide includes a plot summary, discussion topics and questions, an author biography, and supplemental reading. Ask for them at your favorite bookstore, call 1-800-793-BOOK, or download them from our Web site.

And join the Vintage Reading Group on-line, where you can meet fascinating authors...recommend your favorite books...order books on-line and download more than 65 Vintage Reading Group Guides. There's always something new to read and say, so stop back often at **http://www.randomhouse.com/vintage/read**

VINTAGE BOOKS
The Reading Group Source for Book Lovers

__*Absalom, Absalom! / The Sound and the Fury / As I Lay Dying* by William Faulkner 0-676-53803-7

__*All the Pretty Horses* by Cormac McCarthy 0-394-07287-1

__*Altered States** by Anita Brookner 0-676-53017-6

__*American Pastoral* by Philip Roth 0-676-53736-7

__*Anywhere But Here* / *The Lost Father** / *A Regular Guy** by Mona Simpson 0-676-53004-4

__*Asylum** by Patrick McGrath 0-676-53725-1

__*Babel Tower* by A.S. Byatt 0-676-52442-7

__*Birdsong* by Sebastian Faulks 0-676-52440-0

__*Breath, Eyes, Memory** by Edwidge Danticat 0-394-07738-5

__*A Civil Action* by Jonathan Harr 0-676-51731-5

__*The Club Dumas* by Arturo Pérez-Reverte 0-676-53729-4

__*The Confessions of Nat Turner* by William Styron 0-394-07765-2

__*Corelli's Mandolin* by Louis de Bernières 0-676-50441-8

__*The Crossing* by Cormac McCarthy 0-394-07249-9

__*Daisy Bates in the Desert* by Julia Blackburn 0-676-50329-2

__*Dancing After Hours** by Andre Dubus 0-676-52020-0

__*Dead Man Walking* by Sister Helen Prejean 0-676-51488-X

__*Ellen Foster** by Kaye Gibbons 0-676-51131-7

__*The English Patient* by Michael Ondaatje 0-394-07740-7

__*The First Man* by Albert Camus 0-676-51552-5

__*Girl, Interrupted** by Susanna Kaysen 0-394-07240-5

__*God: A Biography* by Jack Miles 0-676-51599-1

__*Hitler's Willing Executioners* by Daniel Jonah Goldhagen 0-676-52016-2

__*Hotel du Lac** by Anita Brookner 0-676-50338-1

__*I Was Amelia Earhart** by Jane Mendelsohn 0-676-52749-3

__*Independence Day** by Richard Ford 0-676-51210-0

__*The Information* by Martin Amis 0-676-51190-2

__*Invisible Man* by Ralph Ellison 0-394-07247-2

__*Last Orders* by Graham Swift 0-676-52664-0

__*A Lesson Before Dying** by Ernest J. Gaines 0-394-07080-1

__*Life Estates** by Shelby Hearon 0-394-07739-3

__*Light Years* by James Salter 0-394-07557-9

__*Lolita* by Vladimir Nabokov 0-676-51335-2

__*Love Invents Us** by Amy Bloom 0-676-53215-2

__*The Lymond Chronicles* by Dorothy Dunnett 0-676-52426-5

__*Martin Dressler** by Steven Millhauser 0-676-53577-1

__*The Moor's Last Sigh* by Salman Rushdie 0-676-52013-8

__*My Ántonia / The Professor's House* by Willa Cather 0-394-07505-6

__*My Own Country* by Abraham Verghese 0-394-07741-5

__*Nobody's Fool** by Richard Russo 0-394-07241-3

__*Open Secrets** by Alice Munro 0-676-50342-X

__*Our Guys* by Bernard Lefkowitz 0-676-54135-6

__*Personal History* by Katharine Graham 0-676-53722-7

__*Possession* by A. S. Byatt 0-394-07507-2

__*Push** by Sapphire 0-676-52449-4

__*Reading in the Dark* by Seamus Deane 0-676-53733-2

__*Remembering Babylon* by David Malouf 0-394-07245-6

__*The Road From Coorain* by Jill Ker Conway 0-394-07242-1

__*Sleeping at the Starlite Motel* by Bailey White 0-676-51295-X

__*Snow Falling on Cedars** by David Guterson 0-676-50337-3

__*To the Wedding* by John Berger 0-676-51178-3

__*Tracks* by Robyn Davidson 0-394-07828-4

__*True North* by Jill Ker Conway 0-394-07504-8

__*An Unquiet Mind* by Kay Redfield Jamison 0-676-52748-5

__*The Unconsoled* by Kazuo Ishiguro 0-676-51567-3

__Vintage Crime/Black Lizard Three Titles in One 0-676-51334-4

__*When I Was Puerto Rican* by Esmeralda Santiago 0-394-07304-5

__Women's Memoir: *The Shadow Man* by Mary Gordon / *First Comes Love* by Marion Winik 0-676-52430-3

AVAILABLE IN SUMMER 1998:

__ *The Best of Ann Beattie** 0-676-54086-4

__ *Cold Mountain** by Charles Frazier 0-676-54074-0

__ *Fugitive Pieces* by Anne Michaels 0-676-54068-6

__ *Midwives** by Chris Bohjalian 0-676-54078-3

__ *Straight Man** by Richard Russo 0-676-54085-6

__ Vintage Spiritual Classics 0-676-54173-9

* Denotes a Vintage Contemporaries title

ISBN	Title, Author	Price
679-74730-3	AIR AND FIRE, Thomson	$12.00p
679-73752-9	ALL STORIES ARE TRUE, Wideman	$12.00p
679-77325-8	ALTERED STATES, Brookner	$12.00p
394-75987-7	ANGELS, Johnson	$13.00p
679-73464-3	ANOTHER YOU, Beattie	$12.00p
679-73738-3	ANYWHERE BUT HERE, Simpson	$13.00p
375-70012-9	AS SHE CLIMBED ACROSS THE TABLE, Lethem	$12.00p
679-75377-X	ASA, AS I KNEW HIM, Kaysen	$12.00p
679-78138-2	ASYLUM, McGrath	$12.00p
679-76796-7	BACK IN THE WORLD, Wolff	$12.00p
679-72327-7	BAD BEHAVIOR, Gaitskill	$11.00p
679-74821-0	BAILEY'S CAFE, Naylor	$12.00p
679-73271-3	THE BEGGAR MAID, Munro	$11.00p
679-73491-0	BIG BAD LOVE, Brown	$13.00p
679-73412-0	BIRDY, Wharton	$13.00p
679-75661-2	BREATH, EYES, MEMORY, Danticat	$11.00p
679-73733-2	BRIEF LIVES, Brookner	$12.00p
394-72641-3	BRIGHT LIGHTS, BIG CITY, McInerney	$10.00p
679-74532-7	BRIGHTNESS FALLS, McInerney	$14.00p
679-76500-X	THE BURNING HOUSE, Beattie	$11.00p
394-72642-1	THE BUSHWACKED PIANO, McGuane	$13.00p
679-75857-7	CARSON VALLEY, Barich	$14.00p
679-72369-2	CATHEDRAL, Carver	$12.00p
679-73891-6	CATHERINE CARMIER, Gaines	$12.00p
679-73234-9	CHILLY SCENES OF WINTER, Beattie	$13.00p
679-73052-4	THE CHINCHILLA FARM, Freeman	$12.00p
394-72633-2	THE CHOSEN PLACE, THE TIMELESS PEOPLE, Marshall	$15.00p
679-73351-5	CITY OF BOYS, Nugent	$9.00p
679-74340-5	A CLOSED EYE, Brookner	$11.00p
375-70075-7	COLD MOUNTAIN, Frazier	$13.00p
679-72174-6	THE COMMITMENTS, Doyle	$11.00p
679-76718-5	THE COUNTRY AHEAD OF US, THE COUNTRY BEHIND, Guterson	$11.00p
679-76075-X	CUBA AND THE NIGHT, Iyer	$12.00p
679-73672-7	A CURE FOR DREAMS, Gibbons	$10.00p
679-78151-X	DANCE OF THE HAPPY SHADES, Munro	$12.00p
679-75114-9	DANCING AFTER HOURS, Dubus	$12.00p
679-72712-4	THE DEBUT, Brookner	$12.00p
679-73049-4	DIRTY WORK, Brown	$12.00p

ISBN	Title, Author	Price
679-74578-5	DOLLY, Brookner	$12.00p
679-76652-9	EDWIN MULLHOUSE, Millhauser	$12.00p
375-70305-5	ELLEN FOSTER, Gibbons	$10.00p
679-74506-8	ET TU, BABE, Leyner	$11.00p
375-70051-X	EXEGESIS, Teller	$11.00p
679-76838-6	EXILES, Caputo	$13.00p
679-73192-X	FALLING IN PLACE, Beattie	$12.00p
679-78164-1	FAMILY AND FRIENDS, Brookner	$12.00p
679-75245-5	THE FAN MAN, Kotzwinkle	$12.00p
679-72076-6	A FAN'S NOTES, Exley	$14.00p
679-75376-1	FAR AFIELD, Kaysen	$13.00p
679-75933-6	THE FERMATA, Baker	$13.00p
679-72239-4	FIRES, Carver	$11.00p
679-74308-1	FRAUD, Brookner	$12.00p
679-72957-7	FRIEND OF MY YOUTH, Munro	$12.00p
679-77270-7	THE FRIENDS OF FREELAND, Leithauser	$14.00p
679-73890-8	A GATHERING OF OLD MEN, Gaines	$10.00p
679-73898-3	GORILLA, MY LOVE, Bambara	$11.00p
679-77621-4	THE GROTESQUE, McGrath	$11.00p
679-77651-6	HARMONY OF THE WORLD, Baxter	$11.00p
679-76795-9	HEARTBURN, Ephron	$11.00p
679-75511-X	HONEY, Tallent	$12.00p
679-75932-8	HOTEL DU LAC, Brookner	$11.00p
679-78135-8	THE HOTTEST STATE, Hawke	$11.00p
679-73477-5	THE HOUSE ON MANGO STREET, Cisneros	$9.95p
679-76942-0	THE HUNDRED BROTHERS, Antrim	$12.00p
375-70152-4	THE HUNDRED SECRET SENSES, Tan	$13.00p
679-75045-2	I SMELL ESTHER WILLIAMS, Leyner	$11.00p
679-77636-2	I WAS AMELIA EARHART, Mendelsohn	$10.00p
679-74523-8	IMPOSSIBLE VACATION, Gray	$12.00p
679-74243-3	IN A COUNTRY OF MOTHERS, Homes	$12.00p
679-72791-4	IN MY FATHER'S HOUSE, Gaines	$11.00p
679-76512-3	INCIDENTS IN THE RUE LAUGIER, Brookner	$12.00p
679-73518-6	INDEPENDENCE DAY, Ford	$13.00p
679-74324-3	THE INFORMERS, Ellis	$12.00p
679-77652-4	INTO THE GREAT WIDE OPEN, Canty	$12.00p
679-73221-7	JACK, Homes	$11.00p

ISBN	Title, Author	Price
679-72768-X	THE JOY LUCK CLUB, Tan	$11.00p
679-73033-8	KEEP THE CHANGE, McGuane	$12.00p
679-73886-X	KENTUCKY STRAIGHT, Offutt	$12.00p
679-74808-3	THE KITCHEN GOD'S WIFE, Tan	$12.00p
679-76657-X	KRIK? KRAK!, Danticat	$11.00p
679-72668-3	LATECOMERS, Brookner	$12.00p
679-73546-1	THE LAUGHING SUTRA, Salzman	$11.00p
679-78149-8	LESS THAN ZERO, Ellis	$12.00p
375-70270-9	A LESSON BEFORE DYING, Gaines	$12.00p
679-76805-X	LET 'EM EAT CAKE, Jedren	$14.00p
679-72944-5	LEWIS PERCY, Brookner	$12.00p
679-75796-1	LIFE ESTATES, Hearon	$11.00p
375-70143-5	LITTLE KINGDOMS, Millhauser	$12.00p
679-75001-0	LITTLEJOHN, Owen	$12.00p
679-74424-X	LIVE GIRLS, Nugent	$12.00p
679-73813-4	LOOK AT ME, Brookner	$12.00p
679-75527-6	LOOSE WOMAN, Cisneros	$10.00p
679-73303-5	THE LOST FATHER, Simpson	$13.00p
394-74418-7	LOVE ALWAYS, Beattie	$12.00p
375-75022-3	LOVE INVENTS US, Bloom	$12.00p
679-72181-9	MAMA DAY, Naylor	$13.00p
679-78127-1	MARTIN DRESSLER, Millhauser	$12.00p
679-72576-8	THE MEZZANINE, Baker	$10.00p
679-77146-8	MIDWIVES, Bohjalian	$13.00p
679-73260-8	MILE ZERO, Sanchez	$14.00p
679-75382-6	MOHAWK, Russo	$13.00p
679-73270-5	THE MOONS OF JUPITER, Munro	$12.00p
679-74579-3	MY COUSIN, MY GASTROENTEROLOGIST, Leyner	$10.00p
679-78132-3	MY LIFE, STARRING DARA FALCON, Beattie	$13.00p
679-77641-9	MY OLD SWEETHEART, Moore	$12.00p
679-72295-5	THE NAMES, DeLillo	$13.00p
679-78155-2	THE NIGHT IN QUESTION, Wolff	$12.00p
679-75289-7	NINETY-TWO IN THE SHADE, McGuane	$12.00p
679-74007-4	NO HEROICS, PLEASE, Carver	$12.00p
394-74738-0	NOBODY'S ANGEL, McGuane	$14.00p
679-75333-8	NOBODY'S FOOL, Russo	$14.00p
679-74778-8	NOTHING BUT BLUE SKIES, McGuane	$13.00p
679-75248-X	OF LOVE & DUST, Gaines	$12.00p
679-74769-9	THE ONE-ROOM SCHOOLHOUSE, Heynen	$12.00p
679-75562-4	OPEN SECRETS, Munro	$13.00p
679-75291-9	PANAMA, McGuane	$11.00p
679-73650-6	PHILADELPHIA FIRE, Wideman	$12.00p
679-73194-6	PICTURING WILL, Beattie	$12.00p
394-72914-5	A PIECE OF MY HEART, Ford	$12.00p
679-72293-9	PLAYERS, DeLillo	$12.00p
679-75443-1	A PRIVATE VIEW, Brookner	$12.00p
679-73814-2	PROVIDENCE, Brookner	$12.00p
679-76675-8	PUSH, Sapphire	$11.00p
394-74118-8	RANSOM, McInerney	$12.00p
679-72292-0	RATNER'S STAR, DeLillo	$15.00p
679-77271-5	A REGULAR GUY, Simpson	$13.00p
679-73812-6	THE REVOLUTION OF LITTLE GIRLS, Boyd	$12.00p
679-72191-6	REVOLUTIONARY ROAD, Yates	$15.00p
679-75383-4	THE RISK POOL, Russo	$14.00p
394-75700-9	ROCK SPRINGS, Ford	$13.00p
679-77016-X	ROCKET CITY, Alpert	$12.00p
679-73440-6	ROOM TEMPERATURE, Baker	$10.00p
679-78148-X	THE RULES OF ATTRACTION, Ellis	$13.00p
679-72294-7	RUNNING DOG, DeLillo	$14.00p
679-74076-7	THE SALT EATERS, Bambara	$12.00p
679-75546-2	SECRETS, James	$10.00p
679-73193-8	SECRETS & SURPRISES, Beattie	$13.00p
679-76730-4	SELECTED STORIES, Dubus	$14.00p
679-76674-X	SELECTED STORIES, Munro	$16.00p
679-74864-4	SHORT CUTS, Carver	$10.00p
679-77624-9	THE SIZE OF THOUGHTS, Baker	$13.00p
679-75539-X	SLEEPING BEAUTIES, Moore	$12.00p
679-72777-9	SLEEPING IN FLAME, Carroll	$13.00p
679-76402-X	SNOW FALLING ON CEDARS, Guterson	$13.00p
679-75926-3	THE SOLOIST, Salzman	$12.00p
394-73156-5	SOMETHING TO BE DESIRED, McGuane	$10.00p
375-70268-7	SPARTINA, Casey	$13.00p
679-75290-0	THE SPORTING CLUB, McGuane	$11.00p
679-76210-8	SPORTSWRITER, Ford	$12.00p
679-72257-2	STORY OF MY LIFE, McInerney	$12.00p
375-70190-7	STRAIGHT MAN, Russo	$13.00p
679-76394-5	STRANGER IN THIS WORLD, Canty	$10.00p
679-75032-0	TERMINAL VELOCITY, Boyd	$12.00p
679-74240-9	THROUGH THE IVORY GATE, Dove	$12.00p
394-75521-9	TO SKIN A CAT, McGuane	$10.00p
679-74521-1	TOOTH IMPRINTS ON A CORN DOG, Leyner	$11.00p
394-75089-0	THE ULTIMATE GOOD LUCK, Ford	$12.00p
375-70306-3	A VIRTUOUS WOMAN, Gibbons	$10.00p

ISBN	Title, Author	Price
679-74211-5	VOX, Baker	$11.00p
679-76944-7	WHAT GIRLS LEARN, Cook	$13.00p
679-73903-3	WHAT WAS MINE & OTHER STORIES, Beattie	$12.00p
679-72305-6	WHAT WE TALK ABOUT WHEN WE TALK ABOUT LOVE, Carver	$10.00p
679-72231-9	WHERE I'M CALLING FROM, Carver	$14.00p
679-77102-6	WHERE LOVE GOES, Maynard	$12.00p
679-77615-X	A WHITE MERC WITH FINS, Hawes	$12.00p
679-73447-3	WILDLIFE, Ford	$11.00p
679-73569-0	WILL YOU PLEASE BE QUIET, PLEASE?, Carver	$12.00p
679-73856-8	WOMAN HOLLERING CREEK, Cisneros	$11.00p
679-77668-0	WOMEN WITH MEN, Ford	$12.00p

AVAILABLE FROM RANDOM HOUSE AUDIOBOOKS
(Vintage Contemporaries Titles)

ISBN	Title, Author	Price
679-41163-1	BRIGHTNESS FALLS, McInerney	$16.00a
679-46069-1	COLD MOUNTAIN (abridged), Frazier	$18.00a
375-40292-6	COLD MOUNTAIN (unabridged), Frazier	$44.95a
679-45200-1	THE COUNTRY AHEAD OF US, THE COUNTRY BEHIND, Guterson	$18.00a
679-43116-0	THE FERMATA, Baker	$17.00a
394-58486-4	FRIEND OF MY YOUTH, Munro	$16.00a
679-44380-0	INDEPENDENCE DAY, Ford	$18.00a
679-45805-0	I WAS AMELIA EARHART, Mendelsohn	$18.00a
679-41059-7	THE LOST FATHER, Simpson	$16.00a
679-46075-6	MEMOIRS OF A GEISHA, Golden	$18.00a
679-43050-4	NOBODY'S FOOL, Russo	$17.00a
679-44775-X	SNOW FALLING ON CEDARS, Guterson	$18.00a
679-46004-7	STRAIGHT MAN, Russo	$18.00a
394-57874-0	WHERE I'M CALLING FROM (unabridged), Carver	$16.00a
679-41210-7	WOMAN HOLLERING CREEK, Cisneros	$16.00a
679-46012-8	WOMEN WITH MEN, Ford ("Jealous," an unabridged story)	$15.00a